Debrett's

THE STATELY HOMES OF BRITAIN

Debrett's

THE STATELY HOMES OF BRITAIN

Personally Introduced by the Owners

SIBYLLA JANE FLOWER

With photographs by

DERRY MOORE

Foreword by Lord Howard of Henderskelfe

An Owl Book

Holt, Rinehart and Winston
New York

Text copyright © 1982 by Sibylla Jane Flower
Illustrations copyright © 1982 by Derry Moore/
Webb & Bower (Publishers) Ltd./Debrett's Peerage Ltd.
All rights reserved, including the right to
reproduce this book or portions thereof in any form.
Published by Holt, Rinehart and Winston,
383 Madison Avenue, New York.New York 10017.

Library of Congress Cataloging in Publication Data
Flower, Sibylla Jane.
Debrett's the stately homes of Britain.
1. Historic buildings - England.   2. Dwellings -
England.   3. England - Nobility - Biography.   I. Title.
II. Title: The stately homes Britain.
DA660.F64   1982   942   82-9337
ISBN: 0-03-061993-9
ISBN: 0-03-002843-4 (An Owl bk.) (pbk.)

First American edition published in hardcover by Holt,
Rinehart and Winston in 1982.
First Owl Book Edition—1985

Designer: Vic Giolitto
Printed and bound in Italy by New Interlitho SpA
1 3 5 7 9 10 8 6 4 2

ISBN 0-03-061993-9 HARDBOUND
ISBN 0-03-002843-4 PAPERBACK

Contents

Acknowledgements

This book could not have been written without the help and co-operation of the owners or occupants of the twenty houses described in these pages. We offer them our grateful thanks. Their patience in answering numerous questions about their houses, their families and themselves is greatly appreciated, as was their warm welcome to Derry Moore and myself.

We would like to thank David Burnett and Sir Roy Strong for the part they played in the conception of this book, George Howard who contributed not only the foreword, but also sage advice and assistance, and the Duchess of Devonshire for her help and encouragement. Sir Iain Moncreiffe of that Ilk, Bt, CVO gave valuable advice on Scottish houses.

We are grateful to the various regional information officers of the National Trust for permission to include four of their houses in the book, in particular Mr Giles Clotworthy and Miss Pam Horner; to the administrators, of whom Mr R. G. Wakeford of Knole was particularly helpful; and to Mr James Stormonth Darling CBE, MC, TD, Director of the National Trust for Scotland, for permission to include Haddo House.

I am grateful to the following owners for allowing me to examine manuscripts in their possession, and to quote from them in my text: the Marquess of Bath (correspondence of the 4th Marquess of Bath); the Trustees of the Chatsworth Settlement (papers of the 6th Duke of Devonshire); Mr David Lytton Cobbold (Knebworth House MSS); Mr Henry Douglas Pennant (the diary of Adela Douglas Pennant); Mr George Howard (Carlisle MSS, from the Castle Howard collection); Mrs L. Mackeson-Sandbach (reminiscences of Lilian Douglas Pennant); the Duke of Northumberland (Syon MSS). Mr Thomas Cottrell-Dormer lent me his notes on the history of Rousham and also Stephen Swift's transcript of the McClary letter quoted on p. 131.

I would like to acknowledge my debt to those writers whose work on the history of various houses and families has proved an invaluable source of material, in particular: the Marquess of Aberdeen (Haddo and the Gordons); G. R. Batho (Syon and the Percys); David Burnett (Longleat and the Thynnes); John Cornforth (Boughton and Chatsworth); Viscount De L'Isle (Penshurst and the Sidneys); Mark Girouard (Carlton); David Green (Blenheim and the Spencer-Churchills); Gervase Jackson-Stops (Ickworth and the Herveys); Tresham Lever (Wilton and the Herberts); Sir Iain Moncreiffe (Scottish family history); J. Martin Robinson (Carlton and the Stapletons); A. L. Rowse (the Spencer-Churchills); V. Sackville-West (Knole and the Sackvilles); F. L. Thompson (Chatsworth); A. C. Wilson (Arbury and the Newdigates).

Thanks are due to the following publishers for permission to quote from published works: William Heinemann (the servants' list at Knole, from *The Diary of the Lady Anne Clifford*, ed. V. Sackville-West); The Hogarth Press (extract from Lady Dorothy Henley, *Rosalind Howard, Countess of Carlisle*); Secker and Warburg (extracts from *Aubrey's Brief Lives*, ed. Oliver Lawson Dick); the Trustees of the British Museum of Natural History (extract from *The Sloane Herbarium*, ed. J. E. Dandy); Yale University Press (extract from *The George Eliot Letters*, ed. Gordon S. Haight).

For contributions to the text, help with photographs of portraits, or assistance in other ways, I am grateful to: the Marquess of Aberdeen; Richard and Mary Carew Pole; Lady Cottesloe; Peter Day and Michael Pearman, Librarians at Chatsworth; Mrs L. C. S. FitzRoy Newdegate OBE; Sybil, Countess Fortescue; Miss Jane Fowles, Librarian at Longleat; Miss Christian Howard; Simon Howard; Mrs Huby at Carlton; Geoffrey Lee; Mrs L. Mackeson-Sandbach; John Pearson; Sir John and Lady Ropner; Mr Hugh Sackville-West MC; Mrs Joan de Salis; Miss Diana Thorne CBE, TD; Lord Christopher Thynne.

I am grateful to my publishers for their patience and also to my long-suffering colleagues at Phillips, Jock Smith, Louise Guest and David Weston-Lewis; and to Doris Kent, Jay Harris and Charlotte Edwards who helped in innumerable ways. Gerald Burdon proved a mine of information and carried out noble work on the proofs.

My principal debt is to Derry Moore, not only for his great skills as a photographer which are evident throughout this book, but also for the humour which enlivened our travels, and the encouragement which lightened my task.

Foreword

Lord Howard of Henderskelfe

The story of historic houses is interwoven with that of the people who built and lived in them; without some account of their lives, deaths and eccentricities it is impossible to understand the significance of the palaces, mansions, castles and manor houses which are the proudest jewels in the British heritage.

Most books on historic houses concentrate on their architectural history, though the irreplaceable *Country Life* articles which have been appearing since 1897 do usually include an account of family history and background. This book, however, concentrates on the human side of the story. Never has it been more important to realize that the future of historic houses lies with individual owners and their determination to survive. Comparison between the hollow magnificence of empty French palaces or châteaux and English country houses may be a cliché, but it is none the less valid. The National Trust does a remarkable job, but cannot accept any more houses without massive endowments, nor could it cope with a flood of accessions even in the unlikely event of Government or the National Heritage Memorial Fund endowing each and every one. Besides, an historic house, still privately owned and lived in as a home, displays an indefinable atmosphere which is clearly appreciated even by the most casual visitor.

As one threat to the future of our historic houses recedes, another seems to loom over the horizon. A few years ago, the axe of a wealth tax hung over the necks of owners; it has temporarily been put back into the cupboard, but may yet emerge sharper than ever. Capital and income taxation looked as if they might destroy the private owner. At the eleventh hour, measures have been introduced in the past five years which greatly alleviate their effects. There is now a tax regime within which owners can hope to maintain their houses: fortunately, the measures have all-party support. There is a recognition on all sides that the best method of retaining houses and their contents is by leaving them in private hands, and that tax arrangements, supplemented by Government grants, should be directed to that end. Unfortunately, grants are still woefully inadequate, so that timely repairs are deferred – leading to much higher expenditure later.

It is a bitter irony that the recession should have begun to take its toll just as the tax environment has been pulled into more or less the right shape. Inflationary pressures have affected everyone during the last ten years, but few more severely than the owners of historic houses. The index of building repairs has risen more steeply than the retail prices index, the cost of the craftsmen who work on historic buildings more steeply still.

The recession of 1981–2 will be, for many, the last straw on the camel's back. It is not only the drop in visitor numbers which bites. Most homes are at the centre of an agricultural estate, and farming profits have plummeted. More than one owner has said that he cannot see any light at the end of the tunnel. So does this mean a wholesale rush of dispersal sales while owners try to salvage what they can, before all their resources are irretrievably committed to keeping their homes going? Shall we see a multitude of homes standing forlorn, empty and useless? The answer to these questions must inevitably be yes, if the recession is prolonged to the end of the decade. Very few houses, or their owners, could withstand for very long the pressures which a deep recession would bring. Historic houses are not immune to the forces which bring about the collapse of great industrial companies as well as the bankruptcies of small firms.

So the future of these treasures depends upon the economic health of the country. But if any hopeful rays do glimmer on the horizon, most houses will survive, perhaps not in quite such good shape, but relatively intact. There is a long history of resilience in the breed. What some might describe as a blinkered reluctance to face unpalatable facts, others would call steadfast optimism. Many owners are prepared to weather severe storms, if there is any hope of calmer waters beyond.

If first the works of art and then the houses themselves disappear, Britain will be an irretrievably poorer, duller and more miserable country. In realistic terms, there is not a great deal more that Government can do. As always, the future depends upon individuals, each varying in his attitude and his circumstances. In the end, the future of historic houses is a human problem.

Introduction

'It was impossible to foresee, in the spring of 1944, the present cult of the English country house,' Evelyn Waugh wrote in 1959 in the preface to a revised edition of *Brideshead Revisited*. 'It seemed then that the ancestral seats which were our chief national artistic achievement were doomed to decay and spoliation.'

This artistic achievement and the decay – actual or threatened – have until recently provided the themes for the majority of books and commentaries on country houses. It is only in the last few years that writers such as Mark Girouard and John Cornforth have tried to redress the balance and to consider the houses from the point of view of the inhabitants.

The life and soul of these great houses were derived from their possessors. It is admitted on all sides that when the family departs they become museums or, stripped of their contents, only monuments.

This book is about the inhabitants of twenty houses in Britain both in the recent and in the remote past. I have described in each instance some of the owners and their families, not forgetting their servants and the artists and craftsmen who built the houses and decorated them or created their gardens.

These stately homes were an integral part of the careers of their owners, not only as residences, but as centres of political and economic power and social prestige and influence. It is hardly too much to say that private life in the modern sense hardly existed in British country houses until the time of Jane Austen. The public careers of the principal owners have therefore been sketched in this book, as well as the part the houses played in their lives.

Each house has a chapter prefaced by an interview with the present owner or occupant, or in the case of properties of the National Trust or the National Trust for Scotland, with the donor or his successor. The object of these interviews is to provide an introduction to the houses and to link the present with the past. Personal reminiscences therefore loom large. While these custodians are naturally concerned with the continued existence of the houses, this book is not about the problems of preservation, and as it relates to the personalities of the inhabitants the architecture of the houses is not described exhaustively. But it is sketched, and I have attempted to show the considerable role played by many of the owners in architectural and decorative schemes.

Similarly, Derry Moore's photographs are intended to evoke the atmosphere of the houses and to suggest the infinite variety of the decoration, rather than to provide a detailed architectural record.

Today country houses are visited by millions yearly. All the houses described in this book are open to the public and at some it has been a tradition for centuries for the owners to admit visitors.

Although Lord Bath is generally considered the founder of what is known as the stately homes business, he has described how this developed as a natural extension of the ancient custom whereby the housekeeper showed visitors round Longleat for a small reward. Great houses such as Chatsworth and Castle Howard have been open to the public since they were built. Mr Howard is fond of quoting a passage from the 1829 edition of *Paterson's Roads* which relates to Castle Howard and reads: 'The Liberality of the noble proprietor, in admitting the public to view this elegant repository, entitles him to grateful applause.' A special gateway was built by William Kent at Rousham for the public to enter the gardens at a respectable distance from the house. Joseph Farington toured Blenheim in 1801 and wrote in his diary: 'We were three quarters of an hour in the house, and five companies arrived to see it before we left.' Edward Bulwer Lytton opened his gardens at Knebworth to the public on certain days advertising the fact in the local Hertfordshire papers, although he himself was not on view and would retreat to London to escape the people who came to catch a glimpse of him. The Herbert family experimented at Wilton in the 1860s with paying visitors, but the receipts amounted to no more than £50 a year and decreased after the novelty had worn off. Syon was open free of charge in the nineteenth century to 'anyone of respectable appearance' who left their card at Northumberland House, the Percy London house near Charing Cross, the day before their intended visit. The gates were open daily between ten and six and the 1851 guide recommended the train from Waterloo to Brentford which ran almost every hour, a boat to Richmond, or the omnibus which provided an enjoyable view of 'the western suburb of the vast metropolis'. But the major tourist attraction in England as far as country houses are concerned has always been Chatsworth. A glance at the nineteenth-century visitors' books which are preserved in the house show that people came from all over the world. In 1910 visitors numbered some 80,000. When it was pointed out to the 8th Duke of Devonshire the wear and tear this involved he remarked, 'I dare say they will bring down the floors some day, but I don't see how we can keep them out.' The crowds have continued to flock to Chatsworth and their financial contributions are now an essential element in the preservation of these floors which the Duke feared they would destroy. But this raises the question of conservation and that subject is outside the scope of this book.

'One cannot be said to have seen anything that a man of curiosity would think worth seeing in this Country,' wrote Daniel Defoe in the 1720s, 'and not have been at WILTON HOUSE; but not the beautiful Building, not the ancient Trophy of a great Family, not the noble situation, not all the Pleasures of the Gardens, Parks, Fountains, Hare-Warren, or whatever is rare either in Art or Nature are equal to, that yet more glorious sight, of a noble Princely Palace, constantly filled with its noble and proper inhabitants.'

Mr John Berkeley of Berkeley Castle is twenty-fourth in descent from Robert FitzHarding, to whom the castle was granted in 1153. From time to time in this long period the Berkeley family has neglected the castle – they did for instance in the nineteenth century – but their hounds have always been cherished. Looking down across the meadows to the south of the castle, visitors see what is apparently an eighteenth-century country house among the trees. It is the kennels and stables of the Berkeley Hunt, one of the most historic and renowned packs of hounds in the country. Mr Berkeley is the Master. There has always been a great feeling of kinship among the Berkeleys; it pervades their whole history, but it still comes as a surprise to hear that Randal, 8th Earl of Berkeley, left the castle at his death in 1942 to Captain R. G. W. Berkeley, a remote cousin who shared with him an ancestor born over 500 years before.

'Will you explain this relationship, and how the bequest came about?'

'Yes, Randal, the last Lord Berkeley, and I had a common ancestor, James, Lord Berkeley, who died in 1463. Randal discovered that my father was his nearest legitimate male heir. He had a great feeling for family history, and felt that there had been enough illegitimacy in the family. My father was aware from about 1924 that he would inherit, and grew to love the place in the 1920s and 1930s.'

'Where did he live before he came here?'

'At Spetchley, near Worcester. Our branch of the Berkeley family established themselves at Spetchley Park in 1605. My father always lived there, and looked on Berkeley as a hunting-lodge.'

'The hunting tradition appears to be stronger here than almost anywhere else in the country. What is the history of the pack?'

'There have been hounds here since Norman times, at first to hunt stag and since about 1770 to hunt the fox. Queen Elizabeth I came to hunt here and the Prince of Wales does from time to time today. The present kennels were built in the early eighteenth century on the site of the earlier ones. And, of course, we wear the distinctive yellow Berkeley livery.'

'As one can see in the Orpen portrait of the last Lord Berkeley in the dining-room.'

'Yes, he much disliked that portrait, and tried to prevent Orpen exhibiting it at the Royal Academy. It was painted when he was still enthusiastic about hunting. But this didn't last and he handed over the mastership and the hounds to my father after eight years.'

'When did you come here to live?'

'I opened the castle to the public for my father in the summer of 1956, and lived here from then until he died in 1969. After I married we lived here continuously for the first two years. We don't any more, we spend the summer at Spetchley, because the crush of visitors here in such a constricted space makes life impossible.

We return as soon as the tourist season is over and cub-hunting begins.'

'Why did your father decide to open to the public, and has this been a success?'

'He felt people would like to see the castle. It has been a success: in 1981 we had 75,000 people. One year we were over the 100,000 mark which is too high and imposes a strain on the place. We have had grants but the visitors pay for the upkeep.'

'You have an excellent guidebook written by Vita Sackville-West. How did this come about?'

'My father was impressed with what she had written about the castle in one of her books. He was a great gardener and he knew her well enough through their mutual interest in gardens to ask her. She agreed.'

'You found the castle in good order when you came here?'

'Yes. Randal was a great eccentric. He removed the mechanisms of all the clocks in the house, for instance – and there are some very good ones – and replaced them with electric parts regulated from one central clock. But at the same time he put in lots of bathrooms, cupboards and wardrobes everywhere, double-glazing, a lift.'

'Have you made any alterations?'

'To the kitchen and laundry. There were after all fourteen servants here even during the war. And we restored the chapel in the keep. The Spetchley family has always been Catholic. Randal made the chapel, but he was an agnostic and filled it with muniments. It is now a private chapel, but used for public Mass.'

'And you have two sons.'

'Yes, they were the first Berkeley sons to be born in the neighbourhood for two hundred years – they were actually born in Bristol – there was great excitement here.'

Towards the west, and within sight of the castle, looms the Berkeley Nuclear Power Station. With luck there will be someone around to celebrate the 1000th anniversary of the Berkeleys of Berkeley Castle.

Berkeley Castle

GLOUCESTERSHIRE

Mr John Berkeley

Berkeley Castle, from the water-meadows to the south.

Berkeley Castle is a fortress. Its massive, rugged presence dominates the Severn Vale. For over 900 years, from the reign of Edward the Confessor, the castle has occupied a position of command, seated firmly on an eminence overlooking the River Severn and the Marches of Wales. The strategic importance of the site faded away hundreds of years ago, but no attempt was ever made to tame the character of the architecture. And yet there is nothing forbidding about Berkeley when viewed from across the meadows or from the terrace on the south front. For the rose-pink and the iron-grey stone of which it is built – Vita Sackville-West likened the colour of the walls to that of pot-pourri – gives an impression of warmth which softens the military aspect.

About 1153 the Manor of Berkeley was granted by Henry of Anjou (Henry II) to Robert FitzHarding, a rich Bristol merchant and ancestor of the present owner of Berkeley Castle. Some years later, FitzHarding's son, Maurice, married the daughter of a previous owner of Berkeley, so pushing back the connexion between family and castle to the middle of the eleventh century.

Berkeley has been owned by the family ever since, although for a period of sixty-two years the castle was in the hands of the Royal Family. William Berkeley, aptly named 'Waste-all', settled the estate for three reigns on Henry VII and his male successors in return for certain favours including a title, and the Berkeleys did not regain their home until after the death of Edward VI.

According to Sir Anthony Wagner, a former Garter King of Arms, one family alone in England is able to show a clear descent from a pre-Conquest Englishman (the Arden family of Warwickshire); the Berkeleys almost share this distinction, but one weak link in the chain in the twelfth century means that their claim is not quite proven; perhaps a record will emerge one day to strengthen it.

From an early date the Lords of Berkeley wielded great power. They were warriors, 'each one of them martially inclyned', who served in all the major wars of the late Middle Ages. Members of the Berkeley family fought with bravery at the battles of Bannockburn, Crécy, Poitiers and Flodden and a host of lesser encounters. The Lords were also statesmen, they attended Parliament, acted as governors and went on embassies to foreign rulers. They dominated the affairs of their own county. And over the generations they built up a great estate, acquiring land from kings, from heiresses and widows, or as a result of negotiation and purchase, for they were shrewd men of business and were slow to forget the example of their ancestor, the rich Bristol merchant. Large flocks of sheep and well-managed farms were the source of great riches.

Berkeley Castle was always their base. The great Norman keep was begun in 1153 by Robert FitzHarding, and encloses an earlier fortified mound. FitzHarding lent large sums of money to Henry of Anjou during his war with Stephen, and in the charter granting FitzHarding the castle,

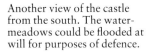

Another view of the castle from the south. The water-meadows could be flooded at will for purposes of defence.

Henry undertook to pay for the building himself. Maurice FitzHarding, Robert's son and heir, added a tower and a guardroom; he also replaced the wooden stockade of the courtyard with a stone curtain against which he built a great hall. Robert FitzHarding is the first feudal Lord of Berkeley (that is, by tenure of the castle; the Berkeley barony, by writ of summons, dates from 1421).

Thomas, the 8th Lord, made extensive additions in the mid-fourteenth century. What is notable about the structure of Berkeley is that few alterations have been made to the exterior since his time. Berkeley escaped serious damage in the Civil War, and was not affected in any major way by eighteenth- or nineteenth-century taste, for the castle tended to be lived in by the family only during the hunting season, and was neglected for long periods; by the early twentieth century, it was in a poor state of repair. In 1916 the castle was inherited by Randal, 8th Earl of Berkeley, who devoted himself with great enthusiasm to the restoration of its mediaeval character.

We are fortunate when we turn to the history of the family, for in the early seventeenth century John Smyth of Nibley, a Berkeley steward, gathered together all that he could find out about it. To illuminate the early periods he made extensive use of the archives, and drew an incomparable picture of a family, full of recondite information and lively detail.

Thomas, 6th Lord Berkeley, was a favourite subject of Edward I, and the King was generous to him with presents of land and money. He was born at Berkeley in 1245. For over fifty years he fought against the Welsh, the Scots and the French ('28 tymes in Armes in the feild'), and he was still in action in his seventieth year at the Battle of Bannockburn where he was taken prisoner. He was known as Thomas 'the Wise'. Smyth calls him 'a man of men; a man of all houres and for all affaires'.

Edward I sent him as ambassador to the King of France in 1295, and to Pope Clement V in 1307. He became Vice-Constable of England in 1297. As long as he could sit in the saddle, he continued to take part in jousts, and to hunt. Smyth refers to his hounds and other dogs 'which hee all his life solaced in; A number so great, that it wold nowe

The alabaster tomb of the 8th Lord and his wife, in Berkeley parish church. Lord Berkeley is wearing the armour in which he fought in the French wars, and his wife Katherine is dressed in the height of fourteenth-century fashion. She is wearing stays which were a mark of nobility, and her headdress is typical of the elaborate style worn by sophisticated ladies of the time.

bee deemed burdensome to a faire estate'.

His household and estate accounts show the meticulous way in which his affairs were run. He was a careful man who would put himself to considerable inconvenience to save money. Smyth reckoned that he had not been nearly so generous in his charitable works as some of his ancestors. Yet at Christmas he kept open house at Berkeley to all comers.

He found the perfect wife in Joan de Ferrers. She was content to remain at home and manage his affairs in his long absences, and was happiest in her dairy or at work on the farm. She found old age and ill-health very hard to bear after her years of activity, but to exercise herself, she took to sawing stakes and kindling wood in her chamber using a small handsaw. When she was sick, one of her sons would send as far afield as Oxford for her favourite doctor. In forty-two years of married life Joan did not travel more than ten miles from the

Berkeley manors. She died in 1309, and was buried in St Augustine's Abbey at Bristol. Twelve years later the old warrior was laid to rest beside her, 'as their two harts in life were tyed togeather with an entire amity'.

Maurice 'the Magnanimous' became the 7th Lord on his father's death. All Maurice's interests in life we are told were 'martiall'. He fought beside his father in Scotland, and rose to be Governor of Berwick-on-Tweed and, later, Seneschal of Aquitaine. He had a passion for tournaments. His career was brought to an abrupt halt when he joined the baronial revolt against Edward II and was imprisoned in Wallingford Castle. He died in captivity at Wallingford in 1326.

At the age of eight Maurice was married to Eve, daughter of Eudes La Zouche. Smyth was shocked to discover that their first child, Thomas, was born before his father was fourteen, and he wrote, after a diligent search of the records, 'I would gladly

The morning-room. This was formerly the chapel of St Mary, and has a timber roof with fourteenth-century painted decoration which includes verses from The Revelation. The translation was made by a Cornishman, John Trevisa, who was chaplain to Lord Berkeley from about 1380. The tapestries are Brussels and depict the stories of Isaac and Rebecca, and Sodom and Gomorrah.

think otherwise, but Truth will not permit mee.'

The castle's long and colourful history is dominated by one sinister event which occurred during the time of this young son Thomas, 8th Lord Berkeley. After his father's death, Thomas, Lord Berkeley, had managed to recover the family estates with the connivance of Queen Isabella and his father-in-law Roger Mortimer, the Queen's lover. In the following year, 1327, the weak and incompetent King Edward II was brought to Berkeley as a prisoner and soon afterwards brutally murdered at the instigation of the Queen and Mortimer.

Edward was held in a minute cell. (The room known today as the King's gallery incorporates this.) He was shown little mercy by the two knights who guarded him, and he complained bitterly of the way in which he was treated to some carpenters who were working near his window. The King was a lover of music and spent his time

singing songs. The air in his room was foul, for putrid carcasses were piled up in the dungeon below in an attempt to asphyxiate him. But the stench, the cold, the damp and the incessant noise which prevented him from sleeping, broke neither his spirit nor his body, and after six months the Queen and Mortimer lost patience.

T. D. Fosbroke put together what he could find out about the King's violent end. He was apparently asleep when his murderers burst into the room, and 'they surprised him, and throwing over him large and heavy feather-beds more than fifteen strong men could carry, partly suffocated and partly burned his entrails'. The shrieks of pain were heard by the townspeople of Berkeley, and prayers were hurriedly said for the repose of the King's soul.

By the time the King's death was examined at an enquiry Thomas, Lord Berkeley, had provided himself with an alibi. He swore that he was some

The King's gallery where Edward II was imprisoned and later murdered. The room was greatly enlarged in the early part of this century but it still gives a strong feeling of a prison cell. The furniture dates from a later period, and during the King's imprisonment would have been spartan in the extreme, though we know he at least had a bed because he was smothered in it.

miles from Berkeley and not only ill but delirious. Smyth was able to show from the household records that this alibi was a fabrication. Fosbroke sums up Smyth's conclusions. 'Lord Berkeley was not sick at Bradley,' he wrote, 'when the King was murdered … nor had he lost his memory, for he sent Gurney the regicide at the very time with letters of the King's death to the Queen and Mortimer at Nottingham Castle.'

Family tradition rather naturally exonerates Thomas, Lord Berkeley, from any role in the imprisonment and death of the King, other than as a host to the prisoner and his jailers. But this is hard to believe in the light of what Smyth tells us. Christopher Marlowe refers to Lord Berkeley in his play *Edward II* as a man of pity. The evidence

suggests that Lord Berkeley has been fortunate; his good name survived intact in his own lifetime as has his reputation in legend and literature. At the enquiry he was acquitted of every fault except negligence, and at no time did Edward III bear him ill-will as his father's captor.

Thomas, 8th Lord Berkeley, is known as Thomas 'the Ritch'. He owned well over seventy-five important manors and is described as a 'landmongre'. He lived in great state at Berkeley Castle and is largely responsible for the building as it stands today. He was first and foremost a soldier. As a very young man he fought against Edward II at the Battle of Boroughbridge and was taken prisoner.

Lord Berkeley's military career prospered. He

became Marshal of the English Army in France in 1342 and later Captain of the Scottish Marches.

He lived in the castle with a 'traine' of about 300 attendants. He had twelve knights drawn from the principal families in Gloucestershire, and as each knight had two servants and a page and there were in addition at least twenty-four squires, with a servant and page apiece, it will be seen how this almost exclusively male household was built up.

He managed his estates with great care. He kept all his farms in hand which was necessary considering the number of people he had to feed. His steward's minutely detailed accounts show the enormous amounts of beef, mutton and pork produced and consumed at Berkeley in his time, together with vast quantities of eggs. One of his pigeon-houses alone provided over a thousand birds for the table in a year. He grew excellent fruit. He was proud of the pears grown on his estate, which were a rarity at the time, and pears were the best present he could think of to take to his mother-in-law at Ludlow. When he journeyed to Scotland, he took nine lamprey pies for the Queen.

Smyth has much to say about Lord Berkeley's love of sport. Jousting, hunting and falconry were his great favourites. So fond was he of hunting that as children he and his brother would spend days and nights on end in the countryside around Berkeley with their hounds, lying in wait for foxes. 'And with this delight of hunting this Lord began and dyed,' he wrote, an epitaph which would serve for many of the Berkeley family over the ages.

Lord Berkeley also found time to extend his castle. He carried out some alterations just before his marriage, presumably to make it more comfortable, but in about 1340 he began to rebuild the great hall, giving it the appearance it has today (the screen is a replacement). The great hall at Berkeley is thus contemporary with the Baron's hall at Penshurst, but very different in feeling and construction.

The Penshurst roof soars to an apex whereas the Berkeley timbers are placed in a curious saddle-like shape. There is a tradition that the roof was extensively repaired in 1497, so it is possible that it was altered at this time. Whatever its original appearance, it is certain that Lord Berkeley favoured a conservative style, and did not think of employing royal craftsmen as Sir John Pulteney most probably did at Penshurst. He also built the massive rectangular tower to the north-west which is known as the Thorpe Tower.

Some years after the death of his first wife in 1337, Lord Berkeley remarried. His bride, Katherine Le Veel, was a rich widow 'fruitfull to her husband both in lands and children'. She presents a striking contrast to Joan de Ferrers, wife of the

6th Lord Berkeley, for we do not hear of Katherine spending her time working on her husband's farms. Her interests were wider, and she is remembered today as the founder of the grammar school at Wotton-under-Edge. Perhaps her husband encouraged her. Years before their marriage, someone had induced Lord Berkeley to make a grant of £5 a year to one William de Stinchcomb, 'an hopefull Scholler'.

Katherine's effigy in alabaster in Berkeley Church gives us another clue to her personality. She was evidently interested in clothes, for under her mantle she is wearing a corset – then the height of fashion – to accentuate her long, slim waist. Beside her lies her husband. He predeceased her by twenty-four years. After his death she went on a

Frederick Augustus, 5th Earl of Berkeley, 1745–1810, by Pompeo Batoni.

The long drawing-room, photographed from under the King's pew, which was formerly in the chapel. The depth of the window recess on the left gives an idea of the thickness of the castle walls. The portrait above the chimney-piece is of Mary Cole, daughter of a Gloucestershire butcher and wife of the 5th Earl of Berkeley, by Hoppner. The room was described as the 'eating-room' in 1811, and the 'great dining-room' about 1600.

pilgrimage abroad, as a mark of her devotion, obtaining a royal licence to travel for a year. Unfortunately we do not know where she went.

Thomas was succeeded by his son Maurice, 9th Lord Berkeley. Maurice 'the Valiant' fought at 'the feirce and cruell battle of Poitiers' where he was badly wounded and taken prisoner. He was ransomed, but his wounds were so severe that he could not be brought home for four years. He never recovered, and died in 1368 at the age of thirty-seven. We know that among his more peaceable activities he planted a vineyard at Berkeley and maintained a vessel which traded with France, exchanging corn and wool for wine.

Thomas, 10th Lord Berkeley, 'the Magnificent', was also a warrior in the family tradition. He entertained Richard II at Berkeley Castle and was one of the Regents of the Kingdom in 1416. He employed as his chaplain at Berkeley a Cornish-man, John Trevisa, who was a distinguished scholar and one of the earliest masters of English prose. Lord Berkeley's patronage enabled him to translate many important works from Latin into English. Trevisa remained at Berkeley until his death in 1412.

The death of the 10th Lord in 1417 brings to a close what one writer has called 'the heroic age' of Berkeley. The 10th Lord left no son, and the estates which had been so carefully built up by the preceding generations became subject to endless wrangling and legal disputes.

As we make a great jump forward to the end of the eighteenth century in our account of the family at Berkeley, it is only fair to add that in the intervening years many members of the family distinguished themselves. The martial arts were not neglected. Thomas Berkeley fought valiantly at the Battle of Flodden. In the seventeenth and

The 'great state'. The bed belonged to James I and the head-piece is carved with his arms. The walls are covered in Cordova leather bought by the 8th Earl of Berkeley in the 1920s.

eighteenth centuries, the Berkeleys appear to have switched their allegiance from the land to the sea, for the marine paintings in the picture gallery at the castle depict ships commanded by members of the family, and the painting by Gainsborough in the Great Hall is of Admiral Sir George Cranfield Berkeley.

Two Berkeleys became colonial governors of Virginia; and the philosopher George Berkeley, Bishop of Cloyne, was a benefactor of Yale and Harvard and ultimately, years after his death, of the University of California.

Several members of the family were rewarded for their support of the Stuarts. In 1658 John Berkeley was made Lord Berkeley of Stratton. He built Berkeley House in Piccadilly in the midst of a twenty-acre garden. This land was developed in later years, and became one of the great Mayfair estates; it remained in the hands of the family until

1919. A kinsman of Lord Berkeley of Stratton was created Earl of Berkeley in 1679.

Legal disputes play a large part in the history of the Berkeley family. The root of the trouble was generally a lack of male heirs. But it was not the lack of sons which bothered the 5th Earl and his wife – for they had eight – but the question of their legitimacy. This exercised their minds for years and resulted in the notorious Berkeley Peerage Case of 1811.

The story of Mary Cole, the Gloucestershire butcher's daughter who after many vicissitudes became the wife of the 5th Earl, has been told with great affection by Hope Costley-White in a book published in 1961 which did much to redeem Mary's reputation among the descendants of her Gloucestershire neighbours. Mary's portrait by Hoppner hangs in the place of honour in the long drawing-room at Berkeley Castle. Her remarkable history begins in a familiar way. The 5th Lord Berkeley caught sight of Mary in Gloucester; he was smitten by her beauty and charm and pursued her to London. He was at that time the Lord Lieutenant of Gloucestershire, nearing forty, indolent, dissipated, and disinclined to marry. Mary was eighteen, sober, industrious and bent on the preservation of her virtue. She resisted his demands, but Lord Berkeley was infatuated and arranged to have her kidnapped. He proposed marriage, she accepted and in 1785 a secret ceremony took place at dawn in the Parish Church at Berkeley; the vicar officiated, for he was willing to fall in with Lord Berkeley's wishes, but the ceremony itself was a humbug. Mary was not of course aware that it was so.

At the end of the following year, Mary gave birth to a son who was given the names William Fitzhardinge Berkeley.

Lord Berkeley was delighted, and installed Mary and the child in his house at Cranford, the family dower-house near Hounslow. Mary's love for her first-born, Fitz as he was known, became a passion.

As 'Miss Tudor', Mary ran the two family establishments, Cranford during the summer months and Berkeley Castle where they moved for the hunting season. She gave birth to six more children. Mary supervised their upbringing with meticulous care, even to the extent – as the House of Lords were told during the trial – of deciding herself when the children should cast their winter clothes and put on their summer ones.

The castle and estates at Berkeley had suffered from years of neglect. Mary began to ride around the estate and note what needed attention, there were gates and fences to repair, and buildings to put in order. She sat in the family pew in Berkeley Church, but her position was equivocal. Although she was on the best of terms with her tenants, the county did not call, and when members of the family stayed, they did not bring their wives.

Lord Berkeley was devoted to Mary but from time to time he was unfaithful and on several occasions he threatened to throw her out. But he accepted her authority. On one occasion his butler Boniface, who had been with him for sixteen years, lost his temper with Mary; Lord Berkeley dismissed him instantly. Mary became aware that her 'marriage' at Berkeley Parish Church was a charade, and for some years she pressed Lord Berkeley to marry her. He vacillated, for there were no means by which he could secure the whole inheritance for their beloved Fitz. But Mary was insistent and in 1796 she succeeded. She was pregnant once more. The ceremony took place in Lambeth Parish Church. No one was informed, but the wily governess at Berkeley noticed that the

sempstress was busily engaged removing an embroidered 'T' (for Tudor) from Mary's under-clothes and replacing it with a 'B' and a coronet. In October Thomas Moreton Berkeley was born. He was, of course, legitimate.

The question of the inheritance was now uppermost in the minds of Lord and Lady Berkeley and so great was their concern for their favourite that they decided upon an extraordinary plan of action. With the co-operation of the pliant Vicar of Berkeley, they forged an entry in the parish register; their 'marriage' of 1785 was now recorded.

Fitz was accepted by everyone as the heir. He was known as Viscount Dursley, and his coming-of-age was celebrated with a large party at Berkeley Castle in the presence of the Duke of Clarence. The great hall was decorated with five thousand coloured lamps; four hogsheads of strong beer were drunk by the tenants, and forty gallons of punch consumed by the dancers.

Lord Berkeley died in 1810. Fitz was left Berkeley Castle, Cranford and the great Mayfair estate which had passed to his father in 1803 under the will of the last Lord Berkeley of Stratton. Fitz applied for a writ of summons to the House of Lords so that he could take his seat. For four months in 1811 the Committee of Privileges investigated his case, the past was raked over in merciless detail, Mary was examined, witnesses were produced from the days of her first encounters with Lord Berkeley. London was agog at the revelations.

The Committee rejected the claim. Fitz and those siblings born before the Lambeth marriage were declared illegitimate. Fitz returned to Berkeley. Mary settled at Cranford and, brave, determined, stubborn woman that she was, continued to fight on his behalf until her death in 1844. She had chosen to close her eyes to her son's defects. He was known as Colonel Berkeley, and Charles Greville went so far as to describe him as 'an arrant blackguard'.

The Colonel divided his time between his castle, the Berkeley kennels and the Cheltenham stage. Mrs Arbuthnot saw him act in *King John.* 'His great pleasure seems to be to act the sort of King of Cheltenham,' she wrote in her journal, 'where all the vulgar Misses make a great piece of work with him.' His brother Grantley was considered an even greater cad by his contemporaries.

Colonel Berkeley rendered certain services to the Whig party, and after his successful efforts to secure the return of no less than four of his brothers to the House of Commons, he was given an earldom in 1841 by Lord Melbourne. It was barter, pure and simple; he chose the title FitzHardinge. The Colonel died in 1857, a

bachelor, and was succeeded by his next il-legitimate brother, Maurice. After the death of Maurice's nephew in 1916, the castle and the earldom were reunited in the person of Randal, 8th Earl of Berkeley, a descendant of the 5th Earl's younger brother. In 1891, Randal Berkeley successfully claimed the earldom which had been in abeyance since the 5th Earl's death in 1810. The Lord FitzHardinge of the time made one last attempt to prove that the 5th Earl and Mary Cole were legally married in 1785, but the Lord Chancellor was not amused by the ludicrous waste of legal time and effort.

Randal, 8th Earl of Berkeley, scientist, autocrat, misanthrope, entered upon his inheritance with a millstone of debt round his neck. This was not due to profligacy, but to his boundless enthusiasms, some of which were expensive. After early years at sea, he settled at Oxford and built himself a laboratory on Boar's Hill where he proceeded to conduct experiments in osmosis which led to his election as a Fellow of the Royal Society. For some years before he inherited the Berkeley estates he had borrowed money, and when he came into his inheritance his creditors forced him to sell the great Mayfair property. In 1919, the date of sale, this comprised twenty acres centred on Berkeley Square, and included most of the houses in the square and the freehold of the garden, practi-cally all Bruton Street, Bruton Place and Audley Square, and much of Farm Street and Charles Street. Lord Berkeley is believed to have received about £2,000,000. He spent a considerable pro-portion of the sum on the restoration of Berkeley Castle.

All his prodigious energy was channelled into various enterprises which were entered into with great passion and then dropped. Golf was one, hunting another. He hunted for four seasons after he took over at Berkeley and then gradually lost interest. The mania for building, however, lasted all his life. He spent years restoring the mediaeval character of the castle, and imported a screen for the great hall from Wales, fireplaces from France, stone window-surrounds, doorways: after a winter abroad, he would return with a trainload of purchases. He introduced heating, lighting and comfortable bathrooms. And every bill and every receipt connected with this work he destroyed.

Inevitably he was criticized for what he did. The architectural historians accused him of not employing experts and of destroying evidence, the archivists complained that he would not allow them to look at the Berkeley manuscripts, the local people thought he neglected them, for he had no interest in Gloucestershire affairs, and questions were asked in the House of Commons about his treatment of his tenants. Lord Berkeley turned his back on them all. 'I loathe humanity,' he told his second wife, Molly, and in the pages of her book of reminiscences *Beaded Bubbles* published in 1967, the 8th Earl of Berkeley comes alive.

Molly Berkeley was his second wife. She married him in 1924 and soon realized what she had undertaken. 'This man is divine,' she decided after a stormy scene in the dining-room of the Ritz at Madrid, 'but may take a bit of handling.' Molly Berkeley was a Bostonian. Her father was a Lowell and she had not *one* but *two* Cabot great-grandmothers. She was well equipped to cope with Lord Berkeley's moods, the formality of English life, the prejudices she found. She loved it all: her weekend house-parties, the beautiful swimming-pool Lord Berkeley built for her on the terrace below the castle, the bathroom they brought from the old Waldorf Astoria, Lord Berkeley's chauffeur-valet Lowe who adored his master and always walked behind him with the palms of his hands turned backwards out of respect.

'Fill the house with your friends,' Lord Berkeley had told her, 'I haven't any.' When Molly Berkeley woke up in the morning and thought that she was going mad, she had only to look down at the old man with his donkey which passed beneath her window each morning pulling the castle rubbish-cart painted in the Berkeley colours (yellow with green stripes), to restore herself to sanity.

When Lord Berkeley died in 1942, the most the local paper could find to say about him was that he sometimes presided at the rent audit dinners of his estate. He left Berkeley Castle, in excellent shape, to his kinsman Captain R. G. W. Berkeley whose son, Mr John Berkeley, is the present owner.

Randal, 8th Earl of Berkeley, 1865–1942, by Sir William Orpen. Lord Berkeley disliked this portrait of himself so much that he tried to prevent Orpen exhibiting it at the Royal Academy.

William, 1st Viscount De L'Isle is steeped in the history of Penshurst and the Sidney family. He has done much to restore the house since the war, and is now at work on a grand scheme to enlarge the gardens which have been famous since the early seventeenth century.

Lord De L'Isle was Secretary of State for Air 1951–5, and Governor-General of Australia 1961–5, and has been Chairman of the Freedom Association since its foundation in 1975.

'Your ancestor Robert Sidney became Viscount Lisle in the seventeenth century. You became Lord de L'Isle and Dudley after the death of your father and you are now Viscount De L'Isle. Will you explain the history of these titles?'

'The Lisle viscountcy died out with the last Earl of Leicester in 1743. My great-great-grandfather, Sir John Shelley-Sidney, was granted a baronetcy in 1818. And then his son Philip married the eldest natural daughter of the Duke of Clarence and the actress Mrs Jordan. After the Duke had become William IV, his daughter badgered him to give her husband a peerage. It was not easy but eventually he became Lord De L'Isle and Dudley in 1835. I inherited the barony and the baronetcy from my father, and was created Viscount De L'Isle in 1956.'

'There is one impression which the visitor carries away from Penshurst, and that is the good shape the building is in.'

'Thanks to my grandfather! And Aunt Adelaide who inherited a coal-mine. My grandfather restored the house, the paintings, the furniture. He had excellent taste, and worked with George Devey as his architect. He redesigned the gardens. He bankrupted himself, and at the end of his life his housekeeper said she would give up her pension for him. In 1910 my eldest uncle Philip had the roof of the Baron's hall carefully restored, and my Uncle Algernon continued the work after the First World War by restoring the long gallery. And of course we must mention Lady Albemarle. She was John Shelley-Sidney's sister-in-law, and when he suggested demolishing the Baron's Hall, she told him he could pull it down around her ears. We owe her a lot.'

'Were you born here?'

'No, in Chelsea. My father was a barrister and concerned in local politics in London.'

'What are your first memories of the house?'

'My uncle Philip lived here for four months in the year and then spent the other eight in Yorkshire. We were here as children. I remember coming here in June 1914. My sister and I were given strawberries by the head-gardener, Mr Bridger, who wore a large straw hat and was then in his eighties. I didn't realize until later that his father had been head-gardener before him. He would have known my great-great-grandfather – a link with the eighteenth century.'

'When did you come to live here?'

'My uncle Algernon died in April 1945. We moved in five months later. Three flying-bombs had landed about a quarter of a mile away and brought down the ceilings and shattered all the windows.'

'Had your uncles modernized the house?'

'Yes, electric light and hot water were introduced in the early 1920s but the kitchens needed attention. My uncle Algernon was a bachelor, ninety-one when he died. He lived in the state dining-room during the war and kept going with a butler, chauffeur and housemaids.'

'Do you mind the public in your house?'

'Not a bit. We are fairly well protected in this wing. We opened seventy years ago at a shilling a head, but people visited the house throughout the eighteenth century. The first Visitors' Book by the way is dated 1818.'

'The deer park here has always been famous. Is the estate a large one?'

'The maximum was probably about 4400 acres in the nineteenth century. It is just under 3000 now, and farmed by my son.'

'Another Philip Sidney.'

'Yes. And in 1986 it is the four-hundredth anniversary of the death of Sir Philip Sidney.'

Penshurst Place, the south front and gardens.

Penshurst Place

KENT

The Viscount De L'Isle VC, KG, GCMG, GCVO, PC

In 1752, Horace Walpole made a pilgrimage to Penshurst. He went in a spirit of reverence to visit a shrine, the birthplace of Sir Philip Sidney and the childhood home of Dorothy, Countess of Sunderland, the poet Waller's 'Sacharissa'. He was disappointed. The park looked forlorn, the grand apartments were furnished in 'a tawdry modern taste' and the family portraits 'seem christened by chance, like children at a foundling hospital'.

Penshurst was then in the possession of Elizabeth Perry, a niece of the 5th, 6th and 7th earls of Leicester, and the last member of the Sidney family in the direct line to own the house. She inherited in 1743 from the 7th Earl whose extravagance and negligence had greatly impoverished the estate. Elizabeth married William Perry, a rich, vulgar man with antiquarian tastes, whose measure we can gauge from the enormous painting he commissioned in 1752 from David

Luders of himself, his wife and his five children which now hangs in Queen Elizabeth's room. Perry sits, evidently well pleased with his lot, his waistcoat straining at the buttons, showing off not only his own family and Penshurst Place which appears in the background, but also his wife's ancestors. Four of the most distinguished are depicted in grey monochrome as garden statues, ghostly spectators of the bourgeois scene. The sash windows and other 'improvements' Perry introduced throughout the mediaeval house have been painstakingly removed by later generations.

Elizabeth Perry was not improvident. She was beset with lawsuits which were not of her own making, and the financial difficulties which forced her to neglect Penshurst were due almost entirely to muddleheadedness. Many of the rooms had been stripped of their treasures long before she took over, the library and the contents of the

The Baron's hall, built by Sir John de Pulteney about 1340. It measures 62 feet × 39 feet and its magnificent roof rises some 60 feet above the ground. The worn tiled floor and central octagonal hearth are probably original. The smoke rose to the roof and escaped through a vent. Sir Philip Sidney's funeral helm surmounted by a porcupine crest is preserved on the table at the far end, and the trestle tables to the left and right date from the middle of the fifteenth century. The hall is one of the finest surviving examples of the work of fourteenth-century craftsmen.

armoury had been dispersed, and paintings, prints, drawings and sculpture had disappeared to the London auction rooms.

In the long years of Elizabeth Perry's widowhood and during the minority of her grandson, Sir John Shelley-Sidney (the great-great-grandfather of the present Lord De L'Isle), Penshurst reached the nadir of its fortunes. The house had become a romantic ruin, a place at which to picnic on an afternoon's excursion from Tunbridge Wells.

But Penshurst was more than the sum of its remains. The legend of Sir Philip Sidney, poet, man of learning, and warrior, drew visitors to the house from far and wide, for the brilliance of his star, which so dazzled his contemporaries, had not diminished. Whigs came to Penshurst to pay tribute to their hero, Algernon Sidney, who was executed for treason in 1683, and lesser mortals to muse perhaps on the beauty of Sacharissa.

Three members of the Sidney family presided over the fortunes of Penshurst before the decline: Sir Henry Sidney, KG, who inherited the house in 1554 and died, worn out in the royal service, in 1586; Sir Robert Sidney, 1st Earl of Leicester, KG, who inherited the house from his brother, Sir Philip, and died in 1626; and Robert Sidney, 2nd Earl of Leicester, who died in 1677.

The Manor of Penshurst had been granted in 1552 to Sir William Sidney by Edward VI, the boy-king, whom Sir William had served faithfully as tutor, steward and chamberlain.

The house and the Sidney family are so inextricably linked it is easy to forget that the house was over two hundred years old before the family settled there. The building is not monastic in origin as Longleat or Syon, but secular: the builder, Sir John de Pulteney, was a merchant with a princely fortune derived from successful finan-

Above: The entrance porch of the original fourteenth-century house which leads into the Baron's hall, from beneath the King's tower and across the inner courtyard.

Left: The house from the south-west.

cial speculations. Pulteney bought the Penshurst estate in 1337 and began to build the house in the local sandstone, rich in colour and streaked with reddish brown. The core of Pulteney's house, the Baron's hall, was a symbol of his enormous worldly success; the roof of chestnut timbers rises sixty feet above the tiled floor and may well have been the work of the king's carpenter.

Pulteney's retinue of family and retainers probably numbered between one and two hundred people. It is easy to imagine them seated at long tables in this hall, Pulteney himself at the centre of a table raised on a platform at one end.

He did not live to enjoy his house for he died, a victim of the Black Death, in 1349. Penshurst was altered and enlarged by various owners after Pulteney, so that the house Sir William Sidney received from his grateful sovereign in 1552 was a well fortified manor house. Sidney died in 1554; his son, Sir Henry Sidney, transformed Penshurst into a palace, not in the innovative manner of great Elizabethan builders such as Sir John Thynne of Longleat, but in the familiar, old-fashioned style of his predecessors.

Sir Henry's place in the affections of Edward VI made him an influential figure at court and led to his marriage with Lady Mary Dudley, eldest daughter of the powerful John Dudley, Earl of Warwick (later, Duke of Northumberland), and sister of Robert Dudley, Earl of Leicester, the favourite of Queen Elizabeth.

He was present at the death of Edward VI in 1553, but as a shrewd and cautious statesman he retreated to Penshurst, and avoided the machinations of his father-in-law in his attempt to place Lady Jane Grey on the throne. The Duke and Lady Jane and her husband, Guildford Dudley, who were respectively Mary Sidney's father, sister-in-law and brother, were executed.

The air of despondency which must have hung over Penshurst lifted in the following year, 1554, when Lady Mary gave birth to a son. Sir Henry had pledged his loyalty to Queen Mary and the King of Spain stood godfather to the child, bestowing on him the name of Philip.

More children were born to the Sidneys over the years: Robert, Thomas, and a daughter, Mary, who later became the Countess of Pembroke and a distinguished patron of the arts. To Mary, Philip addressed his *Arcadia* and Robert a volume of manuscript verse which has recently come to light.

Sir Henry's career prospered. He was appointed Lord President of the Marches of Wales in 1559, a position he held for life, and he served twice as Lord Deputy of Ireland between 1565–71 and 1575–8.

His wife remained with her children at Penshurst or at their official residence, Ludlow Castle.

In 1562, she helped to nurse Queen Elizabeth through smallpox and caught the disease herself. She was greatly disfigured and became a recluse, hiding her face from 'curious eyes'. Philip cherished the memory of his mother; after her death he wrote, 'that, for his own part, he had had nothing but light from her.'

We know that Sir Henry was an indulgent husband and father from his meticulous accounts; no difference was made by the Receivers General who kept them for him between public and private expenditure, so that the solemn expenses of state business are listed beside entries such as:

To your Lordship to play at Tables with my lady, which your lordship lost and gave to her, 20s.

Charges and expenses – Riding charges, hawks, surgery, alms, lost in play (*total*, £13.13s.4d, *including* by Mr. Philip at the Tenys, 3s. 4d.).

Edging your daughter's gown with seventeen white lambskins, 6s.8d.

One entry reveals Sir Henry's efforts to establish his family's antiquity. We learn that he spent £6 on a pedigree which was concocted at his request by the herald Robert Cooke. The true ancestor of the Sidney family, a Surrey yeoman of the late thirteenth century, was evidently not of sufficient distinction. Cooke evolved a long line of Sidney knights dating back to the reign of King John; some of the documents he used to forge this descent are still preserved by the Sidneys.

Lady Mary had a yearly allowance of £300. Sir Henry himself paid for some of her dresses such as the velvet dress with petticoats and kirtle which cost £17 in 1574, a modest enough sum. She was evidently a hypochondriac. Her bills for drugs came regularly to £40 or £50 a year. One account shows that she bought:

rose water (a pint)   1s.
carraway comforts   8d.
A sartayne cordiall water
stilled with goat's milk,
ginger, pistacks, pines,
and bitter allmons and divers
other things   £1.6s.8d.
A sartayne potion to
provoke rest   16d.

Sir Henry was an amiable character. Fulke Greville described him as 'a man of excellent natural wit, large heart and sweet conversation'. He was devoted to his children. Just after Philip was sent to Shrewsbury to school his father wrote him a letter, the first he had ever sent his son. 'Marke the sence and matter of that you doo reade as well as the words,' he wrote, 'so shall you both enrich your tongue with wordes, and your wit with matter, & judgement will grow, as yeares groweth in you.'

Robert was eight years younger than his brother Philip; his father urged him to 'imitate his virtues, exercises, studies and actions.' Sir Henry's accounts throw some light on Robert's childhood. At the age of nine, he was given crimson satin stockings and purple canvas breeches which cost 10s, a bow and arrows (2s), and a book for his Latin exercises (1s 4d). At the age of ten, in 1575, he followed his elder brother to Christ Church, Oxford.

Supper cost him 8d, his battels for the first quarter amounting to £4 11s 10d. His clothes were sumptuous. His brother Philip gave him a velvet hat with a gold band and white and blue feathers as a Christmas present in 1576. He had an assortment of hats, doublets of white satin and carnation satin, a French cloak of black velvet and a Spanish cape of black satin. When he came down from Oxford, his possessions, mostly clothes and books, weighed 35 cwt and cost 35s to transport to London.

From an early age the children had allowances though these were constantly exceeded. Sir Henry thought well of his sons as the estimate he made of them as young men demonstrates. Philip he described as 'of excellent good proof', Robert 'of great good hope' and Thomas 'not to be despaired of'.

It is possible that Sir Henry had had plans in mind for Penshurst from the moment that he inherited the house. We do not know whether it was for lack of money or opportunity that he waited for twenty years before he began work. He and his father were hardly typical of the men the Tudors raised to power; while others amassed vast fortunes, the Sidney family made very little from their royal appointments. But Sir Henry had enough money to make his mark on Penshurst. From about 1573 until his death in 1586, he made extensive additions to the house. He began the state rooms for grand occasions and built or rebuilt three ranges of apartments to the north of Pulteney's Hall, for family life was beginning to assume a more intimate character. The style he chose was that of his predecessors with one notable exception. In the south front of the north range he built one of the earliest classical loggias in England. This is dated 1579. Is it fanciful to suggest the hand of his son Philip in the design? He was apparently supervising the building works at Penshurst that summer for his father, and his travels in Northern Italy would have introduced him to the architecture of the Italian Renaissance.

Sir Henry was anxious to retire to Penshurst and devote himself to his house and family. He successfully resisted his recall to Ireland. 'I am now fifty-four years of age,' he wrote, 'toothless and trembling being £5000 in debt, yea, and £30,000 worse off than I was at the time of my most dear King and master, King Edward VI.' His last three years were spent as he desired at Penshurst. He died in May 1586 and was followed three months later by Lady Mary. Mercifully, they were spared the news of the death of their son Philip in the autumn of that same year.

Philip Sidney, 'the god-like Sidney' as Ben Jonson called him, died from a wound received at the Battle of Zutphen: he was thirty-two. The story of how as he lay wounded and parched with thirst, he refused the water offered him and gave it to a dying man, has become a national legend. His body was brought back to England for burial, not to Penshurst but to St Paul's Cathedral. Seven hundred mourners followed his funeral procession and Queen and country mourned the death of a hero. Penshurst became the property of his brother.

Sir Robert Sidney was born at Penshurst in 1563 and died there in 1626: he was a soldier by profession and a courtier, a calling he found much to his taste. But he also loved Penshurst, his marriage brought him happiness, and his letters are full of lamentations about the miseries of separation and absence from home.

After Oxford, he travelled abroad, became an army officer and, in 1588, Governor of Flushing. He held this post for twenty-eight years and heartily disliked his exile.

Lady Sidney (Barbara Gamage), wife of Sir Robert Sidney (afterwards Earl of Leicester), and six of their children, by Marcus Gheeraerts the Younger, 1596. She was a great Welsh heiress.

Sir Philip Sidney, 1554–86, by an unknown artist.

At an early age, he married a great heiress from Glamorganshire, Barbara, daughter of John Gamage of Coity. They spent much of their lives apart but were devoted to each other. 'You are married, my dear Barbara,' he wrote, 'to a husband that is now drawn so into the world and the actions of it as there is no way to retire myself without trying fortune further.'

The tide of Sir Robert's fortune turned with the accession of James I in 1603. He was created Baron Sidney of Penshurst and he found favour with Queen Anne who appointed him her chamberlain. He was made a Knight of the Garter and created Viscount Lisle. In 1618, the earldom of Leicester which had been extinct since the death of his uncle was revived in his favour.

Despite his preoccupations as soldier and courtier, Sir Robert was able to carry out alterations at Penshurst. These were supervised by his wife. Her portrait by Marcus Gheeraerts the Younger shows her surrounded by six of her children. Perhaps the painter has caught in her glance something of the exacting nature we deduce from her husband's correspondence. A long series of letters has survived from Sir Robert to his 'Sweetheart' which express his affection for her and his concern when they are parted. He sent her presents, her favourite Rhenish wine for instance, and a motley selection on another occasion: 'your cotche and the picture I told you of, and your petigree and a fayre piece of parmesan.' London life was expensive and debts were always pressing. Lawrence Stone has described how quickly the

London 'season' developed in the period between 1590 and 1620. Barbara Sidney was no exception in longing for London society. 'There is no reason to leave you where you are at Penshurst without company in the winter,' her husband wrote to her. They inherited Leicester House, but Barbara's household grew to such extravagant proportions in London that her husband insisted she cut down the number of her ladies. The Penshurst servants disliked London; the steward reported that they would stay three days and then 'they steal home again'.

In the summer months it is easy to picture Barbara Sidney happily directing the work at Penshurst. She had a banqueting house in the garden and we are told by Dugdale of the delight she took in feeding the deer in the park from her own hands.

Sir Robert's steward, Rowland Whyte, kept his master informed of all that was happening at Penshurst. In 1600 he reported: 'My Lady takes great pleasure in this place, and surely I never saw a sweeter. All things fairly prospering about it. The garden is well kept.'

The garden was Sir Robert's delight. Although a garden undoubtedly existed before his time at Penshurst, the orchard was his creation. When John Evelyn attended the second marriage of Sir Robert's granddaughter, Sacharissa, at Penshurst in 1652, he described the house as 'famous once for its Gardens & excellent fruit'.

In 1604–05, Sir Robert was occupied in drawing up plans for the garden. The fruit which Barbara sent to him at court, apricots, peaches, cherries and plums, was much in demand and he distributed varieties of quince which had been sent up at his request from Penshurst by the gardener. In return, he sent home red-deer pies and salmon.

He was also an excellent poet. A recently discovered book of manuscript verse in his 'nervous and highly individual Italic' contains a collection of sonnets and other poems written for his sister but, as was customary among Elizabethan noblemen, never published.

The expenses of court life proved a heavy drain on Sir Robert's resources. The bill for his costume for the Christmas masque in 1603 came to £220. At Penshurst, he built and decorated the long gallery which the steward reported was 'reddy to be matted' in 1607. In 1611 his steward was forced to protest when Sir Robert put forward plans to enlarge and replant part of the park. He wrote frankly to Sir Robert telling him that he could not afford it: 'You have alreadye a very fair and sportelyke a park as any is in this part of England; the making of it soe hath abated £100 a yere of your living alreaddy, it is lardge enough to mayntaine 400 deer, which will afford hunting sufficient for your honourable freinds.'

Barbara died in 1621. Her son Robert and his wife came to live at Penshurst after her death, but her husband did not long outlive her, or his master King James, and died at Penshurst in 1626.

Robert, 2nd Earl of Leicester, was not a man of action and lacked the skills needed to keep afloat at a time of rapid political change. Clarendon described him as 'very conversant in books and much addicted to mathematics ... rather a speculative than a practical man'. He married in 1616 Lady Dorothy Percy, a woman of wit and beauty whose mercurial temperament was at constant odds with his own contemplative nature.

Lady Dorothy was a daughter of Henry, 9th Earl of Northumberland, the 'Wizard Earl'. She married a man who shared her father's wide interests but lacked his resolution. She evidently found this failing unforgivable. Their married life began at Penshurst where most of their children were born.

With two brief interruptions they remained in England until 1636, when Leicester was appointed Ambassador to the King of France. He took with him his eldest sons, Philip and Algernon, leaving his younger son Henry at school and his eight daughters with their mother at Penshurst.

Lady Dorothy was miserable alone. She pined for her friends, for her Percy relations and for political speculation and intrigue. She was prepared to remain in London when the plague was raging rather than return to imprisonment in the country. She and her husband quarrelled constantly about money, and she made efforts throughout their married life to gain control of his financial affairs. For a man of his literary inclinations, the fact that she mocked his 'old inclination to reading' must have been intolerable. A lively exchange of letters to and from France reveals their incompatibility. One provoked the other. In one letter Lady Dorothy regrets that the gloves she had sent him were not to his liking, in another she thanks him for pictures, a looking glass and a coffer he had sent to Penshurst 'which are all so pretie as I conclude that eather your jugement is extraordinarie good or ells thear is nothing ill in France'. She felt that he neglected her and the house. In 1639 she complained bitterly that the beds at Penshurst were 'so olde so out of fashion and so rotten as I would faine give some amendment to that decaie'. Finally, in the same year he allowed her to join him in France.

Leicester drew up a long series of complaints against his wife but decided against leaving her 'being loth to dissolve my family as a thing dishonorable and prejudiciall to my children'. Dorothy Osborne relates that after forty years of patient suffering Leicester finally turned upon his

wife: 'he has now taken up the Cudgells,' she told William Temple, 'and resolves to Venture for the mastery.'

In 1641 the family returned from France. Leicester attempted to come to terms with the political situation in England and to serve the King to whom he remained loyal. Unable to cope with the disorder of the time, he retired to Penshurst where he remained throughout the Civil War. His sons Philip and Algernon were zealous republicans; Algernon was severely wounded at the Battle of Marston Moor. Both were appointed judges for the trial of Charles I but avoided signing the death warrant, appearing unexpectedly at Penshurst and remaining there for the week during which the fate of the King was decided.

Penshurst became a refuge. Sacharissa returned to her father's house after the death of her husband, the Royalist, Lord Sunderland, at the Battle of Newbury in 1643. She was twenty-five and had been married for four years. 'I doubt not but your eyes are full of teares,' her father wrote to her when the news of Sunderland's death reached him, 'and not the emptyer for those they shed.' Sacharissa spent seven years in seclusion at Penshurst before she returned to her husband's home, Althorp. The apartment she occupied, set apart from the other family rooms, is still known as 'Lady Sunderland's Lodging'. When she was very young Edmund Waller had paid court to her at Penshurst and immortalized her beauty in the poem 'Go, lovely Rose'. Years after her death, Steele wrote: 'The fine women they show me

Dorothy Sidney ('Sacharissa'), eldest daughter of Robert, 2nd Earl of Leicester, by Sir Anthony Van Dyck. Her childhood was spent at Penshurst. Her husband, Henry, Earl of Sunderland, was killed at the battle of Newbury in 1643. The earls Spencer of Althorp descend through this marriage and Lady Dorothy is thus an ancestor of the Princess of Wales.

This life-size figure appears to support the massive moulded wall-plates of the roof of the Baron's hall. The timbers and the figures are constructed of chestnut rather than oak which is more usual. The figure has lost both his legs and the stone corbel on which he stood.

nowadays are at best but pretty girls to me, who have seen Sacharissa, when all the world repeated the poems she inspired.'

When Sacharissa was at Penshurst, Charles I's children Henry, Duke of Gloucester, and Princess Elizabeth were placed under the guardianship of her mother. They arrived in June 1649 a few months after their father's execution. Parliament ordered that the children should be treated during their stay at Penshurst without ceremony and should sit at table as children of the family. As far as we know, their visit was as agreeable as their pathetic circumstances would allow. They remained just over a year, and were then transferred to Carisbrooke Castle on the Isle of Wight where the little princess died.

Algernon withdrew to Penshurst after he had broken with Cromwell and did not return to public life until after the Protector's death. After a long period of exile on the continent, he returned to bid farewell to his father. Leicester died in 1677. In 1683 Algernon was arrested, convicted of complicity in the Rye House plot and executed on Tower Hill. His portrait by Justus van Egmont shows the stern, uncompromising republican he remained to the end of his life. His brother Philip succeeded their father as 3rd Earl of Leicester, and although he received a general pardon at the Restoration, his political ideals remained unchanged. We catch a glimpse of him in the memoirs of Lord Ailesbury as an old man out of sympathy with the politics of the time, refusing to be drawn on the dreams of his youth.

His youngest brother Henry, on the other hand, was one of the six signatories to the letter summoning William of Orange to seize the throne

The long gallery, completed about 1607 by Sir Robert Sidney (later Earl of Leicester), the brother of Sir Philip. This was restored by the 4th Lord de l'Isle in the mid 1920s. He removed the chocolate paint from the panelling and put up the plaster ceiling adorned with Sidney emblems.

from James II and was created Earl of Romney in 1694.

The history of Penshurst in the eighteenth century as we have seen was one of decline, the nineteenth century one of slow revival. The architect John Biagio Rebecca created for Sir John Shelley-Sidney the private apartments which are still used by the family. George Devey carried out sensitive restoration of the mediaeval part for the 1st and 2nd Lords De L'Isle. Crace reconstructed the library in 1870.

Penshurst has grown over a period of 600 years; few houses owe more to the characters of successive owners.

The private apartments created by John Biagio Rebecca in the north and west ranges for Sir John Shelley-Sidney between 1818 and 1830.

Henry, 6th Marquess of Bath, is the founder of the 'stately homes business' in Britain, for Longleat was the first house in the country to be opened on a regular commercial basis. Many of his fellow peers and other country-house owners were quick to criticize or mock his efforts. Lord Bath was never discouraged by them, quite the contrary, and before long he was amused by the rush to follow suit. Lord Bath has devoted his life to restoring and maintaining Longleat.

'Were you brought up at Longleat?'

'Yes, I lived here during the school holidays. There were seven of us. My parents, elder brother and three sisters. When I was eleven in 1916 I was told that my brother had been killed and that I would one day inherit Longleat. It came as rather a shock. But even at that age I loved the house dearly.'

'And you don't live here any more?'

'I haven't since I was twenty-one. I married and moved away and now have a house four miles away. I knew if I did move back it would have been into a corner. Longleat's great days were over. My father lost heart after my mother's death in 1927 and entertained less and less; he kept the house up – the roof for instance – but he did very little to the inside. During the war the Royal School moved here from Bath. When I took over the house needed so much doing to it and the park was in a shocking state. My eldest son lives in part of the house now.'

'How much time do you spend at Longleat?'

'I come to the house every day but forestry is my particular interest and I spend half my time in the woods. We have about 5000 acres of woodland here and run it as a business. Trees are my hobby.'

'And the approach to Longleat through the woods must be one of the most beautiful to any house in England. When did you decide to open Longleat to the public?'

'As soon as I inherited the house from my father in 1947. My sister had had some success opening Longleat to visitors for charity, and there is a long tradition in this country of housekeepers showing houses to visitors. So we decided to develop that and to remain open permanently, on a commercial basis, every day of the year except Christmas Day. We opened in April 1949, to much criticism, charging 2s 6d for a ticket, half price for children. The night watchman's wife ran a small café in the basement of the west wing and the family helped with car parking.'

'How many visitors did you have through the house in the first year and what is the greatest number you have had since?'

'We had 135,000 in 1949 and 320,000 in 1972 but numbers have dropped back. In 1981 for instance 150,000 toured the house. Attendance had begun to level off in the 1960s so when Jimmy Chipperfield suggested a safari park in the grounds of Longleat, I realized almost at once that was the answer. We became partners and the Lions of Longleat Safari Park opened in 1966. The publicity was world-wide, it was a great success, and we've extended it twice since then.'

Longleat from the east, with the lete from which the house derives its name in the foreground.

Longleat House

WARMINSTER, WILTSHIRE

The Marquess of Bath ED

John Thynne made his own fortune. As a young man he seized the opportunity to leave his father's Shropshire farm and head for London where his uncle William Thynne was clerk of the kitchen to Henry VIII. He made good use of his uncle's introductions and before long had gravitated towards the household of the powerful Earl of Hertford. For better or worse John Thynne attached himself to Hertford; he served him as steward, and remained in his service after Hertford became Duke of Somerset and Protector during the minority of Edward VI. Thynne accompanied the Duke on his Scottish campaign, and was knighted after the battle of Pinkie in 1547. Two years later when Somerset was arrested, Thynne was thrown into the Tower. He was released, only to find himself imprisoned again two years later. When Somerset died on the scaffold, Thynne extricated himself from his difficulties and retired to the country; he had learnt his lesson. He was now in a position to work for himself, for in the years he had served Somerset he had let no opportunity to enrich himself pass by. He was acquisitive by nature and bought extensive monastic lands, woods, farmland, orchards and houses, carefully noting down the details of each purchase in a large ledger. But the property he prized above all others was the tumbled-down Wiltshire priory of the Augustinian canons at Lange-lete which he had bought for £53 from Sir John Horsey in 1540. By the time Thynne died in 1580, he owned 6000 acres and bequeathed to his family the finest Elizabethan house in England.

John Thynne was twenty-five in 1540. Eight years later he made a most advantageous marriage with Christian, daughter of Sir Richard Gresham, Lord Mayor of London, and half-sister of Thomas Gresham, who later built the Royal Exchange. How was it possible that this ambitious, cunning, pugnacious acquisitor could have built a house of such startling originality as Longleat? As the Duke's steward, Thynne would have supervised his master's extensive building works which included the construction of Somerset House; and it appears probable that Thynne's own interest – which later became a passion – was kindled at this time. For in 1546 he appointed his own steward and began to build on the site of the priory at Longleat. At that time he was almost certainly in charge of his own building works. The house burnt to the ground in 1567 and with great courage and determination John Thynne began again. By the end of the year a new model was prepared and by 1572 the façades had been planned. Thynne decided to build in the finest Bath stone and bought a quarry to ensure a constant supply. When Queen Elizabeth announced – much to

The great hall. This is the one room at Longleat which retains its original Elizabethan character. The set of sporting paintings is by John Wootton, about 1740, and includes portraits of the 2nd Lord Weymouth and other members of the hunt. In each picture appears the young stable boy, an orphan found in the Longleat woods who was killed aged fourteen separating the two fighting stallions depicted on the right. The fireplace dates from about 1600.

The state drawing-room. This shows the Italian decoration added by
J.D. Crace and the 4th Marquess of Bath in the 1870s with some of Lord Bath's
collection of Italian old masters which includes a Titian, seen to the right
of the door, the centre one of three smaller paintings under a cassone panel. The
sixteenth-century frieze was bought by Lord Bath from a palace in Venice and
most of the furniture is French eighteenth-century.

Sir John Thynne, the builder of Longleat,
in 1566, by an unknown painter.

Thynne's dismay – that she intended to visit him in 1575, the house had reached the level of the second floor. Thynne had been experimenting by that time for nearly thirty years and, for the second stage of his building, had the assistance of a young man who was later to play a very considerable role in English architecture, Robert Smythson. Sir John Summerson refers to the French mason, Allen Maynard, who was employed by Thynne on the earlier house but who also worked with Smythson on the design of the new. 'The ordenanse thereof,' wrote Smythson, 'came from us.' But Thynne's own contribution to the design of his great palace – one of the 'prodigy' houses of Elizabeth's reign – cannot be underestimated.

For twenty years, from the time of his appointment in 1546, John Dodd served John Thynne as steward. In his history of Longleat, David Burnett describes the thanklessness of his task. Thynne was a bully and interfered at every stage, he wanted in his own words, 'a pennyworth for a ha'penny'; the unfortunate Dodd was accused of the theft of lead and timber, the labourers who began work at five in the morning and finished at seven at night were ordered to cut their meal-breaks, the masons were told to work on through the winter. Nothing was accomplished fast enough; David Burnett pictures the scene as Thynne rampaged around his unfinished house, his spaniels, Quail and Ludlow, most probably at his heels; his gimlet eye penetrated every nook and cranny for no detail was too small to escape his attention. 'If I shall find any fault with the workmanship or seasoning of the stuff,' he wrote to Dodd about the preparation of timber for some new doors, 'it shall be made again.' John Thynne was a perfectionist.

In Thynne's extensive correspondence, David Burnett found only two instances where a spark of humanity enlivens a letter; the second occasion was a letter of congratulation to his wife, Christian, at the birth of a son and was accompanied by a request to make certain that his heir did not catch cold.

By 1562 Thynne's household at Longleat numbered fifty-six and included a cook, a gardener, a falconer and huntsmen. Thynne had established himself as a West Country landowner by that time, for he had become MP for Wiltshire in 1559 and served as high sheriff of the county, although his long-established neighbours eyed him with mistrust, contempt and envy. One local peer forced Thynne to account to the Privy Council for his great accumulation of riches. Was it treasure trove, or 'indirect means', his enemies wondered? Industry, frugality and marriage, answered Thynne, and 'a good master the Duke of Somerset'. In 1572, Thynne and his second wife,

Dorothy Wroughton, another Lord Mayor's daughter, moved back into Longleat five years after its destruction by fire. The great hall, the long gallery, kitchen, parlours and bedrooms were finished and Thynne was able to spend the last eight years of his life surrounded by his enormous family directing the army of joiners, glaziers, masons, plumbers and bricklayers who numbered some 112 in all. By the time of his death in 1580, he had spent £8016 13s 8¼d on his palace of Longleat.

Thus John Thynne created one of the great monuments of the Elizabethan age, perhaps the greatest, Sir John Summerson suggests. And, strangely enough, he laid the foundations of the library at Longleat. His uncle William Thynne began the family tradition of book collecting. He had a passion for the works of Chaucer; one manuscript at Longleat which contains four poems by Chaucer is inscribed in faded ink with the name of William Thynne 'Clerke of the Kechin'. From 1566 books appear in John Thynne's household accounts, and by 1577 he listed eighty-five items in his library, a sizeable collection by the standards of that time. We know he kept these books in his 'closett' which was probably a small room adjoining his bedroom. John Thynne's descendants added to his collection, and the books at Longleat today fill seven or eight large libraries and form the greatest collection in private hands in the country.

When Sir Thomas Thynne unexpectedly succeeded his cousin 'Tom O' Ten Thousand' after his brutal murder by Count Königsmark in 1682, Charles II granted him a viscountcy, and as 1st Viscount Weymouth he presided over Longleat's fortunes for a period of thirty-two years. He was a highly intelligent man: his tutor William Burton was an antiquary who bequeathed him some of his books and manuscripts, and, at Oxford, he was a friend of Thomas Ken who lived at Longleat for many years after he was deprived of his bishopric.

Thomas Weymouth had joined the household of the Duke of York at the Restoration and was sent as ambassador to Sweden in 1666. In 1672 he married Lady Frances Finch, daughter of the 2nd Earl of Winchilsea, who inherited extensive estates in Ireland.

As soon as Thomas Weymouth had established his claim to the Longleat estate towards the end of 1682, he set out with Frances and two small children one winter's day to take possession of his inheritance. The distance from London to Longleat is one hundred miles but the journey took them three miserable days sitting cramped and frozen in a hired coach which had wooden shutters instead of windows. When they arrived Longleat presented a sorry spectacle. It was cold, damp, neglected – and empty – for Tom Thynne had bequeathed the furniture to his brother-in-law. Thomas and Frances may have succumbed to depression that winter, but they did not despair, and by the spring of 1683 Longleat was a hive of industry. Thomas appointed Thomas Allen as steward and plans were drawn up to modernize the house, add fireplaces and a new kitchen, and to make urgent repairs to the roof. Frances organized her household; she engaged maids, footmen, a butler named Brotherton, and a 'boy at the back door' who doubled as a chimney sweep. She even designed a livery for her staff: muslin caps and printed chintz dresses for the maids and mustard-yellow coats and black waistcoats with silver trimmings for the footmen.

In later years, Thomas made some alterations to the structure of the house. He had the battlements 'new railed and balustraded' and he also added the stone statues of Alexander the Great, Henry V, Boadicea and the other figures he deemed appropriate who still decorate Longleat's skyline. His removal of the mullioned windows in the long gallery had a definite purpose, for he wished to obtain a better view of the magnificent garden he created. Alas! no trace of Thomas Weymouth's garden survives, but an engraving made by Leonard Knyff in 1704 gives us some idea of its ordered beauty.

Between 1683 and the end of the century Thomas Weymouth spent £30,000 on the construction of this vast garden which covered an area of seventy acres. The indefatigable Thomas Allen supervised the army of labourers who were employed moving earth, digging, widening the leat with a formal canal, and building the wall which stretched for miles round the perimeter. The garden was designed and stocked by a man supplied by George London who was a partner in the Brompton Nurseries near London, and Thomas Thynne entered into an agreement by which the Brompton Nurseries continued to plant and maintain the garden until 1694.

Thomas Weymouth made his garden to the east of the house. A terrace 215 yards long was constructed, from which steps led down into embroidered parterres bounded by hedges or trees and, at the far end, the elaborate canal system; there were also a wilderness, bowling-green and labyrinth, extensive orchards with fruit trees arranged like soldiers on a parade ground, and beyond, a grove planted with beech and chestnut to form rides which converge at a central point which terminates a great axial avenue. The elaborate waterworks were Thomas Weymouth's especial delight and included a cascade and fountains linked by hundreds of yards of hand-bored alder pipes. The gardens could be viewed from the house or the terrace, or from the hills to

the east and from all view-points must have presented a delightful spectacle. Some distance from the house Thomas Weymouth made an eleven-acre kitchen garden where the formality was retained: 'the very gooseberry and currant bushes . . . drilled to grow in squares or parallelograms, trimmed up as stiff and stately as lords and ladies at the court of the Hague.'

Thomas Weymouth was also a bibliophile and some of his booksellers' bills are preserved at Longleat together with many of the books he collected. In his account of the great library at Longleat, John Collins refers to a bill of 1693 which shows that Thomas rearranged his library and had 995 volumes lettered on their spines (at 12s a hundred) to enable him to identify them readily; for early books were not lettered but either kept flat or placed on shelves with their spines at the back and the edges of the pages outwards. He bought books at auction and one elaborate bill shows a large number of very early printed books obtained on his behalf in Venice.

Thomas Ken took refuge at Longleat with his own great library after he had been deprived of his bishopric for refusing to take the oath to William and Mary. Thomas Weymouth gave his old friend rooms at the top of the house which are preserved as he left them, and 'in that retirement he lived, wrote hymns, sang them to his viol, prayed, and died'. Thomas also filled the house with treasures of all kinds, tapestries, furniture, clocks, silver, paintings and glass. His brother, Henry Frederick Thynne, visited him in 1689, and was delighted by all he saw. 'The condition of the house,' he wrote, was 'so excellent it makes my mouth water.'

One day in June 1685 when Thomas Weymouth was in London to sit for his portrait, Frances received alarming news at Longleat. The Duke of Monmouth, the illegitimate son of Charles II and Lucy Walters, had landed at Lyme Regis and was marching through the West Country towards London. He had attracted an army of 5000 and had been proclaimed king at Taunton. Frances was terrified, she was alone with Thomas Allen and a few servants, and feared for Longleat's safety and her own, for one of Monmouth's officers, Captain Kidd, had been a steward and a gamekeeper at Longleat and he knew that the armoury was well stocked. Brotherton, the butler, hurriedly packed up two chests of silver and plate and took them to Salisbury, and some of the labourers in the garden downed tools and left to join the rebel army. 'I believe Myles the warrener is gone over to the rebels,' Allen wrote to his master, 'I can never find him at house of late.'

Eventually Frances could bear the suspense no longer and, with her daughter and a maid, she set off for Salisbury herself, escorted by armed

The bath was installed by the 3rd Marchioness in 1840 and was in constant use by the 5th Marquess up to the time of his death in 1946.

keepers and a groom. The faithful and imperturbable Thomas Allen remained at Longleat. He went to Frome to catch a glimpse of Monmouth himself and heard the local militia toast the Duke's health in Warminster. He rounded up the horses and sent them off to Gloucestershire for safety and waited for the rebels to appear at Longleat. He had already made up his mind, when the rap was heard at the front door, that he would surrender the keys of the armoury if threatened with death. But instead of the large armed band he expected on the doorstep

he came face to face with two soldiers, whose somewhat imprecise demands were swiftly drowned by Lord Weymouth's claret. News arrived that Monmouth was on the march with his army, and later Allen heard rumours that they had encamped at King's Sedgemoor on an outlying part of the Longleat estate. Allen worried about the hay, for the lives lost on that battlefield as the rebels' hopes were smashed were not after all his concern.

Thomas Weymouth outlived his three brothers, his two sons and his wife, Frances. He lived on at

Below: Katherine Lyte-Howard. She married Sir Thomas Thynne, grandson of the builder, in 1613. She was a wicked stepmother, and made life very difficult for her stepson after he inherited Longleat.

Above: The 4th Marquess of Bath by Sir George Richmond. He succeeded at the age of eight and later devoted himself to transforming the interior of Longleat in the Italian style. He was a great picture collector and with his wife Frances made yearly visits to Italy.

Longleat, crippled by gout, until one day in 1714 he died in his bedroom and was succeeded by his great-nephew, Thomas, who alas allowed weeds to grow in the garden and the roof to leak.

The profligate Thomas, 2nd Lord Weymouth, was succeeded by his son, another Thomas who came into the Longleat estate when he was twenty-one in 1754. The house was in a pitiful state and the contents mortgaged. Old Lord Weymouth's garden, so dearly prized, was lost beyond recall – the walls had collapsed, the fountains had been smashed – and, in 1757, 'Capability' Brown arrived to sweep away the bones. Three years later Mrs Delany found no evidence at all of the old gardens. 'They are succeeded by a fine lawn,' she wrote, 'a serpentine river, wooded hills, gravel meandering round a shrubbery, all modernized by the much sought-after Mr Brown.' Brown's work at Longleat, which included levelling the meadows round the house and making a ha-ha half a mile long, cost Thomas £8000. Apart from various emendations made by Humphry Repton in the time of the 2nd Marquess of Bath, the landscape we see today at Longleat is Brown's creation.

The saloon. This was originally the long gallery of the Elizabethan house, transformed out of all recognition by the 4th Marquess in the style of the Italian Renaissance. The coffered ceiling is copied from an original in Rome and the marble fireplace is a replica of one in the Palazzo Ducale in Venice. The tapestries on the left are late sixteenth-century Brussels and depict scenes from the life of Cyrus, the conqueror of Babylon, and the liberator of the Jews.

When Alexander, 4th Marquess of Bath, succeeded to Longleat in 1852, the estate had been so carefully nursed by his mother that the family finances were in an unprecedented state of good health. David Burnett gives an idea of this prosperity which increased through the first decades of his long reign at Longleat until by 1883 his annual income totalled £68,000. This figure included annual profits of £5000 from a lead mine on the Shropshire estate, and substantial amounts from the Irish land; it also reflected the steadily increasing rents from the middle of the century in England and the flourishing state of agriculture. And then the prosperity began to wither as the great depression overtook every landed estate in the country and Alexander was forced to sell the Irish estates and at one moment to think of closing

Longleat and going to live in London. He had no capital reserves because he had spent his income. Most of it had gone on the embellishment of Longleat, for he was a noted collector of works of art and a bibliophile. After his marriage in 1861 to Frances Vesey, daughter of Lord de Vesci, he visited Italy on numerous occasions with her and always returned with some new acquisitions. His most considerable undertaking was the remodelling of the state rooms at Longleat.

This decoration was undertaken by J. D. Crace and carried out by a team of his craftsmen who worked under the direction of the Clerk of the Works, Mr Buckinham. Every detail was planned and supervised by Alexander in consultation with Crace. For thirteen years he lavished attention on these intricate decorations, travelling to Italy probably once a year to seek inspiration and to collect more paintings and works of art. From his first visit to Italy on his Grand Tour, he had fallen for the art and architecture of sixteenth-century Venice. 'I am fully convinced that for two hundred and seventy years there has been nothing original that has been really good,' he wrote to Crace in 1874, 'except perhaps some of the Adams and such like works.' The correspondence shows that Crace had great respect for Alexander and that the partnership was harmonious. He paid numerous visits to Longleat. 'Lord Bath has made no alterations with anything since you left,' wrote one of the workmen to Crace, with feeling, no doubt.

The remodelling of the state drawing-room was begun in 1873. The paintings on the ceiling were copied at Alexander's request by a Venetian from paintings in the library of San Marco in Venice. The frieze which arrived at Longleat in 1874 depicts stories from the life of Circe and was removed from a Venetian palace; the chimney-piece is sixteenth-century Italian and carved in Istrian stone with the upper storey and the accessories added by Crace; he also mounted and arranged the door dressings which Alexander obtained from a dealer, and designed the curtains, much of the furniture and details such as the damascened steel lock-plates and handles. The carpet was made at Wilton and the design taken from a Persian example in the Victoria and Albert Museum. 'I have had great pressure put on me to have the Drawing room carpet all of one color,' Alexander wrote to Crace, 'but I have resisted it, I may proved to be wrong but am at present strongly of opinion that a Persian pattern such as we have decided on will be the right thing.' It was later dyed green.

The saloon – the old Elizabethan long gallery – is dominated by the enormous coffered ceiling derived from one in the Palazzo Massimi in Rome, also a large white marble chimney-piece which Alexander had copied in Venice from an original in the Palazzo Ducale in Venice. Alexander bought the Brussels tapestries depicting the history of Cyrus and the pilasters, but the original curtains with appliqué embroidered borders were designed and made by Crace.

And thus Alexander worked round the house room by room until in September 1882 Crace's last bill arrived. The interior of Longleat had been transformed out of all recognition.

The life led in these rooms was as sumptuous as the decoration. Longleat's staff towards the end of the nineteenth century consisted of fifty indoor servants, thirty gardeners, fifty farm workers, fourteen grooms and coachmen, fifty woodmen, twenty gamekeepers and fifty labourers under the direction of the Clerk of the Works.

Domestic life at Longleat did not change much over the years. The 3rd Marchioness installed a bath in 1840 and the 5th Marquess electricity in 1928.

Daphne Fielding, the first wife of the present Lord Bath, gives an account in her book *Mercury Presides* of the rigid hierarchy which existed at this time below stairs. The head butler, the cook, the lady's maid, the valets and the groom of the chamber would eat their evening meal as upper servants, in the steward's room, at a table which was presided over by the house steward and the housekeeper, and they would have tea in her sitting-room; the liveried servants and the under maids had their meals in the servants' hall under the eye of the second butler and the head laundry maid. A visiting servant was accorded the rank of his or her master or mistress: a duke's valet would arm in the housekeeper to dinner in the steward's room and be seated at her right; a royal lady's maid entered with the steward. A visiting upper servant who neglected to bring evening dress was sent to eat in the servants' hall.

At the midday meal, the under servants would file into the servants' hall and stand by their places until the upper servants entered in order of rank and were seated. As soon as the joint, which was carved by the steward, was eaten, the remainder was removed by the steward's-room footman who carried it out, followed by the upper servants who then retired to the steward's room for the remainder of the meal.

At Christmas time a ball was given in the dining-room for servants and local tradesmen who dealt with the house. Lord Bath invariably opened the ball with the housekeeper and Lady Bath danced with the steward, and this was followed by the lancers. When Daphne Fielding attended the ball for the first time as the wife of the son of the house, the butler partnered her for the opening dance and the head groom for the lancers.

Gradually this life began to diminish in the 1920s and 1930s, and World War II swept away every vestige of it at Longleat. The present Lord Bath succeeded in 1947; the difficulties of maintaining this great Elizabethan house seemed almost insurmountable. In April 1949 he opened Longleat to the public and, as Humphry Repton wrote in 1803, 'This magnificent estate, so far from being 'locked up to exclude mankind from partaking of its scenery, is always open, and visitors are allowed freely to amuse themselves, which circumstance tends to enliven the scene, to extend a more general knowledge of its beauty to strangers; and to mark the liberality of the noble proprietor, in thus deigning to share with others the good he enjoys.'

Lionel, 6th Lord Sackville lives in the private apartments at Knole. His father was a younger brother of the 3rd and 4th Barons and he maintains the tradition of an unbroken family occupation of the house since his ancestor, the 1st Earl of Dorset, established himself at Knole in the first few years of the seventeenth century.

'When did you come to live here?'

'My uncle – the General – offered my wife and me a cottage on the estate. I was working in London and we came down for weekends. After he died in 1962 we moved into the north side of the house – the old guest bedrooms – while the National Trust restored the south side of the house. We had to wait four years and then there were only two bedrooms in this side so we had to make some more in the attic.'

'What are your earliest memories of Knole?'

'I remember as a child how terrified I was sleeping in the north wing, and feeling abandoned when my parents went over to join the other grown-ups for dinner. All I could hear was the plod of the night-watchman's feet.'

'Was it inevitable that Knole passed to the National Trust?'

'Every occupier of the house since Mortimer, 1st Lord of Sackville, said it would be impossible for any future member of the family to live here. We were all sad but we accepted it as inevitable. Yes. Of course in those days, it was possible to negotiate a very good arrangement with the Trust. The Trust is responsible for the upkeep of the entire structure for instance.'

'What is left in family hands now?'

'The estate – and the park which covers 1000 acres – but so much land has gone over the years. My brother Hugh manages this side; he is agent for the family and the National Trust. We still own the paintings and some of the silver – that in the King's room for instance.'

'You don't manage any of it yourself?'

'No. I was a commuter until 1965. After Oxford I joined Jardine Matheson and then after the war I began at Lloyds.'

'Your immediate predecessor Edward, Lord Sackville, is an intriguing figure, his biography of Thomas de Quincey is written with such sympathy, but it is impossible not to think of that superb portrait of him by Graham Sutherland which Benedict Nicolson called "this magnificent image of controlled distress".'

'Yes, a very remarkable man, a musician and a conversationalist too. But Eddie never felt strongly about the house. He didn't want the responsibility. His father – the General – set him up in a flat in the tower but he was very unhappy there in the thirties. His American stepmother had been an actress and gave very smart parties.'

'There was no passion for Knole comparable with Vita Sackville-West's?'

'No. Vita never came here publicly after the death of her father in 1928 until we invited her to a lunch party about 1960, and she came. But she hated the changes which had been made. Nigel Nicolson says that she had a key to the garden which the General gave her.'

'You are fairly well insulated from the public here. Do you mind so many people so near?'

'I made a concession and allowed the public to come into our private garden once a week on Wednesday afternoons. The garden is in fact owned by the National Trust and I make a contribution to its upkeep but it has never been open before. The lawn comes right up to the windows. I'll tell you what I call the public days – black Wednesdays.'

Knole: the garden front. The chapel is on the extreme right, and the middle window of the bay to the immediate left was Vita Sackville-West's bedroom.

Knole

SEVENOAKS, KENT

The National Trust:
The Lord Sackville

Knole is the creation of two men, Thomas Bourchier and Thomas Sackville. Bourchier acquired the estate in 1456 and built the original mediaeval palace; Sackville humanized his predecessor's work a century and a half later, and added the great series of state rooms. Both had reached the pinnacles of worldly success when they came to Knole, for Bourchier was Lord Chancellor and Archbishop of Canterbury, and Sackville – created 1st Earl of Dorset in 1604 – was Lord High Treasurer; they were men of peace, and lovers of music and learning, Chancellors of the University of Oxford, rich beyond dreams, and far above the competition for place and patronage. The serenity of old age which Knole acquired so young probably owes as much to these two men as to later generations of the Sackville family who cherished what they found and did not feel the need for change.

As long ago as 1673 John Evelyn described Knole as 'A greate old fashiond house', and in the following century Walpole spoke of its 'faded splendour'. Today, the richness of Thomas Sackville's decoration is a little more sombre, and the silk velvets, the damasks, the silver spangles on the crimson satin, the cloth of gold and the russet fringes are duller than when Walpole saw them. But nothing very much has happened at Knole to disturb the venerable atmosphere, for this was respected in the eighteenth and nineteenth centuries, and jealously guarded in the twentieth.

Bourchier spent much time at Knole during the thirty years he owned it. He enclosed the park, and built on the site of an old house the fortified mansion of grey Kentish ragstone whose outlines survive today. First impressions of Knole give no idea of its size, for it is very large, more of a village than a house when viewed from the north, and grouped round 7 courtyards, with, as legend has it, 365 rooms and 52 staircases to correspond to the days in the week, and the days and weeks in the year.

At his death, Bourchier bequeathed Knole to the See of Canterbury, and it remained in the possession of the archbishops until Cranmer was persuaded to give it up to Henry VIII. Queen Elizabeth gave Knole to Thomas Sackville in 1566, but, as the house was let, he did not gain possession until 1603.

The Norman family of Sackville was based from about 1200 at Withyam in East Sussex. The main branch is still there, and other members of the family scattered far and wide, including those at Knole, have returned to be buried in the parish church by the window whose inscription proclaims with pride and certainty: 'The noble family of the Sackvilles here await the Resurrection.'

Thomas Sackville was born with two great advantages: his father, Sir Richard Sackville, an astute lawyer known as 'Fill-sack', had raised the family from the rank of Sussex gentry to a position of considerable national power; and he was a

The entrance front.

The inner wicket or gatehouse tower built by Archbishop Bourchier in about 1460. The tower to the right led to the apartments of Madame Baccelli, mistress of the 3rd Duke of Dorset. It was called 'Shelley's Tower' by the Knole servants who were unable to pronounce her name.

cousin of Queen Elizabeth, for his grandmother was a Boleyn. He was a few years younger than the Queen; he served her faithfully throughout her life, and died in the service of her successor.

As a very young man he wrote poetry, and he fills an honourable position in English literature between Chaucer and Shakespeare, for as a law student he wrote part of *Gorboduc* – the first respectable tragedy in the English language – which was produced in 1561 at the Christmas Revels in the Inner Temple. Thomas Sackville soon abandoned such frivolities, and turned his attention to politics. His father died in 1566, leaving him a princely fortune, and in the following year the Queen made him Lord Buckhurst of Buckhurst. For most of his life he enjoyed the royal favour; he was a man of tact and patience who could be entrusted with foreign embassies, and he was even given the melancholy task of telling Mary, Queen of Scots, that she had been condemned to death. In 1599 he succeeded Lord Burghley as Lord High Treasurer of England, a position he held for life, and in 1602 was made Lord High Steward. He was created 1st Earl of Dorset by James I in 1604. About this time he was ordered to put a tax on tobacco which the King felt

was a great evil, and a drug whose use must be discouraged for 'the Healthe of a great nomber of our People is impayred and their bodies weakened and made unfit for Labour'. The tax was raised from twopence a pound to 6s 8d, a rise which no Chancellor of the Exchequer has ever dared to equal.

The portrait at Knole depicts him, sage and inscrutable, clutching his white wand of office, the insignia of the Order of the Garter alone enlivening his sober dress. His private chaplain spoke at his funeral in Westminster Abbey of his service to the Queen and of 'the continuall, and excessive paines, and care which his Lordship did take in her business, his fidelitie in his advices, his dexterity in advancing of her profit'. And his will gives an idea of the immense fortune he built up in land, houses and precious objects. He was also happily married, for he speaks of his wife Cicely with more feeling than the conventions called for, and described her after fifty years of marriage as 'my most vertuous, faythfull, and dearly beloved wife'.

There is evidence to show that Thomas Sackville personally lived a life of extreme modesty, but the surroundings he created at Knole

The great staircase.

were certainly sumptuous. His household numbered over two hundred and included the musicians of whom he spoke in his will, 'some for the voice and some for the Instrument ... who have often given me, after the labors and paynefull travells of the day, much recreation and contentacon with theire delightfull harmony'.

The Venetian Secretary in England reported to the Doge and Senate that Thomas Sackville and the other great ministers of the crown lived 'like so many Kings'. The vestiges of this splendour can be seen in the state rooms Sackville created at Knole between 1603 and 1608. When he turned his attention to the old mediaeval palace he did not destroy the exterior, but to soften the severity of the plain, grey walls he built gables, and added finials, to embellish their gentle curves. He also put

in mullioned windows and much fine lead-work. On one side of the second great courtyard he built a graceful colonnade with an open gallery above, which is seen now, as in the past, by all visitors as they pass through into Bourchier's hall. Beyond this hall whose timbers Thomas Sackville hid behind a plaster ceiling, is the great staircase painted in yellowish-green, grey and white by Paul Isaacson who worked for Queen Elizabeth at Greenwich Palace. A visitor in the early seventeenth century would have been startled by the novelty of this decoration, particularly the illusory effect of the painting of some of the balusters and moulded plasterwork, but even more surprising was the idea of a staircase confined in one room. This makes a grand approach to the principal state room – the great dining-room – which is now known as the ballroom. Here the frieze of the painted oak panelling is alive with mermen and mermaids, winged horses and other fantastic creatures, and the plasterwork is decorated with flowers. The magnificent chimney-piece of alabaster and variegated marbles is the work of the royal master mason, Cornelius Cuer. In the past this room was a combination of presence chamber and dining-room, and of all the state rooms is the only one which was in regular use up to World War I. Bourchier would have eaten at a high table in the great hall with his attendants and retired to this room afterwards; Thomas Sackville evidently used it as a dining-room, and did not eat with his household except on special occasions.

Sackville also created in that short space of time before his death in 1608 the brown gallery, the Leicester gallery, the magnificent ninety-foot long cartoon gallery and some of the bedrooms. It is estimated that he spent between £10,000 and £15,000 on Knole in the last three years of his life. By the end of 1607 the accounts for plaster, glass, nails and other materials of this sort, give way to items such as twenty-six yards of yellow and white damask which he bought at 13s a yard, and twenty-two pieces of gilt leather hangings at £3 2s 6d a piece.

Thomas Sackville was very conscious of the fact that he was creating a dynasty. The heirlooms he left in his will to his successors, the 100 white silver vessels, the ring given him by the King of Spain with 'a great Table Dyamonde being perfect and pure and of much worth', the insignia of the Order of the Garter, the miniature of Queen Elizabeth in agate set with rubies, all of which he lists so carefully, were to form a reminder to his heirs of their benefactor 'by whose greate travell, care and industry they receive greate honour and possessions'.

The old man took infinite pains over the education of his little grandson, Richard, who was born in 1588. Richard became 3rd Earl of Dorset in 1609 when he was just twenty-one, for his father hardly outlived his grandfather and just as soon as the young man could lay his hands on his grandfather's money, he began to spend and then to squander his inheritance in riotous and extravagant living. He loved to tilt, to bowl, to go cock-fighting and horse-racing, to play for high stakes and to give sumptuous entertainments; he adored fine clothes and women. According to John Aubrey his name was linked with that of Venetia Stanley, 'a most beautiful desirable creature ... sanguine and tractable, and of much suavity', and he was a bosom friend of Henry, Prince of Wales. Clarendon writes of his 'excess of expenditure' which was evidently notorious and to pay his enormous debts he sold his lands, the

London estate and almost Knole itself. By the time he died in 1624 at the age of thirty-five there was little of Thomas Sackville's great inheritance left for his successor. As for his wife, however hard he tried, however impossible he made life for her, whoever he ranged against her from the King downwards, he was unable to force her to give up her claim to her father's estates in the north, which would have provided him with another fortune to scatter.

Richard Sackville married Lady Anne Clifford when he was twenty and she nineteen. Her father George Clifford, 3rd Earl of Cumberland, was an Elizabethan buccaneer who combed the seas for treasure. His family estates in Cumberland and Westmorland were immense, and when he died he left a will which provoked endless lawsuits. Lady Anne fought for her share, but not for her husband to spend. He begged and bullied her to settle the dispute over the land with her uncle, they met, fought, made up and separated again. On one

Detail of a wall-bracket in the ballroom.

occasion she sent back her wedding ring, and on another he took away their daughter.

Lady Anne was a little dour and melancholy, but of decided character. She kept careful accounts, and would ask her secretary to copy out texts and maxims culled from her voluminous reading which she pinned up inside the curtains of her bed. She was singularly unfitted to be the wife of Richard Sackville although she always speaks of her moody, pleasure-loving husband with affection and respect. For, apart from his dissipations, he was a patron of writers, and a friend of John Donne and Henry King. And some of his letters to Lady Anne suggest that – but for the question of her lands – they would have lived together tolerably happily.

Vita Sackville-West, who edited Lady Anne's

Right: The great staircase.
This was built by the 1st Earl
of Dorset between 1605 and
1608. The Sackville leopards
recur throughout the
decoration at Knole. The
lady reclining on her couch is
Madame Giannetta Baccelli,
the Italian dancer who lived
at Knole for many years with
the 3rd Duke of Dorset.

Above: Charles, 6th Earl of
Dorset, by Sir Godfrey
Kneller, painted about
1690–95. He was a notorious
libertine in his youth but was
a great patron of the arts and
invited many men of letters
to Knole.

Far right: John Frederick,
3rd Duke of Dorset, by Sir
Joshua Reynolds. The Duke
was Ambassador in Paris
during 1783–8. He had a
passion for opera and ballet
and was a patron of
Reynolds and other painters.
He also employed
professional cricketers who
played on the famous Vine
cricket ground at Sevenoaks.

diary, tells how she quarrelled with everyone, with
her second husband Lord Pembroke, her servants,
the tradesmen and the tenants. Her marriages took
her to Knole and Wilton, 'oftentimes but the gay
arbours of anguish'; but only in her second
widowhood did she return to her own broad acres
and achieve great happiness and contentment as a
matriarch of the north. She restored her castles in
Westmorland, and entertained her numerous
grandchildren. She would set forth on progresses
with a retinue of 300 and sit on the bench with the
judges as the hereditary High Sheriff. She survived
until 1676, when she died at the age of eighty-six
and the memory of her is (or was until recently)
strong, for Vita Sackville-West tells the delightful
story in *Knole and the Sackvilles* of how the offer
of electric light to the almshouses in Appleby in
1956 was turned down on the grounds that Lady
Anne would not have approved.

How she must have disliked the 'fruitful and

tender' countryside of Kent after the dales and fells of her own wild north! From her diary we gain a vivid picture of her at Knole, she plays cards with the steward, she gathers cherries and makes rosemary cake, she talks with the French page who tells her that all the men in the house love her, and she keeps an account of all that happens to her daughter Margaret 'the child', who was put into whalebone corsets at the age of two and three-quarters.

Lady Anne was evidently not interested in dress, but she made efforts for her husband's sake and altered two of her dresses – one of sea-water green satin and another of damask embroidered with green – to accord with French fashion. There are also many details of life at Knole such as the removal in early April from 'the little room' where they supped and dined in the winter, to the great chamber, but nothing evokes the atmosphere of Knole in Lady Anne's time more vividly than the list of attendants and retainers.

Of the Household and Family of the Right Honourable Richard Earl of Dorset in the year of our Lord 1613; and so continued until the year 1624, at Knole, in Kent.

At My Lord's Table
My Lord My Lady
My Lady Margaret My Lady Isabella
Mr Sackville Mr Frost
John Musgrave Thomas Garret

At the Parlour Table
Mrs Field Mrs Willoughby
Mrs Grimsditch Mrs Stewkly
Mrs Fletcher Mrs Wood
Mr Dupper, *Chaplain*
Mr Matthew Caldicott, *my Lord's favourite*
Mr Edward Legge, *Steward*
Mr Peter Basket, *Gentleman of the Horse*
Mr Marsh, *Attendant on my Lady*
Mr Wooldridge
Mr Cheyney
Mr Duck, *Page*
Mr Josiah Cooper, *a Frenchman, Page*
Mr John Belgrave, *Page*
Mr Billingsley
Mr Graverner, *Gentleman Usher*
Mr Marshall *Auditor*
Mr Edwards, *Secretary*
Mr Drake, *Attendant*

At the Clerks' Table
Edward Fulks and John Edwards, *Clerks of the Kitchen*
Edward Care, *Master Cook*

William Smith, *Yeoman of the Buttery*
Henry Keble, *Yeoman of the Pantry*
John Michall, *Pastryman*
Thomas Vinson, *Cook*
John Elnor, *Cook*
Ralph Hussey, *Cook*
John Avery, *Usher of the Hall*
Robert Elnor, *Slaughterman*
Benjamin Staples, *Groom of the Great Chamber*
Thomas Petley, *Brewer*
William Turner, *Baker*
Francis Steeling, *Gardener*
Richard Wicking, *Gardener*
Thomas Clements, *Under Brewer*
Samuel Vans, *Caterer*
Edward Small, *Groom of the Wardrobe*
Samuel Souther, *Under Baker*
Lowy, *a French boy*

The Nursery
Nurse Carpenter Widow Ben
Jane Sisley Dorothy Pickenden

At the Long Table in the Hall
Robert Care, *Attendant on my Lord*
Mr Gray, *Attendant likewise*
Mr Roger Cook, *Attendant on my Lady Margaret*
Mr Adam Bradford, *Barber*
Mr John Guy, *Groom of my Lord's Bedchamber*
Walter Comestone, *Attendant on my Lady*
Edward Lane, *Scrivener*
Mr Thomas Poor, *Yeoman of the Wardrobe*
Mr Thomas Leonard, *Master Huntsman*
Mr Woodgate, *Yeoman of the Great Chamber*
John Hall, *Falconer*
James Flennel, *Yeoman of the Granary*
Rawlinson, *Armourer*
Moses Shonk, *Coachman*
Anthony Ashby, *Groom of the Great Horse*
Griffin Edwards, *Groom of my Lady's Horse*
Francis Turner, *Groom of the Great Horse*
William Grymes, *Groom of the Great Horse*
Acton Curvett, *Chief Footman*
James Loveall, *Footman*
Sampson Ashley, *Footman*
William Petley *Footman*
Nicholas James, *Footman*
Paschal Beard, *Footman*
Elias Thomas, *Footman*
Henry Spencer, *Farrier*
Edward Goodsall
John Sant, *the Steward's Man*
Ralph Wise, *Groom of the Stables*
Thomas Petley, *Under Farrier*
John Stephens, *the Chaplain's Man*
John Haite, *Groom for the Stranger's Horse*
Thomas Giles, *Groom of the Stables*

The cartoon gallery. This is named after the set of copies of Raphael's tapestry cartoons which were presented by Charles I to Lionel, 1st Earl of Middlesex, and brought to Knole by his grandson, the 6th Earl of Dorset. The chimney-piece is another example of the work of Cornelius Cuer. The gallery is ninety feet in length and the floor is formed from oak trees split in half with the rounded sides underneath.

Richard Thomas, *Groom of the Hall*
Christopher Wood, *Groom of the Pantry*
George Owen, *Huntsman*
George Vigeon, *Huntsman*
Thomas Grittan, *Groom of the Buttery*
Solomon, *the Bird-catcher*
Richard Thornton, *the Coachman's Man*
Richard Pickenden, *Postilion*
William Roberts, *Groom*
The Armourer's Man
Ralph Wise, *his Servant*
John Swift, *the Porter's Man*
John Atkins
Clement Doory   *Men to carry wood*

The Laundry-maids' Table
Mrs Judith Simpton
Mrs Grace Simpton
Penelope Tutty, *the Lady Margaret's Maid*

Anne Mills, *Dairy-maid*
Prudence Bucher
Anne Howse
Faith Husband
Elinor Thompson
Goodwife Burton
Grace Robinson, *a Blackamoor*
Goodwife Small
William Lewis, *Porter*
    Kitchen and Scullery
Diggory Dyer
Marfidy Snipt
John Watson
Thomas Harman
Thomas Johnson
John Morockoe, *a Blackamoor*

Richard, Lord Dorset, was succeeded by his brother who became the 4th Earl. He supported the Royal cause and fought at the Battle of

Edgehill while his wife was for a time governess to the Royal children. The Parliamentarian troops sacked Knole in 1642. They were looking for arms, but they also broke about forty locks, and stole twelve long cushion-cases embroidered with satin and gold, and the plumes from Lord Dorset's bed. In 1645 the Parliamentary commissioners were installed in the house, and much else was stolen. This was not the end of Lord and Lady Dorset's suffering, for their eldest son, Lord Buckhurst, was taken prisoner near Oxford and murdered by a soldier shortly afterwards at Abingdon. Lord Dorset himself died in 1652.

In the next generation, some of the depredations suffered by Knole during the Civil War were made good, for the 5th Earl of Dorset married a great heiress, Lady Frances Cranfield, who inherited the estates of her father the Earl of Middlesex, treasurer to James I. Much of the fine furniture now at Knole, with tapestries, good paintings and other treasures, was brought by the wagon-load from Copt Hall, the Cranfield family house in Essex.

Their son Charles became 6th Earl of Dorset on the death of his father in 1677. Lord Buckhurst, as he was known during the wild years of his youth, weaves his vinous way through the memoirs of the Restoration period. He was a rake, his tastes depraved and licentious, and his drunken escapades ended in horse-play, riot and even murder. And yet he was a poet, the author of the charming song *To all you ladies now at land* (he was at sea) and the friend and patron of literary men, for his rake's progress was punctuated from time to time by munificent gestures.

'My grandfather Charles, commonly called the witty Earl of Dorset,' wrote a descendant, with feeling, 'was during his whole life the patron of men of genius and the dupe of women ... Bountiful beyond measure to both.'

Lord Buckhurst was about twenty when Charles II returned from exile, and for ten years he was a ring-leader in wild scenes and orgies, protected from any untoward consequences by his sovereign's friendship.

Pepys gives the lurid details (expurgated by all but the latest editors of his diary), of one drinking bout in 1663 which ended in a riot at the Cock Tavern in Bow Street, London. This was a favourite haunt of the rakes, run by a woman known as 'Oxford Kate'. Buckhurst and his cronies, the poet Sir Charles Sedley and Sir Thomas Ogle, ended up at this tavern one day and Sedley, aided and abetted by the others, lurched on to the balcony, stripped off his clothes, and 'acting all the postures of lust and buggery that could be imagined' proceeded to draw a crowd of spectators. They stood below, stunned by the sight of

further lewd actions (specified by Pepys), accompanied by a stream of profane and obscene language so gross that the crowd, unable to bear this performance any longer, stormed the building. Sedley was hauled in front of the Lord Chief Justice and fined £500 for riot, but Buckhurst sheltered behind the throne.

At the age of twenty-five Buckhurst fell in love with Nell Gwyn who was then seventeen and an actress at Drury Lane. How John Evelyn disapproved of the Restoration theatre, and the actresses who appeared on stage for the first time! He specifically mentions Buckhurst 'who fell into their snares, to the ... ruine both of body & Soule'. Buckhurst and Nell lived openly together until she was wrested from his protection by the dexterous

The Venetian Ambassador's room. The magnificent bed with the hangings of blue-green Genoa velvet, and the set of armchairs and stools were made for James II in 1688 by Thomas Roberts, and form one of the finest and best preserved sets of furniture of that period in existence. The room is named after Niccolò Molino who was Venetian Ambassador to the court of James I and is believed to have stayed at Knole. The tapestries are Flemish, late sixteenth- or early seventeenth-century, and depict scenes from *Orlando Furioso*.

hands of the King. Buckhurst was sent on a mission to France while this was accomplished, but Nell remembered him always with affection, and is said to have referred to him as *her* Charles I. He was also consoled with an earldom, for he was created Earl of Middlesex in 1675, and two years later he inherited his father's title, and became 6th Earl of Dorset.

Marriage, middle age and the accession of James II appear to have calmed Lord Dorset. He withdrew from court where he found the atmosphere uncongenial, and he was replaced as Lord Lieutenant of Sussex by a Catholic. He spent much time at Knole where he entertained his friends Dryden, Shadwell, Wycherley and many others including Matthew Prior, whom he discovered as a child reading Horace in his father's tavern and sent away to school. Kneller portrayed him about this time, in deshabille, the lines of

The ballroom. This was formerly known as the great dining-room and was planned by the 1st Earl of Dorset as the principal reception room. The panelling with its elaborate decoration of miraculous men and beasts, the plaster ceiling decorated with sprigs of flowers and the chimney-piece are all contemporary; the latter was the work of the royal master mason, Cornelius Cuer, and is of alabaster and variegated marbles. The portrait is of Lady Anne Clifford, wife of the 3rd Earl of Dorset, a painting attributed to William Larkin. Lady Anne lived most unhappily at Knole for many years with her spendthrift husband and she left a diary which gives a vivid picture of Knole in her time. Her second marriage took her to Wilton where she was equally miserable. She was a woman of many accomplishments.

dissipation hanging loose about his face. He supported William III, and became his Lord Chamberlain, but the consequences of his wild youth began to overtake him. He drank heavily, and became very fat. The bills preserved at Knole tell their tale, for in the months between July 1690 and November 1691, £598 19s 4d was spent on drink, when a gallon of canary wine cost 8s, of sherry 6s 8d and of red port 5s 1d. He died at Bath where he was kept a virtual prisoner by his third wife, 'a woman of very obscure connections', but contrary to his family's fears he left the bulk of his fortune to his eldest son Lionel, 7th Earl and 1st Duke of Dorset.

The 1st Duke of Dorset is said to have 'preserved to the last the good breeding, decency of manners, and dignity of exterior deportment of Queen Anne's time'. In other words, he was dull and worthy, he was also a leading Whig and a rather unsatisfactory Lord Lieutenant of Ireland.

John Frederick, 3rd Duke of Dorset, succeeded his uncle the 2nd Duke in 1769. He is one of the most agreeable and romantic characters in the history of Knole. He loved the house, women and cricket, but not necessarily in that order. In the year that he succeeded we learn that 'his raven

looks and milk-white vest had begun to allure a crowd of feminine spectators to the new pastime'. He was a man of taste, not over-endowed with brains; women melted under the gaze of his wistful grey eyes, and his liaisons were notorious. As a very young man he set out on his Grand Tour with the daughter of a Bond Street tailor called Nancy Parsons and a motley crew of actors, dancers and musicians, for he had a passion for opera and ballet and was the most generous of men. After his return he dropped Nancy and is said to have disguised himself as a gardener at Knowsley to pursue his intrigue with Lady Derby. After a visit he paid to Chatsworth in 1777, the Duchess of Devonshire told her mother, 'I always have look'd upon him as the most dangerous of men, for with that beauty of his he is so unaffected, and has a simplicity and a persuasion in his manner that makes one account very easily for the number of women he has had in love with him.'

The Duke cut a splendid figure in Paris where he went as British Ambassador in 1783 and amazed the French with his lavish expenditure on good living. He does not appear to have noted that anything was astir in France, and the Secretary of State was moved to write to the Secretary of Legation in Paris, 'either prevail upon our friend the Duke to write something worth perusal, or else suppose your principal absent, and let your own zeal and abilities have fair play.' There were other matters on his mind in Paris – he met the Italian dancer Giannetta Baccelli who later returned with him to live at Knole. For a number of years she reigned supreme and had her own apartments in what the other servants, in an attempt to pronounce her name, called 'Shelley's Tower', and she caused a great scandal in the county by wearing the Sackville family jewels at a ball in Sevenoaks. The Duke was a great patron of the arts, and commissioned many works from Gainsborough and Reynolds, both of whom painted the Baccelli; she was also sculpted lying on her couch, naked except for a single rose in her hair and after languishing in the attic for many years, she is now restored to the place of honour at the foot of the stairs. Their liaison lasted until 1789 and when she left Knole she is said 'to have behaved very well'; she went to live with Lord Pembroke, and in the following year the Duke married. His bride, Arabella Diana Cope of Bramshill, brought him £140,000 but he was by now in his mid-forties and soon fell a prey to the Sackville family complaint – melancholia. He began to economize, and he grew disagreeable and taciturn. He was soothed, it is said, by listening to the sound of music played in an adjoining room, and he died in 1799 at the age of fifty-four.

His love of Knole led him to spend money on its

repair and embellishment and, according to a guide-book to the house published in 1839, he 'would not suffer the primitive form and character of its exterior to be altered', so posterity owes him a debt of gratitude. His patronage of the arts brought to Knole paintings and works of art from the continent, and the portraits by Reynolds of Dr Johnson, Goldsmith, Garrick and the Duke's Chinese servant, Wang-y-Tong, whom he educated at Sevenoaks Grammar School. His Duchess survived him until 1825. She left two daughters, one of whom married Lord de la Warr, and Knole eventually passed to her grandsons, first to Mortimer, 1st Lord Sackville and then to Lionel.

Lionel, 2nd Lord Sackville, who inherited the house in 1888, is the old, silent, inscrutable grandfather of Vita Sackville-West's reminiscences of Knole, who hated people but took quiet delight in the company of his granddaughter (who married the Hon. Harold Nicolson, but preferred to be known simply as V. Sackville-West). And, as Vita sat playing draughts with him in that great empty house, she had no idea that the old man who was so rude to his neighbours, and spent hours gazing vaguely at the flowers in the garden in the company of two demoiselle cranes had, as a young diplomat, fallen in love with a beautiful Spanish dancer; and, in defiance of all the rules, had acknowledged the seven children he had by her, and taken his eldest illegitimate daughter Victoria to act as his hostess when he went as British Minister to Washington. This Vita learnt later. Victoria returned from Washington with her father to Knole, and married her cousin, Lionel Sackville-West, who was her father's heir. She set about putting Knole in order, she repaired the house, put in electricity and bathrooms, and

bought a very early car, doing very much as she liked because neither her father nor her husband interested themselves in such matters. And later, as Lady Sackville, she bewitched the genial and good-natured Sir John Murray Scott, the secretary and adopted son of the great collector Sir Richard Wallace. Sir John loved Knole, and supported it for years with a steady financial subsidy. Vita Sackville-West, Lady Sackville's daughter, loved Knole passionately and, but for the vagaries of men's laws, would have inherited it. She knew it as no one will ever know it again, silent and empty, for she wandered as a child through the state rooms after nightfall with a candle, saw the chapel during midnight thunderstorms, for a flight of steps lead directly from her bedroom to the family pew, and came face to face with a startled deer who had roamed into the great hall on a summer evening. On her father's death, Knole passed to her uncle, Major-General Sir Charles Sackville-West who became 4th Lord Sackville, and he began the negotiations with the National Trust which distressed her so deeply; the house passed to the Trust in 1946, and she died in 1962.

Years before, in 1928, Virginia Woolf published a historical fantasy, *Orlando*, which was inspired by Knole, its history, and her friendship with Vita Sackville-West. Thus, her name is linked with Knole through her own writings, and through *Orlando* as certainly as if she had never left. For as Orlando mused as she wandered through the great empty galleries at Knole, brushed her hair with King James's silver brushes, stirred the aged rose petals, and pressed her cheek against the worn silver counterpane that lay on the King's bed, 'The house was no longer hers entirely ... It belonged to time now; to history; was past the touch and control of the living.'

Above: Family group at Knole in the early twentieth century. Vita Sackville-West is seated on the ground, her mother at the tea-table (left), and her grandfather, Lionel, 2nd Lord Sackville, is the old man standing to the right.

Above left: The back staircase. The paintings in *grisaille* depict trophies of weapons and the crest and motto of the 1st Duke of Dorset.

Henry, 17th Earl of Pembroke is a film director. Most of his work is now concerned with television drama, but he spends as much time as possible at Wilton where he farms 3000 acres.

'Were you brought up at Wilton?'

'No, sadly I hardly knew the house until 1960 when my grandfather died. We lived at Iver from the early 1940s until 1953 because my father was equerry to the Duke of Kent and later private secretary to the Duchess so my childhood was spent there. We moved to a house near Wilton about 1953, but my grandmother was a very alarming person and when we visited the house it was to have tea with her.'

'How much time did your father spend at Wilton before he took over in 1960?'

'He was effectively running the estate for years before that—from the early 1930s in fact—Wilton was his whole life. He published his first book on the family before the war and his catalogue of paintings just before he died in 1969. It was tragic; he waited all those years to take over and then only had nine years to enjoy it.'

'Did he encourage you to take an interest in the history of the house and family?'

'Yes, in a general sort of way. But his knowledge was very specialized and he never expected me to share his interest in the paintings—in fact, he took it for granted that I didn't. Fortunately he never tried to force this. I love the place and am interested in the history of it and the family, but people expect me to know details about the paintings for instance which I don't!'

'So the house was in good order when you took over?'

'Oh yes! My parents redecorated extensively with the help of John Fowler from 1960 on. The paintings were in an immaculate state of repair, my father had them restored. I was looking through the bills the other day and saw what my father paid, a fraction of what it would be today, fifteen years later. The ceiling of the double cube room was restored after the war. The house was taken over by the army—in fact some of the D-Day landings were planned there—and the cables were run over the gutters and blocked them. When the mushrooms appeared on the ceilings in the double and single cube rooms the damage was discovered—dry-rot—it took two years to repair.'

'Have you got extensive archives at Wilton?'

'The early material has disappeared. We don't know what happened to it. And there was very little for the eighteenth century until my father discovered a room below the estate office. It had been completely forgotten and there he found a mass of eighteenth-century letters on which he based his books on the family.'

Wilton House from the south-east. The south front is half
the length which was originally planned and when work was
interrupted by the Civil War Inigo Jones made the venetian window
the centrepiece and added the towers to balance the design.

Wilton House

WILTSHIRE

The Earl of Pembroke and Montgomery

Sir William Herbert KG, Master of the Horse, had his portrait painted in 1551, the year he became Earl of Pembroke. He is dressed most elegantly, with the Garter he had received two years before at his knee, his staff of office in his hand and a small dog at his feet. John Aubrey described him as 'very Cholerique ... strong sett, but bony, reddish-favoured, of a sharp eie, sterne looke', so it comes as no surprise to hear that years before when he had just gained a foothold on the first rung of the ladder at the court of Henry VIII, he killed a man in a fight in Bristol and had to flee to France. His family were Welsh and by the end of the fifteenth century prominent in the counties of Glamorgan and Monmouth. His father Sir Richard Herbert, a kinsman of the Herberts of Raglan, was a gentleman usher to Henry VII and Constable of Abergavenny Castle. Aubrey recounts how 'black Will Herbert' joined the French army after his flight and by a combination of courage and good sense commended himself to Francis I who interceded on his behalf with Henry VIII.

Shortly after he returned to England and royal favour, he married Anne, the younger of the two daughters of Sir Thomas Parr, Comptroller of the household of Henry VIII. Parr had died some years previously leaving his family in moderate circumstances, but in 1543 there occurred an event which radically altered all their fortunes: Anne's sister Catherine became the sixth wife of Henry VIII.

The King showered honours and rewards upon his brother-in-law in the next few years. Herbert was knighted and appointed Captain of the town and castle of Aberystwyth, Keeper of Baynard's Castle and a steward of much royal property in the west; he was granted Cardiff Castle and the manor of Hendon and, most significant of all, he received in 1544 the extensive estates of the Abbey of Wilton.

On the death of Henry VIII in 1547, Sir William became an executor of the King's will and one of the guardians of Edward VI. He was appointed in the following year Master of the Horse and a Knight of the Garter, and two years later President of Wales. His great loyalty to Edward VI was rewarded when he was raised to the peerage in 1551 as Baron Herbert of Cardiff and Earl of Pembroke, and by the time Queen Mary came to the throne he was one of the most powerful noblemen in the country. His attitude towards the Queen was equivocal, but he was much liked by Philip of Spain and he was appointed Captain General of the English force sent to France in 1557.

Lord Pembroke was one of the noblemen who went to Hatfield to greet the young Queen Elizabeth and he carried the Queen's sword in the procession into London. He stood very high in the Queen's favour; he was a supporter of the Secretary of State Sir William Cecil and he became Lord Steward in 1568. It is evident that Lord Pembroke's heart did not lie at court. The Venetian Ambassador reported to the Doge and Senate in 1555 during a war-scare that Philip of Spain had sent for Lord Pembroke, 'one of the chief noblemen of England, who, as usual with him, was living in retirement at his country seat'. This country seat was, of course, Wilton.

As soon as Lord Pembroke was granted the Abbey of Wilton, he began to think in terms of building a house on the site. There had been a monastic settlement there for some 800 years before the dissolution of the monasteries by Henry VIII, but it appears that Lord Pembroke demolished whatever remained of the old Abbey.

According to Aubrey, the nuns returned to Wilton when Queen Mary came to the throne but his story of their treatment by Lord Pembroke is probably apocryphal. He describes how Lord Pembroke fell on his knees before the Abbess and nuns with the word *peccavi* – I have sinned; but upon Queen Mary's death, he came to them 'like a Tygre' and turned them out with the cry 'out ye Whores, to worke, to worke ye Whores, goe spinne'.

Lord Pembroke put up between 1545 and 1555 a quadrangular brick building of some magnificence. The house was in a fit state to receive Edward VI in 1552 when he progressed through the West Country accompanied by Lord Pembroke and fifty members of his household; and two years later he entertained Philip of Spain's ambassador, the Marquis de las Navas, at Wilton in great style.

When he died in 1570 at Hampton Court he left the Queen his 'best jewel, named the Great Ballace' and his richest bed. Lord Pembroke's much loved mongrel, 'none of the Prettiest' according to Aubrey, the successor of the little dog with whom he was portrayed in 1551, 'would not goe from his Master's dead body, but pined away, and dyed under the hearse'.

Henry, 2nd Earl of Pembroke, does not emerge with any clarity from the shadow cast by his wife. As a widower in his early fifties he married one of the most remarkable women of her age, Mary Sidney of Penshurst, the sister of Philip, whom Aubrey describes as 'the greatest Patronesse of witt and learning of any Lady in her time'.

Wilton in her day was 'like a College, there were so many learned and ingeniose persons', though how much part Lord Pembroke played in this it is difficult to say. Certainly Mary mourned him deeply when he died. He was well known for his prowess in the tilt-yard. He was interested in heraldry, collected heraldic manuscripts and

Left: The east front. The Tudor centre survived the disastrous fire of about 1647 and was preserved in the new design by Inigo Jones and Isaac de Caus.

Far left: Looking through into the double cube room. The portrait shows Philip, 4th Earl of Pembroke, by Sir Anthony Van Dyck. He was responsible for the rebuilding of Wilton and the decoration of these rooms.

was greeted by Lady Pembroke accompanied by 'divers ladies and gentlemen'. On the following day a hunt had been arranged with a feast prepared under canvas, but it rained so hard that this had to be called off.

Lord Pembroke became President of Wales in 1586 and thus followed in the footsteps of both his father and his father-in-law, Sir Henry Sidney, but much of his time appears to have been spent at Wilton. Mary Pembroke spent twenty-four years of married life there with occasional visits to London or other houses owned by her husband.

Mary, Countess of Pembroke, was renowned as a poet and translator of verse and prose. Aubrey says she had a laboratory at Wilton and studied chemistry, and that she laid the foundations of the library. She was well educated and read Latin, French and Italian. She and her brother Philip were exceptionally close and had been from childhood, and when he fell from favour at court in 1580 he went to stay with her at Wilton. Both Philip and Mary had time to spare, for she was very shortly to give birth to her first child, William, and at her suggestion he began his romance, *The Countess of Pembroke's Arcadia*, part of which was written at Wilton that year and the rest dispatched to her page by page as he completed it. It was dedicated to Mary, 'most dear Lady'. They also began their translation of the psalms at this time, a task which Mary completed after her brother's death and circulated in manuscript among friends as was the custom at that time. It was praised, and inspired some lines by John Donne.

Gabriel Harvey commended her translation of *Le Excellent Discours de la Vie et de la Mort* by Philippe Duplessis-Mornay; she also translated *Marc Antoine*, a tragedy by Robert Garnier, and wrote a poetical rendering of Petrarch's *Trionfo della Morte*, and other works. After the tragic

employed a secretary, Henry Sanford, who was a scholar and a poet. Lord Pembroke and his wife lived in great splendour at Wilton with a household of over 200. Queen Elizabeth appointed him Lord Lieutenant of Wiltshire just after his father died and honoured them in 1574 with a visit of three nights in the course of one of her progresses. This was a great success, apart from the weather; Lord Pembroke rode out with a host of horsemen brilliantly dressed to meet the Queen and escorted her for the last five miles to Wilton. She entered the gateway to a burst of cannon and

The double cube room designed by Inigo Jones and completed by John Webb about 1653. The room is sixty feet long, thirty feet wide and thirty feet high and is double the size of the adjoining room whose measurements form a perfect cube. It was designed to display the collection of paintings by Sir Anthony Van Dyck. His portrait of Charles I's children, Charles II, James II and Queen Mary as they later became, hangs over the chimney-piece.

death of her brother, she devoted herself for some years to the literary tasks which he had left unfinished.

She is now remembered as a patron. Nicholas Breton compared her with the Duchess of Urbino, and her patronage extended to both the leading men of letters of the day and to lesser lights; Ben Jonson addressed to her his *Epigram to the Honoured Countess* and Edmund Spenser dedicated his *Ruines of Time* to one 'to whom I acknowledge myself bounden by manie singular favours and great graces', to name but two. Philip's old friends treasured her for the memories of her brother which she embodied; in one of the sonnets prefixed to the *Faerie Queene* Spenser speaks of Sir Philip's 'goodly image' which lives on 'in the divine resemblance of your face'.

Mary outlived her husband by twenty years; she died at her house in London in 1621 of smallpox and 'was carried with great show of coaches and torchlight towards Wilton'. She was buried in the family vault in Salisbury Cathedral and a plaque bearing the following epitaph was attached to her coffin:

Underneath this sable Herse
Lyes the subject of all verse,
Sydneyes Sister, Pembroke's mother.
Death, ere thou hast slain another
ffaire & Learn'd & good as she,
Tyme shall throw a Dart at thee.

William, Lord Herbert, succeeded his father as 3rd Earl of Pembroke in 1601. He was a scholar and he loved poetry; he followed in his mother's footsteps and became a great patron, 'the greatest Maecenas to learned men of any Peer of his time' according to Aubrey. As a young man William showed a marked lack of enthusiasm for life at the court of Queen Elizabeth though he had been, in his father's words, 'reared to her Service'; he was considered 'melancholy', and was reluctant to marry the girls his parents suggested to him. He was banished for a time from court by the Queen, for he committed an almost unpardonable sin, in her eyes, when he seduced one of her maids of honour, Mary Fitton, and then refused to marry her. He found life in the country at Wilton insufferable. 'If the Queene continue her displeasure a little longer, undoubtedly I shall turn clowne ... I have as little to do here as any man living,' he groaned to Sir Robert Cecil. Fortunately the Queen gave him permission to travel abroad.

Three years after he succeeded, he took the plunge and married, but not for love. His bride was the rich but singularly unattractive Mary Talbot, daughter of the 7th Earl of Shrewsbury. There was a great tournament at Wilton and other festivities to mark the occasion. Clarendon said, 'he paid much too dear for his wife's fortune by taking her person into the bargain,' but he adds that Lord Pembroke was always 'immoderately given up to women' and to 'pleasures of all kinds, almost in all excesses'. The Pembrokes had two children but both died in infancy.

Lord Pembroke returned to court when James I came to the throne. Although he did not have the success of his brother Philip who became the King's especial favourite, Lord Pembroke was made a Knight of the Garter in 1603, Lord Warden of the Stannaries, High Steward of the Duchy of Cornwall and, in 1615, Lord Chamberlain. He took part in all the activities of the Jacobean court such as the masques, and the tournaments in which he excelled. At the investiture of the Prince of Wales in 1610 Lord Pembroke acted as the Prince's server at the banquet, his brother Philip was the cup-bearer and Lord Southampton the carver; on the following day there was a masque which continued until dawn and on the third day tilting, 'a gallant sea-fight' in the evening, and 'many rare and excellent fire-works'. He travelled ceaselessly as the court moved from palace to palace. In one breathing space, he wrote to his father-in-law, 'These holidays have brought us some rest, as welcome as to schoolboys, for till Christmas Eve we have been in perpetual motion; and as soon as Twelve tide is past, we shall begin our *voyage* again I am afraid.' King James visited him twice at Wilton, in 1620 and 1623.

Whatever Lord Pembroke may have thought of country life when he was a very young man, he later lavished care and money on the embellishment of Wilton. We do not know much about the improvements he is said to have made to the house, but he created a remarkable garden which was described in some detail by John Taylor, the water-poet, who visited Wilton in 1623.

Gardens were created on an unprecedented scale during the Jacobean period so it is hardly surprising that Lord Pembroke was affected by what amounted to garden mania. The design of the gardens at Wilton was of a geometric and symbolic nature and the thought which went into the plan is typical of a man of Lord Pembroke's scholarly turn of mind. He was also fortunate to have a gardener, Adrian Gilbert, who both understood the elements of the design and had the necessary horticultural skills. Taylor describes Gilbert as 'an ancient gentleman ... continually toiling and tilling' who found his garden 'so pleasing and ravishing to the sense, that he calls it "Paradise"'. The garden was planted with fruit trees which framed walks, hedges and arbours, in shapes which brought to mind 'both divine and moral remembrances'. There were for instance an arbour emblematic of the Trinity and a circular labyrinth; however, Taylor does not tell us what it led to.

It is evident that Lord Pembroke was easy-going and with little worldly ambition. Bacon said that he was 'not effectual'. He was a very rich man and generous to his friends and his household. He was a patron of George Herbert, Philip Massinger (whose father was steward at Wilton), George Chapman, Samuel Daniel (whom his mother chose as his tutor), Ben Jonson to whom he gave £20 every New Year's Day to buy books, and many others. He was interested from the early 1600s in the New World and was a member of the council of New England. In 1615 he was appointed Lord Chamberlain; he was Chancellor of the University of Oxford from 1617 and he was a generous benefactor of the Bodleian Library. Pembroke College is named after him.

Lord Pembroke died in 1630 and was succeeded by his brother Philip.

Philip, 4th Earl of Pembroke and 1st Earl of Montgomery, was born in 1584 and named after his illustrious uncle Sir Philip Sidney. He was four years younger than his brother William, and nineteen when James I came to the throne. The brothers were remarkably handsome and the King was captivated by Philip. He is described as 'the first who drew the King's eyes towards him with affection'. Honours and rewards were showered upon him, including the earldom of Montgomery in 1605. The year before he had married Lady

Susan Vere, a granddaughter of Lord Burghley. The bride was given away by the King and the banquet and festivities at Whitehall were sumptuous.

But Philip was a much rougher diamond than his brother William. He was hot-tempered and foul-mouthed and lived for hawking and hunting, the bowling alley, the tilt-yard and the gaming table. Aubrey says that he was a shrewd judge of character – a quality which the King appreciated – and though he did not share his brother's interest in books or poetry, he 'exceedingly loved Painting and Building, in which he had singular Judgement'. He was responsible for the creation of Wilton as we know it but the garden he made, which Sir Roy Strong has described as 'the greatest Renaissance garden in England', disappeared and is known only from engravings.

In 1626, Philip became Lord Chamberlain. He and his brother were on good terms with Charles I and Queen Henrietta Maria and before William's death the King and Queen visited Wilton. According to Aubrey, the King 'did love Wilton above all places, and came thither every summer'; and Aubrey goes on to relate that 'It was he that did put Philip ... Earle of Pembroke upon making his magnificent Garden and Grotto, and to new-build that side of the House that fronts the Garden with two stately pavilions at Each end, all al Italiano'.

The King advised him to approach Inigo Jones but he was too busy with the royal works to help; Jones recommended a French architect then working in England, Isaac de Caus, who carried out the work at Wilton under Jones's supervision.

Sir Roy Strong has made a detailed study of the great garden at Wilton and he draws attention to the role of Lady Pembroke in the plans. In 1630 Philip married again. His bride was Lady Anne Clifford, the widow of Richard, Earl of Dorset, who thus exchanged life at Knole for that at Wilton and found even less happiness in Wiltshire than she had in Kent. Why she married Lord Pembroke is something of a mystery; she swore when she was a widow that she would never marry again because her complexion was 'martered' by smallpox, but she appears to have been infatuated by him and she needed a protector because the question of her large inheritance in the north remained unresolved. She managed to live with Lord Pembroke for a few unhappy years. Years later she recalled her two marriages. 'I lived in those my Lordes great familyes,' she wrote, 'as the river of Rhone or Rhodanus runnes thorow the Lake of Geneva, without minleinge anie part of its streames with that Lake, ffor I gave myselfe wholly to Retyredness, as much as I could, in both those great families, and made good Bookes and

Above: Sir William Herbert KG, and his mongrel in the year he became 1st Earl of Pembroke, 1551, by Hans Eworth. He founded the family fortunes and is depicted holding his staff of office as Master of the Horse.

Below: Mary Sidney, sister of Sir Philip, who married Henry, 2nd Earl of Pembroke. Sir Philip was devoted to his sister and wrote part of his romance *The Countess of Pembroke's Arcadia* when he stayed with her at Wilton in 1580. She was one of the greatest patrons of literature of her time.

The upper cloisters completed in about 1814 to the design of James Wyatt. The sculpture forms part of a magnificent collection made by the 8th Earl of Pembroke between 1690 and 1730.

vertuous thoughts my Companions.' Lady Anne was a passionate builder; in the latter part of her life she restored her northern castles and, as Sir Roy points out, her influence on the rebuilding of Wilton and its gardens may have been immense. Work began in 1632, two years after her marriage. In 1632–3 £200 was spent on 'construction of new gardens' and in 1634–5 £1292 was paid 'for construction of the Lord earl's new garden and house'.

We can gather some idea of the miraculous gardens de Caus made at Wilton from engravings and the descriptions of visitors. This garden enclosed about nine and a half acres; it extended 1000 feet southwards and 400 feet across and ingeniously hid the River Nadder which wound awkwardly across the site. At the far end was a balustraded terrace which stretched the entire width from which visitors could look out over the gardens or outwards into the park. The focal point

at the end of a broad central walk was the grotto. The interior of the grotto was alive with all manner of contrivances engineered by de Caus. The first room had a table from which jets of water could lift and toss into the air objects such as crowns; statues wept tears on to the unwary visitor and showers of rain descended from the ceiling; at the same time, water-pipes reproduced the sound of bird-song, 'the melody of Nightingerlls and all sorts of birds'.

The design of the garden was strongly influenced by Venetian architecture, with Inigo Jones as the intermediary. Steps led from the house to the first section which consisted of parterres in clipped box, the corners and edges accentuated by cypresses which centred on four fountains with statues by Nicholas Stone. The second part was the wilderness, carefully cultivated around two eight-foot high statues of Bacchus and Flora; beyond lay two rectangular ponds with elaborate waterworks and an arrangement of formal walks planted with cherry trees with arbours at the sides and, in the middle of the broad walk, a statue of the Borghese Gladiator. Sir Roy explains that this statue was selected as an appropriate tribute to the martial spirit of Lord Pembroke and he contrasts this section of the garden with the first where the theme of the embroidered parterres – love and chastity – suggests Lady Pembroke. The interpretation of the elaborate symbolism would have been apparent to an intelligent visitor of the Jacobean period; Sir Roy suggests that if we see in this garden an expression of the marriage of Anne Clifford and Philip Pembroke, 'we might not be so far off part of its intent'.

What we see at Wilton today is the eastern wing of a projected building which was to have extended for some 400 feet, the two wings flanking an applied portico of six Corinthian columns. This vast scheme was never completed and the half-front was provided with two pedimented towers; the Venetian window with the shield and figures became the focal point of the design. Although built by de Caus, the design owes much to Jones.

Wilton was badly damaged by fire about 1647. Philip again consulted Inigo Jones about the rebuilding, but the work was carried out by John Webb, his nephew. Together they designed two of the most splendid rooms in England, the double cube and single cube rooms. The double cube room which is sixty feet long, thirty wide and thirty high was designed to set off the magnificent portraits which Philip commissioned from Van Dyck. The walls are of pine, painted cream, and elaborately decorated with swags of fruit, flowers and foliage gilded in different shades which provide a perfect foil for the paintings. The plaster cove was elaborately painted with cartouches, vases, garlands and figures by Edward Pierce and the flat ceiling with moulded panels contains scenes from the legend of Perseus painted by Emanuel de Critz.

This work was finished, but any further building was interrupted by the Civil War in which Philip sided with the Parliamentarians. He died of 'a pestilential fever' in 1649.

Wilton was greatly enriched by Thomas, 8th Earl of Pembroke, who was born in 1656 and died in 1733. He made many visits to the continent to buy pictures, sculpture, coins and books and he formed the magnificent library of books and drawings. His greatest coup was the purchase of the Arundel marbles, the first great collection of its kind in England. He is largely responsible for the art collection at Wilton as it exists today. He also imported French weavers and founded the famous Wilton Carpet Factory.

His son Henry who succeeded as 9th Earl was an architect of some importance and a friend of Lord Burlington and William Kent. He and Roger Morris constructed the bridge at Wilton which crosses the Nadder, and landscaped the garden; this resulted in the total loss of the 4th Earl's great gardens. The latter's house remained intact until 1800 when the 11th Earl called in James Wyatt who, Sir John Summerson remarks, respected Inigo Jones but nothing else about Wilton. His alterations, in the Gothic style, which took eleven years to complete were planned to make the house warmer and more convenient and to provide more space for display of the collection of sculpture and paintings. They included the construction of a double-tiered cloister inside the quadrangle, and a new main entrance to the house and forecourt. He

brought from the park the triumphal arch designed by Sir William Chambers, surmounted by the equestrian statue of Marcus Aurelius, and placed it to form a grand entrance.

The 15th Earl of Pembroke removed some of Wyatt's decorations, including his entrance porch, in the 1920s, but it is Sidney, 16th Earl of Pembroke, to whom the credit is due for restoring the house to its present glory. No other family in England has been so liberally endowed with gifts over the centuries as the Herbert family, and the 16th Earl of Pembroke was well favoured. He was a man of taste and discernment; he compiled a scholarly catalogue of the paintings and published books on the history of his family. 'This curious seate of Wilton and the adjacent countrey is an Arcadian place and a Paradise,' wrote John Aubrey in the seventeenth century; none of Wilton's owners loved it more passionately than the late Lord Pembroke.

The 4th Earl of Pembroke and his family. This is Van Dyck's largest family group. Lord Pembroke is shown with the children of his first marriage and his second wife, Lady Anne Clifford. She was formerly married to Lord Dorset, and her portrait hangs in the ballroom at Knole. The children who died in infancy are shown as angels.

John, 9th Duke of Buccleuch, leads a peripatetic existence, for he travels during the year from one of his great estates to the next, following a pattern established by his parents. He has inherited the houses, land and treasures of three great families, two Scottish – Scott and Douglas of Drumlanrig – and one English – Montagu of Boughton. He was MP for the North Division of Edinburgh for many years. Bowhill is the principal family home today. Dalkeith, near Edinburgh, is leased to a computer company and the Duke and Duchess spend part of the autumn at Drumlanrig.

The Duke's attitude towards his estate at Boughton is reminiscent of the great 'improving' landlords of the eighteenth century. A visitor to Boughton cannot fail to be impressed by the meticulous way in which the house and estate is maintained and to admire the skills which are variously devoted to the care of the hedgerows, the thatching of the cottages or the preservation of the earliest carpets in England.

'Boughton is always thought of as a sleeping beauty which had hardly been disturbed over the past two hundred years. Has it always been cherished, or was it neglected?'

'No, the house was always cared for but was never altered in any serious way. My grandfather put up the panelling in the Great Hall and carried out some restoration and my parents removed the nineteenth-century plate-glass windows on the west front in the 1950s. Most of the house is just as Duke John left it in 1749.'

'How has your family managed to keep together these great estates and to administer them so efficiently?'

'My father was an excellent businessman and set up a company in 1923 long before other people thought of such a scheme. So I don't personally own any of it though of course I have the casting vote when it comes to decisions. Adam Smith was the 3rd Duke's tutor and he taught us that the properties should be run on a commercial basis.'

'And they are?'

'Most certainly, but with clear long-term objectives. We have here 11,000 acres, of which 2000 are woodland, 2500 are in hand and the rest tenanted; there are also five villages. Boughton is the centre of an active agricultural community, and we are able to harmonize the often conflicting interests of food and timber production, conservation and recreation. This is impossible to accomplish on a small scale and with trees taking anything up to 150 years to mature, plans must be made that span several generations. I believe that the survival of an estate such as Boughton is in the national interest. Our land resources are so limited they must be put to the fullest and widest use.'

'As soon as one crosses the boundaries of the Boughton estate, one is aware of the activities of Duke John the Planter and other tree-planting members of your family. Were there many elms here?'

'I'm afraid so. We replanted a two-mile avenue for Jubilee Year, limes alternating with southern beech. We made a great occasion of it; the children from the school at Geddington did the planting, and they will remember that day all their lives.'

'How much time do you spend here?'

'We are here in August. There is no central heating which has helped to preserve the house, of course, but it is bitterly cold in winter – you cannot imagine how cold it is. This means that we have to close the house to the public in August as we cannot combine living in the house and opening it; the public walks through the rooms we live in.

We opened the house on an experimental basis – if we don't have enough visitors we'll have to think again.'

Boughton House showing the
façade in the French style which
Ralph, 1st Duke of Montagu,
added to the old Tudor house.

Boughton House

KETTERING, NORTHAMPTONSHIRE

The Duke of Buccleuch and Queensberry KT

In October 1695 William III went to Boughton to dine with Ralph, Earl of Montagu. It was an important occasion, for Ralph Montagu was anxious to impress his sovereign and to show off the additions he had made to the old Montagu house.

The five state rooms which he had planned with just such a royal visit in mind had taken him nearly ten years to build and decorate. The new north front was very grand and quite foreign in appearance, for the design reflected his passion for contemporary French taste.

The King was no doubt flattered by Montagu's attentions. But he was not prepared to grant him his great desire in life – a dukedom. The year before Montagu had written to ask for one, but without success. William had given him an earldom in 1689 to add to the barony he had inherited from his father, the 2nd Lord Montagu of Boughton, and the King presumably considered this was adequate recompense for the support Montagu had given him in his efforts to secure the crown.

Ralph Montagu was a controversial figure, but it is difficult to judge from this distance in time how justified was the mistrust of his contemporaries. His worldly success provoked much envy. He was a younger son who had to make his own way in the world. He did not live in an age noted for probity in public life, and he was by no means alone in seeking power through all the means at his disposal.

What he had in abundance was a sense of style which when recognized is, sadly enough, so often resented. And he had great charm, 'so much Adress', in the words of a contemporary.

His greatest claim to fame is as a patron of the arts, and he was much influenced by what he saw in France. At the time of the Restoration, Montagu was in his early forties. He quickly attracted the attention of Charles II, who sent him to Paris in the spring of 1669 as ambassador to Louis XIV. In France the art and architecture, the decorations and the gardens captivated him. He was instrumental in bringing French artists and craftsmen to England and was generous in his support of Huguenot refugees. For a time he owned and directed the Mortlake Tapestry Manufactory. Years later, William Congreve dedicated to him his comedy *The Way of the World* which was produced in 1700 and partly inspired by the conversation of Montagu and his friends during a stay in the country. Congreve wrote, 'Poetry is almost the only Art, which has not yet laid Claim to Your Lordship's Patronage. Architecture and Painting, to the great Honor of our Country, have

Detail of the entrance front.

florished under Your influence and Protection.'

It is wholly appropriate that he should have held the court appointment of Master of the Royal Wardrobe to Charles II, a role he took most seriously, for this entailed responsibility for both the King's outfits and the furnishings of the royal palaces.

Charles II sent him on two further embassies to Louis XIV, in 1676 and 1677, but the King never really took his ambassador into his confidence. The honours and rewards which Montagu might have expected failed to materialize, and his efforts to advance himself eventually lost him his privy councillorship and the respect of both Charles II and the Duke of York (later James II).

Montagu took up the cause of the Duke of Monmouth, and after the discovery of the Rye House plot in 1683 decided to depart for France and to lie low for a while.

After the accession of James II in 1685, he made his peace with the King. Although he never retired from public life, he had no hope of advancement in that reign, and he had to wait for William and Mary to come to the throne in 1689 before he was readmitted to the Privy Council.

The visits to France had fired Montagu's imagination and he sought for an early opportunity to indulge in building. Although the death of his brother in action against the Dutch in 1665 had left him heir to Boughton, his father was very much alive, but Montagu's marriage in 1673 to Elizabeth, widow of Joceline, 11th Earl of Northumberland, greatly enhanced his means. Two years later he was in a position to start building a London mansion for himself in the French style which he named Montagu House.

A decade passed before he started work at Boughton. In 1684 his father died, and by that date he had the time and the money to devote himself to the adornment of his Northamptonshire home.

Montagu was proud of his origins and he left intact the rambling old Tudor house centred on the great hall. The visitor today can see from the inner windows the numerous small courts (there are seven) round which the rooms are grouped. Much of this house was built by Sir Edward Montagu who acquired the Boughton estate in 1528. The site had minor monastic origins but there was little in the way of buildings when he took over.

Sir Edward Montagu was a lawyer who became Chief Justice of the Common Pleas and an executor of Henry VIII's will. He started from modest beginnings and rose to a position of distinction. After the accession of Mary I in 1553, he retired quietly to Boughton. When he died four

The rainbow room. This was originally two bedrooms and formed part of Duke Ralph's suite at the end of his life. The writing table in the centre by André Charles Boulle was given by Louis XIV to Duke Ralph when he was ambassador. The carpet dates from about 1600 and the tapestries are late seventeenth-century English, woven at Mortlake. The series is known as *The Playing Boys*.

Below: Ralph, 1st Duke of
Montagu, by Benedetto
Gennari. Duke Ralph was
ambassador in Paris and his
impressions of French art
and architecture led him to
create a magnificent house in
London in the French style
and later to add a wing to
Boughton which has
survived in a miraculous
state of preservation.

Above: The cloister. The
door on the right was the
grand entrance through
which William III would
have passed into the great
hall.

years later, he left the house to his widow
'provided she live sole and keep house at
Boughton' and, thoughtful man, a bequest to 'fifty
poor maidens forty shillings each towards their
advancement in marriage'.

His son and grandson added to the house; his
son, the second Sir Edward, was the ancestor of
the dukes of Manchester and the earls of
Sandwich; his grandson was a zealous supporter
of the King during the Civil War, and was
imprisoned for a short period before his death in
1644. He was created Lord Montagu of Boughton
in 1621. He is described as 'severe and regular in
his life', characteristics shared by his son, who
remained quietly at Boughton for most of his life,
but not by his grandson. Ralph Montagu was a
startling contrast to his immediate forebears. And
despite his respect for them and for the old house,

The great hall. Duke Ralph added the painted barrel-vaulted ceiling to conceal the timbers of the Tudor roof. The panelling of Boughton oak was installed in 1912.

he was not averse to covering up the hammer-beam roof in the great hall by adding a barrel-vault, richly decorated by Louis Chéron with a painting depicting the marriage of Hercules and Hebe. And the room he used for a time as a dining-room, known as the Egyptian hall, was similarly adorned with a Triumph of Bacchus.

But his principal architectural works at Boughton were the addition he made to the north of the house, and the building of the stable. The façade with its two pavilions at either end and an arcade on the ground floor of the central part, called 'the cloisters' in the old accounts, is described by Professor Pevsner as perhaps the most French-looking seventeenth-century building in England. The name of the architect remains unknown. The fine stables are also of French inspiration.

The main entrance (which William III would

The Egyptian hall. This room was part of the original monastery round which Edward Montagu built his house. Duke Ralph used it for a time as a dining-room.

have used) was through the central door in the arcade which led into the great hall. From there ceremonial approach to the 'Grand Apartment' – the state rooms – lay through the little hall with its carved stone chimney-piece showing the descent of the Montagu family from William the Conqueror, into Ralph Montagu's stone staircase hall decorated by Chéron, and up to the first floor.

The state rooms consist of the great chamber, the drawing-room, the state bedroom (the state bed is in the Victoria and Albert Museum), the blue room (a dressing-room) and a fifth room whose purpose is unknown. They were designed as show-rooms to be used occasionally when very grand or, hopefully, royal visitors came to stay. Apart from the inevitable juggling of furniture over the years, they remain just as they were when William III made his visit.

In 1692, two years after the death of his first wife, Ralph Montagu remarried. His bride was another rich widow, Elizabeth, Duchess of Albemarle. The Duchess was eccentric to say the least. In a mad moment she swore she would marry only a crowned head, and it was rumoured at the time that Montagu wooed and won her by posing as the Emperor of China. She remained at Montagu House, however, and does not figure in the story of Boughton.

Ralph Montagu died in 1709. Shortly before his death he realized his great ambition in life. In 1705 his son John married the daughter of the great Duke of Marlborough and, in the following year, Queen Anne created Ralph Montagu Marquess of Monthermer and Duke of Montagu.

The 2nd Duke is known in the family as 'John the Planter'. He was a distinguished general who became Master-General of the Ordnance in 1740. As his name implies, his interests lay not so much with the house at Boughton as with the landscape. To the house he made only minor alterations; he did not finish his father's north pavilion. Duke Ralph, to give him the title he hankered after for so

Looking through into the great hall. The portrait seen farthest away through the door is a magnificent portrait of Queen Elizabeth painted by Marcus Gheeraerts the Younger in about 1595.

long, had employed a Dutch gardener as early as 1685 to lay out the parterre, the canal, the fountains and other works. Duke John modified his father's garden and set about planting trees on a massive scale. His lime and elm avenues extended at one time over seventy miles. As one travels over the Boughton estate today, great vistas present themselves at the turn of a road or a footpath. The park entirely escaped the influence of the landscape movement, and retains the formality of the late seventeenth century.

Duke John was not only a soldier and gardener but a mediaevalist who corresponded with the antiquary William Stukeley. He also retained the sense of humour of an English schoolboy. His mother-in-law, the Duchess of Marlborough, was plainly irritated by his efforts 'to get people into his garden and wet them with squirts, and to invite people to his country houses and put things into their beds to make them itch'.

Perhaps others found this a refreshing reaction to his father's sophistication.

Horace Walpole tells a delightful story about Duke John's will. He made two codicils, one in favour of his servants, and the other of his dogs, cats and other creatures for he could never resist rescuing strays. As Duke John was writing this, one of his cats jumped on his knee. 'What,' he said, 'have you a mind to be a witness too! You can't, for you are a party concerned.'

Boughton was inherited on his death in 1749 by his daughter, Mary, who married George, Earl of Cardigan. He was created 3rd Duke of Montagu in 1766. Their son, Lord Monthermer, who is seen in the portrait at Boughton by Batoni, holding in his hand the score of a Corelli sonata, was delicate and died young.

Boughton passed once again in the female line through his sister, Elizabeth, wife of the 3rd Duke of Buccleuch. The Montagu titles died out, but the family name of the Dukes of Buccleuch, who have cherished Boughton since it was added to their estates, is 'Montagu Douglas Scott', so keeping alive the link with Duke Ralph and beyond him to Sir Edward Montagu, the builder of the house.

Boughton is filled with the works of art Ralph Montagu collected: paintings, tapestries, furniture – with much original upholstery – needlework, rugs, silver and clocks, together with furnishings of the previous 150 years. Visitors to the house today gain a unique view of interior decoration in England. For time stopped at Boughton in 1749. The house which by then was old-fashioned, fell into a deep slumber, and very little happened to disturb its peace until this century. When the house did emerge from this long hibernation, nothing was done to spoil the atmosphere of the late seventeenth century.

Above: One of Boughton's seven courtyards.

Left: John, 2nd Duke of Montagu 'John the Planter', wearing the orders of the Garter and the Bath. He was Master-General of the Ordnance and the painter, Thomas Hudson, has depicted the Tower of London in the background. He married the daughter of the great Duke of Marlborough and planted at Boughton avenues of trees which at one time totalled seventy miles in length. He had a great passion for animals.

Andrew, 11th Duke of Devonshire, has revived the great family tradition of art collecting which has lain dormant since the death of the 6th Duke in 1858 and he and the Duchess have made some notable additions to the collection, principally of paintings and books. The Devonshire collections are concentrated at Chatsworth, for only Chatsworth, Bolton Abbey in Yorkshire and Lismore Castle in Co. Waterford survive of all the great houses owned by the dukes of Devonshire in the past. The Duke points out that although the family ceased to buy works of art, they did not sell, so that Chatsworth houses the cream of the contents of Devonshire House, Chiswick House, Burlington House, all in or near London, Compton Place in Eastbourne and Hardwick Hall in Derbyshire.

'Did you find the decision to live at Chatsworth a difficult one to make?'

'Yes, it was difficult. You see I was not brought up to inherit Chatsworth. My elder brother was killed in 1944, and I had a few years to get used to the idea before my father died very suddenly in 1950. My mother had just opened the house again, but it was dirty, depressing and gloomy. Nothing had been repainted for years.'

'How long did your parents live at Chatsworth?'

'Hardly at all. My grandfather died in 1938 and by that time my parents had been established for many years at Churchdale, a house nearby. They moved here for the summer but returned to Churchdale for the winter. During the war we had a girls' school here, 300 girls. My parents decided not to come back after the girls had gone in 1946. My father was a great gardener and he had made a start on the gardens after the war but nothing was done about the house.'

'What are your early memories of Chatsworth?'

'My grandparents spent about three months of the year here in the autumn. Their lives were a continuous round; they moved on to Lismore, then to Devonshire House in May and June for the season, perhaps to Compton Place at Eastbourne, back to Chatsworth and on to Bolton. All the houses had some permanent staff, but a staff travelled with my grandparents, one contingent going ahead and one following. My grandfather was Governor-General of Canada between 1916 and 1921. He had a stroke in 1925 and for this reason Chatsworth was not a very happy place in the 1930s. My grandmother kept together the house and the estate. They had some grand set-piece house-parties of forty or so but my grandfather did not care for them. At Christmas there were invariably over 100 people staying in the house and those parties I do remember.'

'Did you and the Duchess carry out much restoration before you moved here or was it a gradual process?'

'Our agent made moves to entice us back in the 1950s. And we made a start in 1958. We put in central heating which had hardly existed before, rewired the house – it took four winters – and made seventeen bathrooms. We moved back in November 1959.'

'When did you begin to collect works of art?'

'When racehorses became too expensive. We have so many books here, so many duplicates. And yet I sent a sale catalogue of good botanical books to one of the librarians here and asked him to mark those which would fill gaps in the 6th Duke's collection; the answer came back – all of them – so we began to buy. And we have sold many of the duplicates to do so.'

'What about other sales? You have been in the news recently as the seller of a painting by Poussin?'

'This has been forced on Trustees – to whom, of course, the house and contents belong. The quarter of a million visitors we have each year help towards the upkeep of the house, but there is a gap which we have to fill. We have set up a charitable trust with the proceeds of the sale of the Poussin and of some more book sales, to preserve Chatsworth as a national monument. We had to take drastic steps.'

Chatsworth

BAKEWELL, DERBYSHIRE

The Duke of Devonshire MC, PC

Chatsworth: the west front. This was probably designed by the 1st Duke of
Devonshire himself, a talented amateur architect.

At the coronation of Charles II in 1661, William Cavendish was one of four young men invited to bear the King's train, for his father, the 3rd Earl of Devonshire, was a prominent Royalist who had been reinstated the year before in the various high offices he had lost at the time of his impeachment in 1642 for 'high crimes and misdemeanours'. Young William Cavendish did not advance in the royal service, for by the end of the 1660s he had developed into a vigorous opponent of the court party. He was an upholder of the rights of Parliament against the arbitrary rule of the King, a scourge of papists and a defender of the protestant succession. He and his friends made determined efforts to ensure that the Duke of York did not succeed his brother. When the Duke came to the throne as James II, the young Lord Devonshire as he had become on his father's death in 1684, was hardly *persona grata* at court. A few months after the King's accession, a Royalist colonel by the name of Colepeper was outraged to see him in the lobby outside the royal bedchamber in the Palace of Whitehall. Colepeper asked Devonshire in a most insolent manner whether it was the time and place for excluders to appear, and a heated argument ensued. John Evelyn witnessed the scene: 'My lord told him he lied, on which Colepeper struck him a box on the ear, which my lord returned and felled him.'

As a result of his bitter quarrel with Colepeper, Lord Devonshire was fined the huge sum of £30,000 and thrown into prison. In vain did his mother show the King the bonds for twice that sum which the Cavendish family had lent Charles I, but the King had netted a formidable enemy and was not prepared to let him go. Lord Devonshire managed to escape, however, and fled the country. When he returned to Chatsworth the Sheriff of Derby took steps to arrest him. Lord Devonshire, who was a resourceful man, imprisoned both Sheriff and attendants, and proceeded to negotiate his freedom from a position of strength.

Right: Detail of the west front.

Above: Miniature of William, 4th Earl and 1st Duke of Devonshire, by Peter Cross. He transformed the Elizabethan house of his ancestors into a baroque palace and created the state rooms. He was one of the English noblemen who invited William of Orange to take the throne, and was rewarded with a dukedom in 1694.

Lord Devonshire remained in retirement at Chatsworth for some years, but in 1697, when the tables had been turned and William III had come to the throne with his support and rewarded him with a dukedom, he met the Colonel by chance and gave him a good thrashing 'for being troublesome to him in the late reign'.

He was not idle during this period of rural exile, for he turned his attention to his family house. He did not intend to replace the old Elizabethan house with a palace, and he set out to modernize one façade, but once he had started he found it very difficult to stop, and by the time building mania had taken hold of him he had the means and the power to build anything he wanted. Furthermore, his position as a Whig nobleman of the first rank demanded an appropriate background; Chatsworth was one of the earliest architectural enterprises undertaken after the Revolution of 1688, and the Duke claimed for himself a setting worthy of a king.

The Duke's character, proud and forceful, was the dominant factor in the creation of Chatsworth and the evidence of his taste and discernment in the arts is apparent throughout the house. He accompanied William III to The Hague and astonished the Dutch with his expensive plate and lavish entertainments. He was said to possess great charm, and one of his innumerable lady admirers was inspired to compose some lines on this Duke:

Whose soft commanding looks our breasts assailed;
He came and saw and at first sight prevailed.

The Elizabethan house which the Duke inherited owed much to the formidable character of the Duke's great-great-grandmother, Bess of Hardwick, who was the true founder of the Cavendish family fortunes. Elizabeth Hardwick was the daughter of a Derbyshire squire; she was born about 1520 and brought up at her father's

The painted hall was decorated for the 1st Duke by Louis Laguerre between 1692 and 1694 with scenes from the life of Julius Caesar, who can be seen in the centre mural. The ironwork was wrought by Jean Tijou. The original gritstone floor was replaced by a marble pavement in the late eighteenth century.

manor of Hardwick. She made four marriages and inherited four estates. Her second, and favourite, husband Sir William Cavendish came from an old Suffolk family and had been richly rewarded with monastic estates by Henry VIII.

In 1549, shortly after their marriage, Sir William Cavendish bought the Chatsworth estate, fifteen miles from Hardwick, and began to build on the site of the present house. When Sir William died, in 1557, this was far from complete, but Bess undertook to finish it, and her massive Elizabethan house enclosing a square court with towers at the corners can be seen in a painting by Richard Wilson, after Jan Siberechts, which hangs at Chatsworth today.

In 1568 Bess made her most spectacular marriage. Her husband, George, 6th Earl of Shrewsbury, was one of the richest and most powerful men in England and when he died in 1590 she inherited his fortune. This enabled her – at the age of seventy – to embark on the house of her dreams, and Hardwick Hall, which was owned by the dukes of Devonshire until 1956 and is now a property of the National Trust, is her monument.

At her death in 1608 she left Chatsworth to her eldest son Henry Cavendish, but he sold the estate shortly afterwards to his younger brother William who became 1st Earl of Devonshire in 1618 and is the ancestor of the later earls and dukes of Devonshire.

The 1st Duke remodelled Chatsworth over a period of twenty years. Each stage he swore would be the last, and because of his piecemeal approach – the demolition of one wing at a time and then its reconstruction – the present house follows the exact outline of its Elizabethan predecessor.

The Duke commissioned a new design for the south front from an architect who was then relatively unknown, William Talman. Mr Francis Thompson, the historian of Chatsworth, suggests that the Duke who was an autocrat and had decided ideas on architecture himself preferred to choose an architect whom he could manage. Talman brought with him a master-mason, Benjamin Jackson, and a master-carpenter, John Creswell, with whom he had worked before, and imported the other craftsmen from London. Most of the materials used were local except for the wood; he had to go further afield for the oak for

View of the garden created by the present Duchess of Devonshire who has planted in box the outline plan of the basement of Lord Burlington's villa at Chiswick. Lord Burlington left Chiswick and his collections to his daughter whose husband became 4th Duke of Devonshire. Beyond is the bridge built by James Paine which crosses the River Derwent, and is set in the landscape replanned by 'Capability' Brown about 1760.

the wainscot in the state rooms and the cedar for the chapel.

By the time William of Orange set foot on British soil in November 1688, the construction of the south front was complete. 'When he had finish'd this part,' wrote Dr White Kennet, his chaplain and biographer, 'he meant to go no farther; till seeing public affairs in a happier settlement, for a testimony of ease and joy, he undertook the east side of the quadrangle.'

In 1689 the Duke began to demolish the east front and to decorate the rooms in the south front behind the new façade. The Duke was impetuous: the east front had been torn down long before the architect had had time to design a replacement and he changed his ideas with great rapidity. Mr Thompson believed that the Duke's inability to visualize any architectural plan led to the constant changes which took place, for he would experiment by building and tearing down what did not please him, much to the distress of architect and builders. By 1690 work was in progress on the state rooms in the south wing, on the decoration of the great staircase and the reconstruction of the old hall.

The chapel was one of the first rooms to be decorated. Caius Gabriel Cibber designed the altar-piece which was executed in alabaster by a young Derbyshire man, Samuel Watson, who worked at Chatsworth from 1689 until his death in 1715 and carved with equal accomplishment in stone, marble and wood. The painted decoration in the chapel is by Louis Laguerre, who then moved on to the decoration of the painted hall. Jean Tijou made the iron-work balustrade of the staircase and trained a young smith from Baslow named John Gardom who took over from the master.

The state rooms were decorated together, and by the time the carvers were finished in the chapel, they moved on to 'carve the ornaments of lime tree worke for the great chamber to the designe aprooved by his Lordsp'. The carvers and their eight assistants finished the state rooms in eighteen months, urged on by the Duke. Antonio Verrio was spared briefly from Burghley by the Duke's brother-in-law Lord Exeter and, together with Laguerre and Ricard, painted the ceilings. Verrio took great delight in including the witch-like features of Mrs Hackett, the Chatsworth housekeeper, among the company on the ceiling of the great chamber, for she viewed the painter with considerable distaste.

In 1696 Talman resigned or was dismissed by the Duke. Their relationship had steadily declined. Talman was maddened by the Duke's constant alterations and the manner in which he removed workmen from one job and started them on another. The house was built under the contract system – a most unusual procedure – which meant that Talman and not the Duke engaged the workmen. In 1699 the Duke could bear this delegation of authority no longer, sacked everyone and reverted to direct labour.

For some time the Duke had suspected that Talman was overcharging him. When the architect appeared at Chatsworth in a coach drawn by four horses with two servants in attendance his suspicions were confirmed, and in 1692 he called in Sir Christopher Wren to arbitrate. But there was a further complication for the Duke himself had fallen behind in his payments. The men threatened to strike, and by 1694 these financial problems seriously disrupted work on the house.

We learn the reason for this in a letter written by the Duke's distracted London agent to the steward at Chatsworth. 'My Lord is now at Newmarket (where most of our cash is gone).' Talman disappeared in 1696 and there was a lull in proceedings, but three years later the same agent reported that 'Our clamorous workmen are now very hott and pretend to petition the House of Lords'. By 1700 the Duke had begun again with

Detail of the wall-painting in the Sabine room. The decoration of this room is a masterpiece of illusionist painting by Sir James Thornhill, who came to Chatsworth in 1706.

Right: Charlotte Boyle, the daughter and heiress of the great collector and arbiter of taste, Lord Burlington, painted by George Knapton in about 1740. She married Lord Hartington, later 4th Duke of Devonshire, and brought to the Cavendish family Burlington House in Piccadilly, Chiswick House and her father's incomparable collection of paintings and drawings.

Below: Details of the decoration of the great stairs.

renewed energy. He built the west front which he almost certainly designed himself, basing it on two famous French buildings, and in 1702 began to tamper with the north wing, enlisting Thomas Archer to make a design for the façade. By 1706 the west wing was ready for occupation complete with the most elaborate system of sanitation devised by the Duke. Celia Fiennes described the bathroom in 1697, 'the walls all with blue and white marble . . . the bath is one entire marble all white finely veined with blue and is made smooth . . . it was as deep as one's middle on the outside, and you went down steps into the bath big enough for two people; at the upper end are two cocks to let in, one hot the other cold, water to attemper it as persons please.' There were also ten water-closets, with a flush mechanism, cedar and brass fittings and bowls in marble for the Duke and Duchess and in alabaster for the rest of the household.

For the decoration of the coved ceiling of the staircase the Duke secured James Thornhill, and he also painted the Sabine room, a masterpiece of illusionist painting.

The elaborate formal garden was laid out for the Duke by George London and Henry Wise with parterres and terraces. The spectacular water-works were fed by the ample supplies of water from the moors above the house; the great cascade was the principal feature with a cascade house built by Archer from which it is possible to see as Daniel Defoe did in 1724 how 'out of the mouths of beasts, pipes, urns, etc., a whole river descends the slope of a hill a quarter of a mile in length, over steps, with a terrible noise, and broken appearance, till it is lost underground'.

When the Duke died in 1707 he had virtually completed his work.

The 1st Duke was not interested in the acquisition of paintings, but he acquired some superb pieces of plate. His son, the 2nd Duke, enriched his father's house with treasures including an incomparable collection of drawings, engravings, engraved gems and coins. He bought a magnificent group of drawings from N. A. Flinck whose father, Govaert Flinck, was a pupil of Rembrandt, and also Claude Lorraine's *Liber Veritatis*, the artist's record of his own compositions. The 2nd Duke created the Devonshire collection.

The 4th Duke was a widower by the time he succeeded, but he determined to make Chatsworth a more comfortable place to live in, and in between his public appointments – Lord Lieutenant of Ireland, First Lord of the Treasury and Prime Minister, and Lord Chamberlain – James Paine built a new entrance court to the north, extensive domestic offices, the stables and the bridge over the River Derwent. He also gave Chatsworth a setting and approach worthy of its splendour. In 1761 he invited 'Capability' Brown to landscape the surrounding countryside and give the home a more dramatic approach than the route over the moor from the east.

The 4th Duke's attentions to the landscape were matched by additions to the collections through his marriage in 1748 with Charlotte Boyle, the daughter and heiress of the 3rd Earl of Burlington. Lord Burlington, architect, patron and collector, sought with his allies William Kent and Alexander Pope to re-establish the canons of classical antiquity which had been obscured in English taste by the prevailing enthusiasm for the baroque. Their efforts were successful and resulted in the creation of the Palladian movement which dominated English architecture in the first half of the eighteenth century. The portrait of Lord Burlington at Chatsworth shows him holding a volume of his own edition of architectural drawings by Palladio, with a bust of his hero Inigo Jones in the background. These designs were well suited to appeal to the taste of English gentlemen, for Palladio's villas were set in the midst of agricultural communities and were easily adaptable to the requirements of English country life. Lord Burlington's ideals were enshrined in the villa at Chiswick, ten miles from London, which he designed and Kent decorated as a setting for his great collections, rich in paintings and drawings by Rembrandt, Velazquez, Van Dyck, Inigo Jones and Palladio together with books, furniture and other decorations which came to Chatsworth with Charlotte Boyle and are there to this day.

The atmosphere of the state rooms at Chatsworth is richly evocative of the aspirations of the 1st Duke – the great Whig grandee – for the rooms were conceived as an apartment in which to receive King William whom the Duke had personally invited to come to the throne. To a similar degree the nineteenth-century decorations at Chatsworth are an expression of the personality of the gifted 6th Duke. Duchess Georgiana, wife of the 5th Duke, has left no similar mark on Chatsworth, for she and her husband spent most of their time in London; we have to turn to the portraits of her by Reynolds and Gainsborough, or read the letters and diaries of her contemporaries, to gain any conception of her qualities. Georgiana is an outstanding character in the story of the Cavendish family; her beauty and wit enslaved London society for the last thirty years of the eighteenth century; she was the greatest political hostess of her time, and, as she lay dying, ordinary mortals thronged the street outside her London house in silent tribute. She attracted in her time the adulation we would accord to a great actress. Her stage was the magnificent London house of the dukes of Devonshire in Piccadilly, the scene of dazzling balls and soirées to which flocked statesmen, ambassadors, men of letters and ladies, and her intimates who included Charles James Fox, George Selwyn and Richard Brinsley Sheridan. This was above all a political coterie, for the Devonshire House circle was High Whiggery incarnate. It was an agreeable world, rooted half in the great country estates and half in London; the men were not idle for they were a governing class, and their party had effectively ruled England for most of the eighteenth century. Their ample way of life derived from this long hold on government, and their education, their manner of speech, and their attitude to life and its pleasures marked them as a race apart.

The carving of the alabaster surroundings to the door and the decoration of the niche are by Samuel Watson, a young Derbyshire man who spent his life working in stone, marble and wood at Chatsworth. The statue of Apollo is by Caius Gabriel Cibber. The ceiling painting is by Louis Laguerre.

The children of the 4th Duke of Devonshire in the grounds of Chiswick House, by Johann Zoffany, 1765. William, later 5th Duke, is on the left.

Georgiana was a Spencer of Althorp and in 1774 she married the 5th Duke of Devonshire, the most eligible man of his generation. Her mother, Lady Spencer, wrote of her at the time, 'She is amiable, innocent and benevolent, but she is giddy, idle and fond of dissipation.' She pleaded with her daughter to watch her reputation, but Georgiana was tempted by the amiable, easy-going life around her: 'Play at whist, commerce, backgammon, trictrac or chess, but never at quinze, lou, brag, faro, hazard or any game of chance.' Her mother pleaded, but in vain, for all their set gambled, and in 1775 Georgiana had to admit to Lady Spencer that she had debts. Georgiana's first gaming debts were settled by the Duke after Lady Spencer had intervened, and when she was next in difficulties she approached Mr Coutts, the banker, and he was most amiable. He lent her money and was so sympathetic that by the end of 1790 she admitted that she owed £60,000 to him. By the end of 1804, however, she was forced to make a full confession to the Duke. When she died two years later, he discovered that her total indebtedness amounted to £109,135.

No less complicated was Georgiana's private life. In the spring of 1782 Lady Elizabeth Foster, daughter of the Earl of Bristol, the Earl-Bishop, took refuge with Georgiana after she had fled from her husband. The Duke and Duchess invited Lady Betty to join them at Bath and they soon became an inseparable threesome. 'Canis', 'Mrs Racky' or 'The Racoon', and 'Mrs Rat' or 'Rat', as the Duke, Lady Betty and Georgiana named each other, went everywhere together. 'Racky' went to France for a time to look after the Duke's illegitimate daughter and after she returned, she settled at Devonshire House as the Duke's mistress and the Duchess's

'angel friend'. It was a most unorthodox situation even by the standards of that time. The Duke had three children by the Duchess, two by Lady Betty, and the Duchess one by Charles Grey, who later became Prime Minister. Most of these children were brought up together at Devonshire House.

After Georgiana died, the Duke married Lady Betty and when she became a widow in 1811 she settled in Rome and carried out excavations there.

William, 6th Duke of Devonshire, succeeded his father in 1811. He was twenty-one and found himself in absolute possession of the four Cavendish country houses, Chatsworth, Hardwick, Bolton Abbey and Lismore Castle, the three London houses, Chiswick, Burlington House and Devonshire House, and land in Ireland and eight English counties which yielded an income of £70,000 in 1813–15. The fact that this vast inheritance was heavily encumbered and under half this sum was available to him did not concern the young Duke unduly. Mr David Cannadine has made a thorough study of the Cavendish family finances and discovered that by 1814 the enormous sum of £593,000 was secured on the Devonshire estates. The figure had been growing in the previous forty years at an alarming rate. Mr Cannadine estimates that £300,000 was secured by 1790, of which sum £170,000 had been spent on the purchase of land since 1773, and £63,000 on the construction of the crescent at Buxton. The expenses of life at Devonshire House and Duchess Georgiana's gambling debts go some way no doubt to account for the balance.

The Duke chose not to concern himself with this gloomy aspect of his inheritance, for there was so much to enjoy. Chatsworth needed his urgent attention; the 1st Duke after all had not finished the interior of the house and it was most uncomfortable, there was nowhere for the young Duke to house Bishop Dampier's great collection of books which he had bought in 1812, the domestic offices were cramped and insufficient, and he did not care for the entrance front whatever pains the 4th Duke had taken to improve it. Furthermore, members of the public could peer into the windows of his private apartment and, as the number of tourists in the summer was by then considerable, he was continuously harassed. The Duke found the gardens neglected and the gardeners demoralized, which is hardly surprising since Joseph Paxton counted eight bunches of grapes in two vineries and a grand total of eight rhododendrons when he took over as head gardener a few years later. The Duke turned his attention first to the architectural problems and then to the horticultural possibilities. He found two partners, Jeffry Wyatville and Joseph Paxton, and, working in perfect harmony together, they increased the ducal liabilities to just about £1,000,000 by 1844. Paxton was aghast when he saw the accounts. 'I have been the cause of Your Grace spending a great deal of money,' he wrote, 'had I been at all aware of your real position, I certainly never should have done so.'

Had the Duke himself any conception of the state of his financial affairs? Perhaps, but somehow the news that a tree had been sighted in the garden of a ruined monastery in Burma, or the knowledge that a copy of the most important of all early Italian illustrated books, the *Hypnerotomachia Poliphili*, was about to come on the market, distracted his attention from more humdrum affairs; he never appears to have taken an objective view of this mighty sum, for, quite literally, tears of happiness obscured his vision.

The Duke is one of the most engaging figures in the history of Chatsworth. He loved the house, 'that villa of mine in the Peak', with passionate

The state bedroom. The bed in which George II died in 1760 was brought to Chatsworth by the 4th Duke and was a perquisite of his office as Lord Chamberlain.

The library. This was originally the long gallery and was refitted by Sir Jeffry Wyatville for the 6th Duke in about 1830 to house his fine collection of books.

The state dining-room, one of the 1st Duke's great state rooms. The carvings of game, flowers and foliage were executed between 1692 and 1694 by Joel Lobb, William Davis and Samuel Watson and the ceiling painting is by Antonio Verrio. The gilt furniture was made by William Kent, the side-tables came from the collection of Lord Burlington, the father-in-law of the 4th Duke, and the centre table was bought by the 6th Duke.

intensity. 'What happiness I have in Chatsworth,' he wrote, 'adorable Chatsworth, happiness beyond words.' His handbook to the house compiled for the amusement of his sister Lady Granville has about it the contagious gaiety which his contemporaries felt in his presence.

The Duke never married, although he delighted in the company of women, who found him most attractive, and he lavished on Chatsworth the affection other men devote to their fellow human beings. He was convivial – the life and soul of every party, 'larking parties' in particular – but also deeply religious, introspective and subject to bouts of melancholia, connected no doubt with his deafness which became worse as he grew older. Political life held few attractions for him. He was Lord Lieutenant of Derbyshire from 1811 until his death, and undertook a special mission to Russia in 1826 to attend the coronation of Emperor Nicholas. Apart from a brief period as Lord Chamberlain to George IV and William IV, he devoted the rest of his life to his artistic and horticultural interests.

The Duke's alterations and additions to Chatsworth began in 1818. Wyatville transformed the long gallery of the old house into a library and then proceeded to build a north wing, with a dining-

room, extensive domestic offices, a theatre and a sculpture gallery to house the Duke's fine collection of contemporary sculpture.

Between 1832 and 1842 Wyatville restored the state rooms, for the Duke did not use them and found their decoration unappealing. 'This great unappropriated apartment,' he wrote, 'which consumes in useless display the best habitable part of the house … this dismal ponderous range of Hampton Court like chambers.' In fact the only occasion on which the state rooms were used for their original purpose appears to have been the visit of King George and Queen Mary to Chatsworth in 1913. The Duke also decorated the rooms below the state rooms and his own private apartments on the west front, employing J. G. Crace in 1839 to redecorate the lower library (the present Duke's study).

If the Duke had less than twenty-two people to dinner guests would assemble in his new antelibrary. 'I find the most formal, weariest, hungriest moment of life less painful,' he wrote, 'when the patients are squeezed together in a small compass; there is less space for their ceremonies, their shyness, and their awkwardness.' Larger parties gathered in the library and on very grand occasions in the drawing-room, but 'the march' from there to the dining-room he found 'awful'. The Duke installed an elaborate heating system in the library, Price's Apparatus, which was situated in the cellar and under the west corridor and was regulated by valves in the room and ventilated by an air-duct in the west front. It also warmed the chapel.

The first stage of Wyatville's decoration was ready just in time for the Duke to receive the young Princess Victoria and her mother in October 1832. The Princess was thirteen and not only was the dinner the first to be held in the new dining-room (apart from the full-scale rehearsal the day before), but it was the first grown-up dinner party the Princess had attended. Inside the house the Princess singles out for special praise in her diary only the new kitchens; their size and cleanliness she wrote were 'superb', but there was much to admire outside – the plants in the conservatory, the fountains, a monkey on a chain and a Russian coachman in full dress. The gardens were looking magnificent and, although it was October, there was not a fallen leaf to be seen in the morning, for Paxton kept a gang of 100 men working through the night to sweep leaves from the paths and lawns. After dinner on the second night the Princess and the large house-party gathered at the windows to look at the fountains and the cascade illuminated in different colours, and to watch a spectacular display of fireworks; almost inevitably, charades ended the evening's festivities.

By the date of the royal visit in 1832, Joseph Paxton had been at work in the Chatsworth gardens for just over six years and the transformation of the wilderness into a spectacular garden was well advanced, for he had twelve acres of kitchen garden under cultivation, thirty new hothouses in operation, three houses stocked with orchids and the planting of an arboretum under way. Violet Markham, Paxton's granddaughter and biographer, describes him as a man of daemonic energy.

Joseph Paxton and the Duke first met at Chiswick, where the gardens of the Horticultural Society which Paxton managed adjoined those of Chiswick House. The Duke was not at that time interested in horticulture but on his walks he would meet and fall into conversation with the young gardener who must have impressed him, for when the position of head gardener at Chatsworth fell vacant in 1826 the Duke offered him the job. Paxton was twenty-three and on the day he arrived at the house the Duke set off for his embassy to Russia and did not return for six months. Paxton left London for Chatsworth by coach and arrived at 4.30 in the morning. He began as he intended to continue, and within a few hours had taken complete command of the situation which he was to retain until he became absorbed in the construction of the Crystal Palace, which he designed to house the Great Exhibition of 1851. 'As no person was to be seen at that early hour,' he recalled, 'I got over the greenhouse gate ... explored the pleasure grounds and looked round the outside of the house. I then went down to the kitchen gardens, scaled the outside wall and saw the whole of the place, set the men to work there at six o'clock; then returned to Chatsworth and got Thomas Weldon to play me the water-works and afterwards went to breakfast with poor dear Mrs Gregory and her niece. The latter fell in love with me and I with her, and thus completed my first morning's work at Chatsworth before nine o'clock.'

Paxton duly married the housekeeper's niece, Sarah, and set about educating himself at Chatsworth. His enthusiasm for horticulture proved infectious and before long the Duke was as passionately interested in the subject as his head gardener. The plants and trees introduced to Chatsworth were legion and expeditions were made all over the world in search of rare specimens. It was above all a great partnership; the Duke encouraged Paxton's interest in glasshouses and new methods of glazing and heating, efforts which culminated at Chatsworth in the construction of the great conservatory (demolished after World War I).

The Duke did not spend all his time at Chatsworth. He was there for a brief period at the beginning of the year and would then return in August for much of the autumn, broken by a visit to Bolton, and odd weekends at Buxton, Castle Howard or elsewhere. His house-parties invariably took place in the autumn and he tended to have between 100 and 200 people to stay each year. Thus in 1827 his guests included Princess Esterhazy, Henry Greville, Sir Thomas Lawrence and Lord John Russell; in 1828, Lords Melbourne,

Georgiana, Duchess of Devonshire, with her daughter Georgiana Dorothy, by Sir Joshua Reynolds. This is one of Reynolds's most celebrated portraits and was painted in 1784. The Duchess was the greatest political hostess of the age, and gave dazzling parties at Devonshire House in London. Her daughter went to live at Castle Howard as the wife of the 6th Earl of Carlisle. Her silver-gilt and coral rattle is preserved in her bedroom there.

The yellow drawing-room in the private apartments, designed by Wyatville in about 1839.

Palmerston and Durham; Sir Edwin Landseer stayed with him for a couple of weeks in the autumn of 1831 and again in 1853; Sir William Hooker came in 1839; and in 1843 he entertained the Queen and Prince Albert and a large house-party which included Lord Melbourne, the Duke of Wellington, Lord Palmerston and the Buccleuchs, Bedfords and Normanbys. Charles Dickens was a welcome visitor in 1851. So the circle of Whig nobility in which he had grown up was gradually expanded to include friends from other worlds, literary, horticultural and artistic. Chatsworth was kept up with the utmost magnificence: the household expenses amounted to over £36,000 a year in the 1830s. The Duke was adding constantly to the library and the art collections, and he rebuilt the village of Edensor between 1838 and 1842. By that date, the financial crisis, which had threatened for so long, erupted

and he was forced to cut back his expenses and to sell land. Apart from his collection of coins and medals which he sold, the other treasures remained intact. In 1854 the Duke had a stroke and four years later he died suddenly at Hardwick.

His debts amounted to about £1,000,000. The nephew who succeeded him as 7th Duke was a businessman who for a time revived the family fortunes. He invested heavily in the development of Barrow-in-Furness at the time of its expansion after the discovery of iron ore, and created modern Eastbourne. The present Duke describes him as a grim man who taught his wife geometry on their honeymoon, and he lived too long, for his investment at Barrow went sour just at the beginning of the great agricultural depression. He neither bought nor sold works of art and was content to own Chatsworth for thirty-three years and do nothing to it but keep the structure in

The lower library, decorated by John G.Crace in 1839, formed part of the 6th Duke's private apartments, and is now the present Duke's study.

reasonably good repair, for after the death of his wife he became withdrawn and did not entertain. The 8th Duke rehabilitated the family finances but he was forced to sell land in Derbyshire and Ireland to do so.

The 8th Duke succeeded his father in 1891. He was a distinguished Liberal statesman, known for most of his life as the Marquess of Hartington, or 'Harty-Tarty'. He had entered the Cabinet as Secretary of State for War in 1866 when he was in his early thirties but though he served as Secretary for India and Lord President, he refused the premiership. When he succeeded to the dukedom, he was unmarried for the simple reason that the woman he loved – and who ruled his life – was herself married to another duke. Duchess Louise was a German countess by birth, and she met her first husband, Viscount Mandeville, when he went to stay with her family to learn the language. She

married him in 1852 and three years later he succeeded as Duke of Manchester. Within a few years Duchess Louise had established herself at the head of a fast London set which Queen Victoria looked upon with supreme distaste. Towards the end of the 1850s, Duchess Louise's eyes had lit upon the young Lord Hartington who had had the most sheltered upbringing, for his father who had been unhappy at Eton decided not to force his son to undergo the same experience. The Duchess had some very uncomfortable moments at the start of her pursuit as Lord Hartington promptly fell head over heels in love with the young courtesan, Catherine Walters, known as 'Skittles'. Skittles had a passion for horses as did Lord Hartington, and she was employed by the keeper of livery stables to parade his horses. Her figure was shown off to perfection in a skin-tight riding habit, and every head turned as she cantered by in Rotten

Row or on the hunting field in Cheshire. She was beautiful, wild and fearless. Later in life she hunted with the Quorn, certainly the only courtesan to do so. Lord Hartington proposed to her and proceeded to ask the old Duke's permission to marry. The Duke was charmed by Skittles, but not to the point of sanctioning the marriage and Lord Hartington was packed off to the United States. When he returned to England, he made for the Duchess of Manchester and not for Skittles (though he behaved handsomely towards her), and thus began a relationship which lasted thirty years and was known to everyone including Queen Victoria who breathed a sigh of relief when she heard of the Duke of Manchester's death in 1890. Two years later 'Harty-Tarty', who had by this time become Duke of Devonshire, married Louise, and the 'Double Duchess' as she is generally known presided over the great Devonshire estate until the Duke's death in 1908. This was the golden age of Chatsworth. The Duke was an intimate friend of the Prince of Wales, and Chatsworth became the setting for raffish Edwar-

The sculpture gallery. The 6th Duke visited Rome in 1819 and began to form an important collection of contemporary sculpture. The two seated ladies by Canova are Napoleon's sister, Princess Pauline Borghese, and on the right, his mother, Madame Mère.

dian house-parties organized by the Duchess.

The Duke was fond of horses – racing, breeding and hunting – and for relaxation he played cards. His political activities stemmed more from a sense of duty than passionate interest, for he was indolent by nature and hated writing or making speeches. He was, however, a man of sound judgement. 'I don't know why it is,' he once said, 'but whenever a man is caught cheating at cards the case is referred to me.' He didn't care a fig for dress and wore the same clothes until they were threadbare. He never remembered people's names: 'Do you know the name of that red-faced man over there?,' he asked a friend one evening in the library at Chatsworth before dinner. And if any arrangement was left to the Duke to make, nothing happened. He never selected the guns from among his guests until late and frequently was too tired to make up a new list. Lord Rosebery once left Chatsworth in a fury after he had come down to breakfast in shooting clothes only to be informed by his valet that his name was not listed. Margot Asquith wrote of the Duke: 'He had the figure and appearance of an artisan, with the brevity of a peasant, the courtesy of a king and the noisy sense of humour of a Falstaff. He gave a great wheezy guffaw at all the right things and was possessed of endless charm.' For thirty years, Harty-Tarty was content to allow his mistress to fight for him, push him and arrange his life. As a young girl she was said to be ravishingly beautiful and this, coupled with an iron will, unlimited ambition and considerable shrewdness enabled her to maintain her position as a leader of London society for years. She never divulged secrets and was much disliked by other women. Her set was fast and there was much cheating at cards among her friends. She and Harty-Tarty kept up the formalities in public and invariably addressed each other by their titles. The Duke of Portland's mother was once delighted to overhear the Duchess forgetting herself for one moment as she sat at a writing table at Welbeck and called out, 'Harty darling, stand me a stamp.'

Louise was the first duchess to reign at Chatsworth since 1811 and from the time of her marriage to the Duke in 1892 until his death in 1908 she presided over the most enormous house-parties. Twelfth Night was always celebrated in style, and in 1903, when Louise was seventy-four, she wore a very *décolletée* dress with a wreath of green leaves in her wig. Vittoria di Sermoneta saw her as a very old lady at the races, stiffly corseted, sitting on a bench, immovable and immensely dignified with a fixed expression on her face. 'One day I was rewarded,' she wrote, 'by seeing her pull up her skirts and produce a purse from a bag secreted among her petticoats. "Put two pounds on *Cream Tart*," she said to one of her satellites. It sounded like the voice of an oracle.'

John Cornforth has described in *Country Life* the elaborate domestic arrangements at Chatsworth about this time. The permanent staff consisted of housekeeper, six laundry maids, a laundry porter and boilerman, six housemaids and a still-room maid, stable staff, about seventy men in the garden, two lodge porters who managed the gate in twelve-hour shifts and worked for a total of ninety hours a week each, a night fireman, a dairy maid, an electrician and his boy, and a coalman who carried a hundredweight at a time up eighty stairs to the top floor. When the Duke and Duchess were in residence they brought with them the house steward, the groom of the chambers, a valet, the under butler, three footmen, the steward's room-man and the travelling usher. When the house was full the housemaids would make a start at 5.00 am on the grates which they first cleaned and polished and then made up and lit. If one of them was on bad terms with the footmen, the fires would not be raked at night and the grates were still hot in the morning. The laundry at Chatsworth also took in the washing for Devonshire House, Hardwick and Bolton Abbey and was well equipped with a steel boiler, which heated a steel table, a drying rack and a hot cupboard. The laundry appliances were driven by water power as were the turbines for the electricity which was put into Chatsworth by the 8th Duke and the Double Duchess soon after their marriage. Chatsworth was, in fact, the first great house to have electric light.

The 9th Duke parted with Devonshire House just after the end of World War I, and, in 1926, all the Devonshire estates and art collections were transferred to a company. After the death of the 10th Duke in 1950, the family was faced with crippling death duties which resulted in the sacrifice of many outstanding works of art, and Hardwick which passed to the National Trust.

Chatsworth and its incomparable collections are now visited by a quarter of a million people a year. They go to see a great country house, a superb assortment of works of art beautifully displayed and the gardens and estate in good order. The present Duke and Duchess of Devonshire have contributed to the restoration, redecoration and further adornment of Chatsworth on such a considerable scale and with such happy results that every visitor must wish most fervently that their efforts to ensure Chatsworth's survival are successful.

Left: William, 6th Duke of Devonshire, depicted at the opera by Sir Edwin Landseer. The Duke inherited Chatsworth at the age of twenty-one in 1811 and added the north wing and made many alterations to the existing house. He was a great book collector and horticulturalist, and his long partnership with Sir Joseph Paxton resulted in the Chatsworth gardens becoming the most celebrated in the country.

Below: The chapel corridor. The 6th Duke wrote, 'The great ancient Greek foot was sold to me by Carlo Finelli, the sculptor at Rome: it belonged to the Quirigi family at Lucca, and was long in their palace.'

For years Mr George Howard has pleaded the cause of his ancestor the 3rd Earl of Carlisle. At one time Lord Carlisle was accorded no credit for the part he played in the conception of Castle Howard which Mr Howard believes was considerable. Gradually the pundits have come to accept Mr Howard's view that Lord Carlisle, Vanbrugh and Hawksmoor worked together as a team. Mr Howard based his view on his intimate knowledge of the house in which he has lived all his life and his insight into the nature of patronage. For Mr Howard is a notable patron of the arts and he has enriched Castle Howard and its surroundings in a manner which is rivalled only by his eighteenth-century ancestor, the 5th Earl of Carlisle. He is Chairman of the Governors of the BBC, President of the Historic Houses Association, former Chairman of the council of the Royal College of Art and connected with a host of other organizations.

'When did you take over at Castle Howard?'

'After the war. My father didn't believe in primogeniture any more than his parents did and he left the house equally to my elder brother Mark, my younger brother Christopher and myself. They were both killed in France, so it came to me.'

'This inheritance presumably had a considerable effect on your life.'

'Yes, I had always wanted to write and I expect I would have ended up as a political journalist. I have never wanted to be an MP. Mark would have carried on the family political traditions.'

'What was the state of the house and the collections when you took over?'

'Terrible! We had had one fire in 1932 when four rooms were burnt and another during the war when the house was let to a girls' school. This was disastrous, for the cupola and the lantern of the dome were destroyed and over two-thirds of the south front was gutted. The trustees decided during the war that the family would never live in the house again and tried to sell it to the school. In 1944 a leading auctioneer advised them that the price of the pictures and works of art would never be higher and they sold paintings – a dozen Canalettos among other things – and books. When I returned from Burma the house was filthy and bare and the furniture and pictures were in store. The dome was covered in concrete! I put an immediate stop to the selling. Cecilia and I married in 1949 – the year the school moved out of the house – and in May 1953 we moved back. My sister Katie's wedding in that year was the first large social event there after the war.'

'Did you set about tackling the restoration at once?'

'Cecilia was as determined as I was to come back and live here. We made our own wing habitable and then we began on the restoration of the Temple of the Four Winds. This was in an appalling state. I could never have attempted it without her, and of course we had Rupert Gunnis to encourage us.'

'And you have accomplished an enormous amount in the gardens.'

'Yes. Jim Russell is a marvellous plantsman. We have been friends for over thirty years. When his nursery closed I offered him a house and he has lived here on the estate for the past twelve years. The rhododendron collection in Ray Wood is now the largest in the country after Windsor – the Savill collection – and our collection of old roses is nearly the largest. I like the china roses and teas the best but we have modern roses too. We began to plant the arboretum in 1979 – it extends nearly a mile on the edge of the park – and were lucky enough to buy all the rarer things on Harold Hillier's list when Hilliers cut back their stock. We are now established internationally, we correspond with botanical gardens overseas and receive bits from expeditions and so on.'

'And you are still full of plans for Castle Howard?'

'Oh yes! I feel I must get on with all the things I have intended to do over the last thirty years.'

The hall. The dome, designed by Sir John Vanbrugh, was finished in 1706. The original decoration by Pellegrini was destroyed by fire in 1940 and was recreated in 1962–3 by the Canadian artist, Scott Medd.

Castle Howard

YORKSHIRE

Lord Howard of Henderskelfe

By the age of thirty-two Charles, 3rd Earl of Carlisle, had secured an enviable position for himself in the Whig hierarchy. He was able to spend as much time away from government and court circles as he pleased, without losing his influence or forfeiting the royal favours which came his way. This suited his temperament, for he could be the most convivial of men; he enjoyed political intrigue and the society of men of wit and intelligence, yet at times he yearned for solitude and the company of his books. And he was drawn away from London to his Yorkshire estates by the great passion of his life – the building and decoration of Castle Howard, which occupied him for thirty-eight years and was unfinished when he died.

Lord Carlisle began with great advantages. Not only did he inherit extensive estates in the North of England with a family seat in Parliament and influence at court, but he was one of the first members of his family for generations to enjoy his patrimony in uninterrupted peace. He was born in the year after the 'Glorious Revolution' of 1688, which banished James II and placed William and Mary on the Throne. As a young man he was able to reap the benefits this brought about and to become a member of a stable Establishment at a time of civil calm.

His ancestors were not so fortunate. Lord William Howard, the 3rd Earl's great-great-grandfather, was eight years old when his father Thomas, 4th Duke of Norfolk KG, was beheaded on Tower Hill in 1572 for the part he had played in the web of intrigue surrounding Mary, Queen of Scots. Lord William's grandfather, Henry, Earl of Surrey, the poet, met a similar violent end.

The Howard line was founded by William Howard or Hayward, an astute young lawyer from King's Lynn in Norfolk, who established himself as a country landowner in about 1277, was

The antique passage. This contains part of the collection of ancient marbles collected by the 4th Earl of Carlisle.

knighted by Edward I, and rose to become Chief Justice of the Common Pleas. His descendant John was created Duke of Norfolk by Richard III. The 1st Duke remained loyal to the Yorkist cause and died at the Battle of Bosworth in 1485.

Lord William Howard was the founding father of the Castle Howard family. He and his brother Philip, Earl of Arundel, sons of the 4th Duke, were married at a very early age to daughters of Thomas, Lord Dacre of Gilsland. Lord William was married to Elizabeth and Philip to Anne and the girls eventually became co-heiresses to the great Dacre estates in the North of England. Elizabeth inherited lands in Cumberland, Northumberland, Lancashire and Yorkshire. She and Lord William made their home at Naworth Castle in Cumberland, but part of Elizabeth's Yorkshire inheritance was the Manor of Henderskelfe which had passed through eighteen generations of her family. So extensive were her estates that she was

known as 'Bessie with the braid [broad] apron'.

Their great-grandson, Charles, followed family tradition and made Naworth his principal seat, but it is evident from his letters that he spent some of his time at Henderskelfe.

Charles Howard steered his way through the Civil War and beyond with great skill. He served Charles I and Cromwell – he was summoned to Cromwell's rather ineffectual House of Lords – and had switched sides in good time to greet the Restoration. This he did with sufficient fervour to impress Charles II who created him, in 1661, Earl of Carlisle.

The 1st Earl rebuilt the house at Henderskelfe presumably with fortifications, as it was known at the time as Henderskelfe Castle. This building was gutted by fire ten years later, shortly after the death of the 2nd Earl which occurred in 1692. It was left to the 3rd Earl to make good the damage. He did so, and indeed lived there for the next twenty

A staircase in the private apartments.

Castle Howard from the
south.

Detail of the decoration in
the hall, showing some of the
4th Earl of Carlisle's
collection of ancient
sculpture.

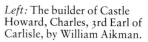

Far left: A corridor in the private apartments. The figure on the right is a plaster cast of the statue of Lorenzo de' Medici by Michelangelo in the church of San Lorenzo in Florence.

Left: The builder of Castle Howard, Charles, 3rd Earl of Carlisle, by William Aikman.

The chimney-piece in the hall. This is an example of the Italian stuccoists Bagutti and Plura.

Lady Georgiana's bedroom. She was the wife of the 6th Earl of Carlisle and she is depicted as a baby with her mother in the Reynolds portrait at Chatsworth. She died in 1858 and this room is largely as she left it, filled with prints, drawings and water-colour portraits of her relations and friends.

years. But he had more ambitious plans in mind, for beside this ancient place, which his ancestors had held for over 600 years, Charles, 3rd Earl of Carlisle, proceeded to build one of the great Baroque palaces of Europe. He named it Castle Howard.

Lord Carlisle was in his early twenties when he succeeded to the title and estates, and had already made his mark in the House of Commons as Whig MP for Morpeth.

He was appointed a Gentleman of the Bedchamber to William III and acted as Earl Marshal of England during the minority of his cousin, the Duke of Norfolk, officiating as such at the coronation of Queen Anne.

Twice Lord Carlisle held the important political office of First Lord of the Treasury: once during the last year of William III's reign, and for a second time, for a few months in 1715, under George I.

Lord Carlisle first consulted the architect William Talman about his plans for Henderskelfe. Talman had worked at Burghley and Chatsworth and was a fashionable choice. But he was a difficult man to work with, and patron and architect soon fell out over money. Lord Carlisle then made an extraordinary decision. He commissioned plans from an acquaintance, Captain John Vanbrugh, a man in his mid-thirties, who was full of ideas but had never designed a building in his life.

Vanbrugh was a soldier turned dramatist. He wrote two sparkling comedies, *The Relapse, or Virtue in Danger* and *The Provok'd Wife* which were produced in 1696 and 1697. The combination of wit, irreverence and bawdy jokes on stage proved irresistible, and Vanbrugh became one of the most popular men about town. Lord Carlisle and Vanbrugh turned for advice to an architect of great skill, Nicholas Hawksmoor, who was Sir Christopher Wren's assistant.

were unique. The dome and lantern, for instance, which crown the central block, had never been seen in England before on a church (the dome of St Paul's Cathedral was still on the drawing-board), let alone a house. And the visitor's first impression of the interior – a vast hall – was overwhelming.

Lord Carlisle lived in the old house until 1712, when he moved into some of the newly completed rooms in the east wing. An army of craftsmen was employed in the decoration of the interiors. Between 1709 and 1712, the Venetian Giovanni Antonio Pellegrini painted the dome in the hall and the wall spaces with frescoes.

In the autumn of 1713, Vanbrugh was able to report on the success of Castle Howard as a place of habitation. Lord Carlisle had been apprehensive about the level of general domestic comfort on Vanbrugh's scale of priorities. He was worried about draughts in the long corridors and the temperature in the high-ceilinged rooms. After some bitterly cold and stormy nights, Vanbrugh wrote in triumph that the candles stayed alight in the corridors and not one needed to be put into a lanthorn, even in the hall; and furthermore, with moderate-sized fires the rooms were like ovens. Vanbrugh had given all the principal rooms a southerly aspect, while the less important rooms in the east wing were sheltered by the hill of Ray Wood.

In 1721 work on the house virtually stopped. Lord Carlisle was unwilling or unable to complete the west wing and he turned his attention to the embellishment of the landscape. Vanbrugh and Hawksmoor continued to work at Castle Howard for the rest of their lives, Vanbrugh dying in 1726 and Hawksmoor ten years later. Vanbrugh designed the Temple of the Four Winds and Hawksmoor the mausoleum, the plans for which he had to defend against the Palladian sniping of Lord Burlington. They added to the landscape a pyramid, an obelisk, elaborate gateways and other outworks, which drew from Horace Walpole the famous description written after his visit in 1772.

'Nobody ... had informed me that I should at one view see a palace, a town, a fortified city, temples on high places, woods worthy of being each a metropolis of the Druids, vales connected to hills by other woods, the noblest lawn in the world fenced by half the horizon, and a mausoleum that would tempt one to be buried alive; in short, I have seen gigantic palaces before, but never a sublime one.'

Lord Carlisle lived at Castle Howard in the company of his youngest daughter, Mary. We do not know when he and his wife separated. Her name was Anne Capel, and she was a daughter of Arthur, Earl of Essex, a man of scholarly interests and a great gardener, who died in the Tower.

In 1700 Hawksmoor joined forces with Vanbrugh to execute Lord Carlisle's commission, and provided the means by which Vanbrugh's dramatic ideas were translated into the technical language of architecture. As Mr George Howard points out, Hawksmoor was not Vanbrugh's partner in the modern sense of the word but his coadjutor. Vanbrugh could not have succeeded without Hawksmoor's professional assistance. Temperamentally they complemented each other; there was no rivalry and almost no jealousy. Probably the presence of a third party helped, for Lord Carlisle's role was far more active than is usually implied by the term 'patron'. The working relationship between the three men was so close that it is impossible to establish the precise nature of their individual contributions. Between them, they conceived and built a house which was startlingly unconventional.

Work began in 1701. As a first bold stroke, Vanbrugh placed the principal façades of the house to face north and south with grand views, choosing a site a little to the east of the old castle of Henderskelfe.

It became apparent as Castle Howard rose from its foundations that the design bore no relationship to any other house in England. The scale, the plan and the original use of architectural detail

John Evelyn saw Anne Capel as a child at her home at Cassiobury and was irritated by the way in which her mother spoiled her.

The Carlisles had five surviving children, two sons – Henry, Viscount Morpeth, and Charles who became a general – and three daughters. Lord Carlisle was especially attached to his daughters Anne and Mary. Anne married Rich, Viscount Irvine, a Yorkshireman and a soldier, who died of smallpox as a young man. Whereas Mary stayed at home helping to entertain the numerous visitors to Castle Howard, Anne lived as a widow in London. She wrote poetry, and kept up a lively correspondence with her father, bringing him up to date with all manner of gossip and political news, and accounts of the latest books and plays. She visited him when she could, but the journey was always hazardous – there was mud to negotiate in the winter, and the threat of highwaymen at all seasons. One day Anne, who was on her way from London to Castle Howard with £160 of her father's money, watched in horror as the York coach was stopped on Finchley Common, only forty yards in front of her, and robbed. The highwaymen did not touch Anne when they saw that her father's coachman, Bulfin, was armed, but they attacked the stage coach 100 yards behind her and got what she called 'a good booty' of two watches and over twenty pounds.

Anne's visits to Castle Howard tended to fall in the late spring, and she would then travel on to Scarborough for the season which began at the end of June; Lord Carlisle sometimes accompanied her, for the waters eased his gout. Anne became in 1736 a Lady of the Bedchamber to the new Princess of Wales.

Elizabeth, Lord Carlisle's eldest daughter, married a Whig lawyer and politician, Nicholas Lord Lechmere, who died of apoplexy in 1727. After her husband's death she returned home. 'I prepose so much pleasure in being at Castle Howard,' she wrote to her father, 'that tho' 'tis very Unreasonable at My Age, to wish Time to Quicken its Natural Motien, Yet upon this Ocasion I can't forbear doing it, till I am there.'

But, despite the enthusiasm of her letter, she and her father did not get on well together. In 1728 Elizabeth married for the second time; she chose Sir Thomas Robinson, an amateur architect. Robinson was fond of imparting advice on every subject to anyone who would listen. He showered Lord Carlisle with letters about Castle Howard, passing on gratuitous advice from Lord Burlington and others.

Lord Carlisle was evidently disappointed in the husbands his daughters chose. But Sir Thomas Robinson did his best for Elizabeth. She was an intelligent woman; her sister Anne described her circle as 'for wit and conversation' rather than cards. But she was a hypochondriac, and had what we would call a nervous breakdown, the effects of which lasted for several years. She would not venture forth from her house, and she and Robinson sat at home playing endless games of piquet.

In 1737 Robinson opened his heart to Lord Carlisle in a long letter asking for help. For Elizabeth was also an alcoholic, addicted to 'both spirituous & other Liq^{rs} & so frequently to such an excess, & so very publickly, that 'tis now too late to conceal'.

Lord Carlisle was too old and frail to assist. Robinson had added that he did not wish to trouble 'your beloved retirement at Castle Howard', for this was rapidly coming to an end.

It was well known that Lord Carlisle was increasingly reluctant to leave Castle Howard, unless to go to Bath for the waters. He did not hold ministerial office again after 1715, but he retained his court appointments. He was Constable of the Tower between 1715 and 1722, and Constable of Windsor Castle from 1723. In 1730, however, George II decided that his Constable must be in attendance at the Castle. Sir Robert Walpole wrote a tactful letter to Lord Carlisle asking him to put the appointment at his disposal, 'both in regard to the state of your health and the retired country life which you seem to make your choice'. He was offered the Mastership of the King's Foxhounds and Harriers instead, at the same salary of £2000 per annum which he had received as Constable, and with a deputy to do the work. Lord Carlisle held the Mastership until his death which occurred at Bath in 1738.

Two thousand pounds was roughly what he had spent each year on Castle Howard. There is an account in his handwriting which gives details of what he had expended between 1701 and 1737 on buildings, gardens, plantations and outworks; this amounts to £78,240 2s 10d. Lord Carlisle raised no mortgages and, although he had gambled heavily as a young man, he left no debts. Castle Howard had been built from the income of the estate.

Daniel Defoe was impressed by what he heard at Castle Howard in 1727: 'they say his Lordship sometimes observes Noblemen should only Design, and begin great Palaces, and leave Posterity to finish them gradually, as their Estates will allow them'. Lord Carlisle was an optimist. For, although the main body of the house was finished, the result was not quite as he had anticipated.

Sir Thomas Robinson persuaded the 4th Earl to allow him a free hand on the unfinished west wing. Robinson had loathed Vanbrugh. Walpole mentions them 'spitting and swearing at one another'.

One of Vanbrugh's endless corridors which the 3rd Earl feared would be unheatable.

Robinson no doubt relished the opportunity to draw up plans and start building the west wing in a Palladian style which bore no relationship whatsoever to Vanbrugh's east wing.

Henry, the 4th Earl, appears to have preferred Rome to Castle Howard. He had taken a close interest in his father's work, but was content to leave its completion in the hands of his brother-in-law. He added to the estates in the 1750s but not in the way his father recommended, for the debts he incurred were a most unwelcome legacy to his successors.

He was however a passionate collector, and in Rome took the opportunity of making a good collection of antique sculpture and gems to adorn Castle Howard and his London house.

His first wife was Frances Spencer, a daughter of Lord Sunderland. She died in 1742 and the year after, he married Isobella, daughter of William,

Lord Byron. Isobella's life was a long saga of debts and indiscretions and, as her son Frederick succeeded his father at the age of ten in 1758, she continued to play a vexatious role in the history of Castle Howard.

Frederick, 5th Earl of Carlisle, was forced to fend for himself at a very early age. His mother remarried, but she made a bad choice and the bickering of mother and stepfather drove her son from home.

Frederick attracted attention throughout his life. His education at Eton and King's College, Cambridge was supervised by a private tutor, Mr Ekins, who, although more than seventeen years Frederick's senior, remained a devoted companion and friend.

At Eton, Frederick met Charles James Fox. They became close friends, Frederick spending much time at Holland House, the Fox family home in London, and looking on Lord Holland as a second father. The Fox family launched Frederick into London society – Whig society – and he became a member of various London clubs such as Brooks's, White's and the Society of Dilettanti.

At White's, Frederick met another father figure, George Selwyn, a wit and connoisseur; their great friendship is commemorated in the double portrait at Castle Howard by Sir Joshua Reynolds.

Frederick made a Grand Tour – an eighteen-month journey through France and Italy – accompanied from time to time by Charles James Fox. At Turin, Frederick was invested by the King of Sardinia with the insignia of the Order of the Thistle which had to be presented by a sovereign. He was made a Knight of the Garter in 1793. In their long history, only about fourteen Knights of the Thistle have subsequently become Knights of the Garter.

He returned to the London life to which Fox had introduced him. He gambled. He became a leader of fashion, and was said to have attempted to introduce 'the foreign foppery' of red heels into England. 'I was afraid I was going to have the gout the other day,' he wrote to a friend. 'I believe I live too chaste, it is not a common fault with me.'

His marriage to Lady Caroline Leveson-Gower in 1770 brought him a father-in-law who was a steadying influence on his life.

In the early 1770s Frederick spent huge sums on improvements at Castle Howard and he built the stables, for he was a passionate rider to hounds. It was not so much his own personal extravagances which wrecked him, but the gambling debts of Fox for which he had stood surety.

Frederick was in 'a scrape'. By the mid-1770s he owed nearly £300,000, although a third of this sum represented his father's debts. In 1775 his estates were conveyed to trustees, and for the next eleven years they were out of his hands. His income was £4000 a year; it was obvious that he must find gainful employment. He chose politics.

In 1778 he headed a commission of five sent to America by the British Government to treat with the rebels. It was strange, Walpole thought, as indeed many others must have done, that 'a young man of pleasure and fashion, fond of dress and gaming ... totally unacquainted with business' should be sent. But the truth was simple. Frederick had offered his services to Lord North, and William Eden, the second commissioner, was adamant that he should go. Although the commission had little power, Frederick emerged with credit from the negotiations and he envisaged a future somewhat akin to the later idea of dominion status.

This incident was typical of Frederick's career. He was probably underestimated by his contemporaries: his reputation for fast living clung to him, his manner which was reserved to an extreme offended those whom he did not know well, and yet those who did, such as the sage William Eden, thought the world of him.

In 1780 Frederick was appointed Lord Lieutenant of Ireland. He remained in Dublin for sixteen months. The position was ideal, for it combined political responsibilities with opportunities for grand entertainments. He took with him a French chef Bertrand and a retinue of servants in smart new liveries. Despite his liberal and conciliatory attitude to the Irish – he was careful, for instance, to wear clothes of Irish origin, especially in public – he was able to achieve little. 'It is beyond a doubt,' he wrote, 'that the practicality of governing Ireland by English law is utterly visionary. It is equally beyond a doubt that Ireland may be well and happily governed by its own laws.'

In 1786 Frederick was released from his trustees and from then on his political interests shifted from national to local Yorkshire affairs. He was able to spend time at Castle Howard. He became Lord Lieutenant of the East Riding. For a glorious decade from the early 1790s he was able to emulate his grandfather, the 3rd Earl. He devoted himself to the adornment of Castle Howard, to his literary interests, and to hunting. Thereafter his health, which he always said had been ruined by the Irish climate, let him down.

The west wing had been completed to the designs of Sir Thomas Robinson during his minority, as his father had left money for this purpose. But it was no more than a lumber room when Frederick commissioned C.H. Tatham to create a new dining-room, the long gallery and a chapel, which were built between 1800 and 1810.

Frederick had bought works of art on the Grand Tour, and in the 1770s he purchased paintings of the Flemish, Dutch and Italian schools. For twenty years he was forced to keep well away from the art market for financial reasons. In the late 1790s he returned. He bought a magnificent *Adoration of the Magi* by Mabuse for 500 guineas. In 1798 he joined his wife's uncle, the Duke of Bridgewater, and his brother-in-law, Lord Gower, to buy the Italian paintings owned by the Duke of Orleans. Frederick kept twelve paintings from this collection which was probably the finest in private hands at the time. These included *The Dead Christ Mourned* known as *The Three Maries* by Annibale Carracci which cost £4000 and works by Giovanni Bellini, Giorgione, Titian and Domenichino. The Mabuse, the Annibale Carracci and the Giovanni Bellini are now in the National Gallery in London.

Frederick's eldest son Lord Morpeth and his wife Georgiana, a daughter of the 5th Duke of

The 9th Earl and Countess of Carlisle in about 1865. He was an accomplished painter and she was a formidable champion of women's suffrage and the temperance movement.

Devonshire, lived at Castle Howard with him. In 1807, Georgiana's sister Harriet stayed at Castle Howard. She was delighted by Frederick; he was awe-inspiring and he ruled his family with a rod of iron, but she appreciated his great kindness and good humour. He took her to see the poultry-yard with which she was most impressed, telling her grandmother that 'it is better to be a Pheasant at Castle Howard than most things elsewhere'.

Later Sydney Smith came to the neighbourhood as Rector of Foston. He was a great addition to the family for there were few agreeable neighbours, and Smith's company leavened Frederick's spirits which his children were not always successful in doing. He told Frederick that 'The pursuits of an English Nobleman should be Politics, Elegant Literature and Agriculture'.

Frederick had retired from politics; he spent time writing plays and poems and he acquired an interest in agriculture late in life. But ill health clouded his last years and the loss of a son at

Waterloo was a bitter blow.

He died in 1825, and was succeeded by his statesman son, George, the 6th Earl.

Sydney Smith was delighted to hear that the 6th Earl and his wife intended to stay at Castle Howard, for she preferred Naworth, the romantic old Dacre castle in Cumberland, which played an increasingly important part in the lives of the Howard family in the nineteenth century.

In the late 1870s, the Howard estates were taken over by George, a grandson of the 6th Earl and a nephew of the 7th and 8th Earls, one a worthy public figure and the other a country clergyman who died in 1889.

George, 9th Earl of Carlisle, was born in 1843. He was a painter of note. He always regarded himself as a professional, working in water-colours using the techniques of the Pre-Raphaelites. He was strongly influenced by Ruskin.

In 1864 he married Rosalind, daughter of Lord

Opposite: Frederick, 5th Earl of Carlisle, in the robes of the Order of the Thistle, by Sir Joshua Reynolds.

Below: In a bedroom at Castle Howard.

A house-party at Castle Howard to celebrate the twenty-first birthday of Mark Howard ten days before the outbreak of war in 1939. The group includes, standing fifth and sixth from the left, the present Duchess and Duke of Devonshire; ninth, Mr George Howard, the present owner; seated second from the right, the Duchess of Northumberland. Mark Howard, seated centre, and Christopher Howard, seated on the far right, were killed in the war.

and Lady Stanley of Alderley. She was a woman of great originality and strength of character who developed advanced political ideas. 'My parents taught me to lisp Liberal watchwords when I hardly knew what they meant,' she recalled.

George and Rosalind Howard spent their honeymoon at Naworth and always preferred it to Castle Howard in later years. Philip Webb designed a house for them in London which was decorated by William Morris and Edward Burne-Jones.

In the 1880s Rosalind Howard became an ardent supporter of Home Rule for Ireland, the most divisive issue of the day, which clouded many family relationships including her own. She held most controversial views. She championed the cause of women and she was a rationalist. She turned her back on London society just as firmly as London society closed its doors on her.

Her husband was perfectly happy to leave the management of the estates to her. She tackled the problem of the mortgages (C.J. Fox's gambling debts still hung over the family finances) and she paid them off by the sale of land in Northumberland.

But her principal interest in life – and this became a crusade – was the temperance movement. In this she was warmly supported by her husband who joined her in closing down all the pubs on their estates. Both became teetotallers in the early 1880s. There was, however, wine for

Stable boys at Castle Howard, 1893, George Tiplady and John Palliser with Tipler. Palliser taught the present Mr George Howard how to ride.

male guests in the house (Lady Stanley of Alderley brought her own flask of brandy), but even the wine disappeared after she became President of the National Women's Temperance Association in 1903.

All sorts of stories circulated about her. She did *not* empty the contents of the cellar at Castle Howard into the lake as was widely believed. She protested vigorously to the *Daily Mirror* when the paper suggested this in 1916, insisting that the only wine she had ever poured away was rubbish and 'Not even a dipsomaniac under the influence of his worst craving would have touched the mixture of fungus and smelly liquid.'

She did stop the brewing of audit ale at Castle Howard after disorderly scenes among the august company of the British Association for the Advancement of Science, who visited the house after their Golden Jubilee meeting in York. And she dispensed with the services of footmen, employing a succession of tall parlourmaids who looked like grenadiers and were less inclined to sample the contents of the decanters.

She made economies at Castle Howard. For instance, she put a stop to the ancient custom whereby the remnants of the 100 candles lit each evening became the butler's perquisites. Despite her thriftiness, she maintained a staff of thirty domestic servants in her three houses.

She was an excellent speaker in public, and addressed meetings all over the country on her chosen subjects. She was full of good works, bringing women and children to Castle Howard from Leeds and Bradford for holidays.

She feuded with her eleven children. They had an unconventional upbringing, for public schools were frowned upon after Charles, the eldest, had been unhappy at Rugby, and a succession of tutors and governesses was engaged. The children were allowed total freedom to climb over the Castle Howard roofs, ride ponies without a groom, or visit the tenants. Christmas was spent at Castle Howard. Rosalind would supervise the decoration of the Christmas tree under the dome in the hall. Everyone was roped in to help, the family, the maids, the vicar's wife, but Rosalind herself would decide on the decoration of every twig on every branch. She was also obsessed with health and health cures. She visited the baths at Nauheim on several occasions and brought two women to Castle Howard to demonstrate to her children the health-posture cure. One of her daughters remembered this vividly: 'We stood in rows (generally including my mother) under the cedars, stuck out our busts and bottoms as far as we could, and breathed deeply from our diaphragms. We intoned "Quoth the raven 'never more, never mo-o-ore, never mo-o-o-ore'", on a single breath for as

long as it could hold (by a stop watch)'. The children accompanied their parents to Italy each year where, after a vigorous day of sight-seeing, Rosalind would tour the local hotels to ensure that she had found the most reasonable. In one hotel in Venice she thought nothing of packing up and moving on when she discovered that the candles were not included in the price. The evenings would be spent reading aloud from Ruskin, Augustus Hare or Mrs Jameson. Inevitably some of her children reacted. Her eldest son married a *Tory*. Another fought in the South African War (Rosalind was pro-Boer). Geoffrey alone of her children remained unswervingly loyal to her and the Liberal cause.

After her husband's death in 1911, Rosalind carried out a suggestion of his and invited the trustees of the National Gallery to take what they wished from the Castle Howard collection; she also sold them the Mabuse *Adoration* at this time. Neither believed in the principle of primogeniture, and when Rosalind died she left Castle Howard, after many vacillations as to whom it should go, to her daughter, Mary. This was hardly a welcome bequest, for Lady Mary was married to the Professor of Greek at Oxford (Gilbert Murray), and both were ardent Liberals. A family conference redivided the estates and Castle Howard became the property of the Honourable Geoffrey Howard passing eventually to his son, Mr George Howard. Naworth became the seat of the earls of Carlisle.

When Mr Howard took over after World War II, he was faced with the almost overwhelming task of restoring the house after the fire in 1940 and the general neglect of the war years. The stonework too was in urgent need of attention for the eighteenth-century building practice of binding one stone with another by an iron cramp had resulted in serious damage to no fewer than one-sixth of the stones. The restoration of Castle Howard was begun by Howard and his wife, Lady Cecilia, and has been going on ever since. After Lady Cecilia's death in 1974, Lord Middleton paid tribute to her in *The Times* describing the energy and enthusiasm with which she threw herself into the task, and 'that wonderful partnership' which preserved the house and 'brought about a miracle of restoration'. In 1978 Mr Howard planted a rose-garden and dedicated it to her memory, placing the following inscription above the entrance-gate:

'Ad Memoriam Ceciliae
Amatae Rosarum Amatricis
Haec Rosaria Dedicavit G. H.
MCMLXXVIII.'

'In memory of beloved Cecilia, lover of roses, these rose-gardens have been dedicated by G. H. 1978.'

John George, 11th Duke of Marlborough, owns the largest private house in Britain. The vast expanse of honey-coloured stone work and the extensive roof, not to mention the 2000-acre park surrounded by seven miles of stone wall, are in constant need of repair and restoration.

'Do you ever feel tempted to give up the struggle?'

'No! never. I *live* for Blenheim. Of course it's a daunting task. I call it my long drawn out Battle of Blenheim.'

'Were you brought up here?'

'No, I was born in London and brought up at Lowesby Hall in Leicestershire where my parents lived before my father inherited. My father hunted there. They moved here in 1935 and lived in the whole house, the saloon for dinner, the breakfast-room, the tea-room and summer luncheon-room, with an indoor staff of about twenty.'

'When did you inherit Blenheim?'

'In 1972.'

'And by then the house was one of the great tourist attractions in the country.'

'My father opened the house four days a week in 1950, but it had been opened on occasions by my father before the war and by my grandfather. We persuaded my father to open five days a week and now of course it is seven days.'

'And your private apartments too. Don't you mind people tramping through your bedroom?'

'I am not there. And the private apartments are very popular, I have to think of that. I have a house not far away where we go for the summer months; we have young children and no private garden at Blenheim, we cannot keep them here with 350,000 people passing through. But we return in September.'

'Apart from your exodus in the summer do you spend most of your time at Blenheim?'

'I'm in London two days a week but otherwise I'm here. Local things interest me – boys' clubs for instance – and I'm a JP. My wife and I hunt and I have a very small stud – four mares – started recently. And I farm 3700 acres.'

'You have recently replanted the northern avenue; was that a victim of elm disease?'

'I'm afraid so. We replanted with limes; it was an enormous job. My grandfather planted the elms in the late 1890s, and wrote a fierce note in the Forestry Book saying that anyone who cut the trees down for the purpose of selling the timber is a scoundrel and deserves the worst fate that can befall him! I fear all "Capability" Brown's beeches are coming to the end of their lives.'

'Will you explain about the quit-rent for Blenheim? Is there one standard which goes backwards and forwards to Windsor Castle or do you send one each year?'

'Indeed we do, *most* carefully! It's the rent! We used to have a standard made each year but what with inflation and so on we tend to order them in small quantities now. The current standard hangs in the Waterloo Chamber at Windsor for the year and is then replaced – most certainly.'

The saloon. The painted decoration is by Louis Laguerre, who depicts himself and Marlborough's chaplain, Dean Jones, between the columns on the left. The marble door-case was designed by Grinling Gibbons, and the over-door is emblazoned with the arms of the Duke and the two-headed eagle to which he was entitled as Prince of the Holy Roman Empire. The saloon was used as a state dining-room until the 1930s and is now used on special occasions such as Christmas Day. The silver centre-piece on the table to the left shows the Duke of Marlborough after his victory at Blenheim writing his famous dispatch to the Duchess.

Blenheim Palace

WOODSTOCK, OXFORDSHIRE

The Duke of Marlborough

In the first state room at Blenheim there is a framed dispatch on view. It is a scribble in pencil on the back of a tavern bill and was sent by John, Ist Duke of Marlborough, to his Duchess. 'I have not time to say more,' it reads, 'but to beg you will give my duty to the Queen, and let her know her army has had a glorious victory.' And thus the news reached England of Marlborough's decisive defeat of the armies of France and Bavaria on 13 August 1704. The battle was fought at Blenheim, a small village on the north bank of the Danube. Marlborough's six-hundred-mile march from the North Sea to the Danube, and the superb victory which crowned the enterprise, have, in the words of the Duke's descendant Sir Winston Churchill, 'always ranked among the finest examples of the art of war'. When the news reached Windsor, it is said that Queen Anne was playing dominoes with Prince George; she began at once to plan a suitable reward for the hero. He arrived in London in December with Marshal Tallard, the defeated French commander, sixteen French generals, other high-ranking officers, and a mass of colours and standards which were paraded around London. By this time Queen Anne had decided upon her gift: the royal manor of Woodstock and a palace which she would build there to commemorate his achievement.

John, Duke of Marlborough, was fifty-four at the time of the Battle of Blenheim, Captain-General of the Queen's Armies and Master of the Ordnance. His wife Sarah, who had been Queen Anne's closest confidante from girlhood, filled the offices of Groom of the Stole, Mistress of the Robes and Comptroller of the Privy Purse. They were the most powerful subjects in the land. John Churchill had been a soldier from the age of seventeen when he was commissioned as ensign in

The great hall. The ceiling was painted by Sir James Thornhill in 1716 and shows Marlborough kneeling to Britannia and presenting a plan of the Battle of Blenheim.

the Foot Guards. His father Sir Winston Churchill, a descendant of a West Country family, became a colonel in the Royalist army during the Civil War and at the Restoration, MP for Weymouth. Sir Winston was introduced at court through the patronage of Lord Arlington so that by the time his children Arabella and John grew up, he had established a position for himself, and an entrée for them. They made good use of it. Arabella became the mistress of the King's brother the Duke of York (later James II) and bore him several children, one of whom became the Duke of Berwick; John, the handsome young Guards officer, began a liaison with Barbara Villiers whose title, Duchess of Cleveland, had been bestowed by a grateful sovereign.

But there was only one woman in John Churchill's life, and that was Sarah Jennings whom he married in 1678 after a courtship conducted by her with great skill. It was a love match, which lasted until the day he died. 'I am resolved ... to be your slave as long as I live,' he had written to her before they married. And she wrote to her soldier-husband, 'Wherever you are, while I have life, my soul shall follow you, my ever dear Lord Marlborough.'

John Churchill was a colonel when they married, and there was little money to spare. 'From the very beginning of his life, he never spent a shilling beyond what his income was,' Sarah wrote years later. 'He began with the first commission of an ensign in the army, and went on regularly through every step in that profession.'

John Churchill's romantic nature was hidden beneath his calm, handsome exterior, but this was to find expression in the disposition of a battle or the planning and embellishment of Blenheim. He was also, as Dr Rowse has explained, 'a fascinating mixture of caution with extreme daring'. Lord Ailesbury observed John Churchill in the Netherlands over a period of time and left his impressions in his memoirs: 'For his natural good temper he never had his equal. He could not chide a servant, and was the worst served possible; and in command he could not give a harsh word, no, not to the meanest serjeant, corporal or soldier.' He was thus ideally equipped to cope with his wife Sarah, a woman of great beauty, who was by nature wilful and determined, practical and careful.

From a very early age, Sarah was close to Princess Anne and soon after the Princess's marriage to Prince George of Denmark she became a Lady of the Bedchamber. The Princess was emotionally dependent on Sarah; indeed so close did the friendship of the Princess and the Churchills become that she suggested they wrote to each other in perfect equality and perfect

freedom using the names Freeman and Morley. The Princess left Sarah to choose which she preferred. 'My frank, open temper naturally led me to pitch upon Freeman,' wrote Sarah, 'so the Princess took the other; and from this time Mrs Morley and Mrs Freeman began to converse as equals, made so by affection and friendship.'

At that time there was very little prospect that Anne would survive her sister Mary and come to the throne. When she did, Mr and Mrs Freeman became Her Majesty's favourite subjects. The great military appointments which had eluded Churchill under James II and William III were eagerly bestowed upon him; he was made a Knight of the Garter and created Duke of Marlborough. 'I hope you will give me leave,' the Queen wrote to Sarah about the dukedom, 'I know my dear Mrs Freeman does not care for anything of that kind nor am I satisfied with it, because it does not enough express the value I have for Mr Freeman, nor nothing ever can how passionately I am yours, my dear Mrs Freeman.' Sarah was adamant that a dukedom was useless without the means to uphold it. The Queen came to their aid with a grant.

Thus when Queen Anne received the news of the victory at Blenheim, she was able to savour the triumph at both a national and a personal level.

The Queen gave to Marlborough the manor of Woodstock and 2000 acres, and signified that she would build him a house there at her own expense which was to be called after the village where he won his famous victory. The quit-rent for Blenheim is one standard which bears three fleurs-de-lis and is presented at Windsor Castle on every anniversary of the battle. Unfortunately the quit-rent was the only arrangement made and that was a token. The Queen never mentioned how much

The 1st Duke and Duchess of Marlborough with their family, painted in 1693 by Johann Baptist Closterman. Their son, on the extreme right, died of smallpox at the age of seventeen.

money she was prepared to pay, no agreement was ever entered into: it was after all a matter between friends. Parliament confirmed the initial gesture as a gift of the nation to the Duke, and John Vanbrugh was engaged as architect. Marlborough himself chose the soldier-dramatist and worked in harmony with him throughout the period that Vanbrugh worked on the palace. The Duchess would have preferred Sir Christopher Wren.

The manor of Woodstock was a royal hunting-lodge, steeped in history and legend, when Vanbrugh visited it in 1704. It was a picturesque ruin barely habitable and overlooking a swamp. Vanbrugh chose a site on level ground to the south of the old house where the land fell sharply away into the valley to the west. He was anxious to retain the manor house and incorporate it into the landscape.

As at Castle Howard, Vanbrugh enlisted the aid of Hawksmoor, and by the spring of 1705 he had produced his initial design and prepared a model which was shown to the Duke and Duchess, the Queen and the Government. Everyone except the Duchess was impressed. The foundation stone was laid in the following June.

Both Vanbrugh and Marlborough envisaged a palace on an heroic scale. Vanbrugh consulted various people about the commission and the general opinion was that although the plan must take into account the fact that the Duke and Duchess intended to live in the palace, the building should be considered a royal and a national monument; '*Beauty, Magnificence and Duration*' Vanbrugh decided were the attributes most fitted to reflect this.

The Duchess on the other hand wanted a private house; the concept, the plan and the model were deeply offensive to her parsimonious spirit. Before long she had fallen out with the architect. 'I made Mr Vanbrugh my enemy,' the Duchess wrote, 'by the constant disputes I had with him to prevent his extravagance.' Marlborough was away on his campaign for months on end; the Duchess was left to supervise the building. He longed for the moment when Blenheim would be inhabitable; nothing was ever accomplished quickly enough. 'Pray press on with my house and gardens,' he wrote to the Duchess, and yet Vanbrugh infuriated her with talk of grottoes and temples and the vast bridge he intended to build across the swamp.

Vanbrugh gathered together an outstanding team of artists and craftsmen to work on Blenheim. Hawksmoor was responsible for most of the detail. Henry Joynes was appointed resident overseer. He was twenty-one when work began and within two months of the laying of the foundation stone had 1500 men on site, but he was

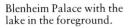

Blenheim Palace with the lake in the foreground.

The entrance front.

Vanbrugh's great bridge over the tiny River Glyme, half submerged by 'Capability' Brown when he made the lake.

not his own master which made his position difficult for he had to work in conjunction with the Duchess's man.

The master-masons included the Edward Strongs, senior and junior, who had worked on St Paul's Cathedral and were responsible for most of the stonework of the main building; two Oxford men, John Townesend and Bartholomew Peisley who built the clock tower, the grand bridge and the east front; and Henry Banckes of Guiting who built the colonnades of the great court.

Grinling Gibbons carved the principal decorative ornaments in stone which were concentrated on the sky-line with dramatic effect; the choice of these was made by the Duchess, a slow and laborious process which involved hoisting numerous models for her to accept or reject. Gibbons also carved the two groups on the clock tower which portray a lion and a cock and symbolize the savaging of France by Britain.

Sir James Thornhill and Louis Laguerre were brought in to paint the hall and saloon, Isaac Mansfield to carry out the plasterwork, and Langley Bradley and John Rowley to provide clocks and sundials. Henry Wise began work on the garden at the first possible opportunity. The planning of the garden was of the greatest interest to the Duke, and Wise designed for him parterres, avenues, plantations and walled gardens. Work started on the grand parterre where 1700 yards of earth had to be moved and replaced.

Slowly the great palace began to take shape. The main block is 480 feet across and contains the hall, stairs, saloon and state rooms flanked by a corridor, an elaboration of the Castle Howard plan. To this were added long side wings, private apartments to the east and a picture gallery (which later became a library) to the west, and kitchens and stables which enclose a deep forecourt. The scale on which it was conceived was unparalleled: the English answer to Versailles. The north front differs markedly from that at Castle Howard, for at Blenheim Vanbrugh has placed at the four corners of the building massive pavilions as high as the attic of the portico on the main block. It evokes an effect of sheer mass and an overwhelming sense of military might. Vanbrugh miraculously sustains the drama of his composition, from the loggias of the kitchen and stable court to the pavilions, through the quadrants to the centre block, up to the pediment, and again up and beyond to the crowning pediment and the finial. The sky-line with the Gibbons figures, the trophies of arms and the grenades on the pavilions is one of the great architectural sights in England.

Sir Winston Churchill wrote: 'About his achievements Marlborough preserved a complete silence, offering neither explanations nor excuses for any of his deeds. His answer was to be this great house.'

And how Sarah, who loved the Duke so passionately, hated his house, 'this wild unmerciful Hous'! For his sake, she accepted it, she helped to build it, she recognized that Blenheim was his passion and his greatest weakness, for Blenheim in the Duke's eyes nothing was too good. But Vanbrugh she would not tolerate. They quarrelled at every stage and about every aspect of the construction. Vanbrugh was not the Duchess's only headache. The unthinkable happened, and she was supplanted in the affections of Queen Anne by her cousin and protégée Mrs Masham. Sarah had her last deeply distressing interview with Queen Anne in the spring of 1710. In the same year the Tories came to power. Marlborough was stripped of all his employments at the end of 1711 and in the following year work at Blenheim ceased. The financial situation was chaotic. £220,000 had been spent on the house and it was not half completed; £45,000 was owed to the contractors. There were furious scenes on site as the workmen realized that there was no money to pay them: the Marlboroughs said they were not responsible for the debts of the Treasury, the Tories were unwilling to come to the rescue. Queen Anne was bitterly hurt. There was nothing on paper. When work began, Lord Godolphin had issued a warrant to Vanbrugh to make agreements with the contractors, and the necessary money was issued by the Treasury to the Duke. This was a most unsatisfactory arrangement because it appeared to make both Vanbrugh and the Duke liable when the money from the Treasury dried up.

For two years the Marlboroughs went into exile. They returned the day after Queen Anne died in 1714. 'My lord Duke,' said George I to Marlborough, 'I hope your troubles are now all over.' The Blenheim debt was acknowledged, but the Duke decided to finish the palace at his own expense. Vanbrugh and Hawksmoor remained with him but some of the craftsmen who had been owed money for years and whose claims had not been settled in full were reluctant to go back. Gibbons and the Strongs had been paid only a third of what was due to them; the Duke then asked them to lower their rates for him. This was the final straw and they refused to return.

Work resumed in 1716, but the Duke had a stroke, and by the end of the year relations between Vanbrugh and the Duchess had broken down. He left. 'You have your end, Madam,' he told her, 'for I will never trouble you more unless the Duke of Marlborough recovers so far as to shelter me from such intolerable Treatment.'

Finally, the Duke was able to furnish the palace with all the treasures he had collected over the

The third state room. The furniture is French. The painting over the chimney-piece shows the 1st Duke of Marlborough with Colonel Armstrong, his chief engineer, studying a plan of Bouchain and the Duchess considered the painting of the Duke 'as like him as ever I saw'. She called in the Colonel to help her plan the waterworks in the grounds of Blenheim.

years and above all with the great tapestries depicting his victories which he had ordered in Brussels. The Duke and Duchess moved into Blenheim in 1720 and he spent his last two summers there. He died in 1722.

The Duchess was left with the palace. Their son John had died of smallpox in 1703 and the dukedom was inherited by their eldest daughter Henrietta. Sarah remained devoted to the Duke's memory until her own death in 1744. She built the great Column of Victory in his honour, and put up a triumphal arch which was designed by Hawksmoor after he returned to Blenheim to work. One day in her widowhood, the 'proud' Duke of Somerset sought her hand. She made this magisterial reply: 'If I were young and handsome as I was, instead of old and faded as I am, and you could lay the empire of the world at my feet, you should never share the heart and hand that once

belonged to John, Duke of Marlborough.'

When Vanbrugh appeared at Woodstock in 1726 in the company of Lord and Lady Carlisle, Sarah gave instructions that he was not to be admitted to the park. He cannot have been surprised; he had thought of her for years as, 'That B.B.B.B. old B. the Dutches of Marlbh'; he had seen his palace on one occasion when he knew she was away but he never saw it again for he died later that year.

At length, even Sarah was reconciled to Blenheim. She delighted in the growing beauty of the surroundings; 'it will be a wonderful fine place,' she concluded, 'and I am glad it will be so, because it was the dear Duke of Marlborough's passion to have it done.'

After the death of Henrietta, Duchess of Marlborough, in 1733, the dukedom passed to her sister's child Charles Spencer, Earl of Sunderland,

The west gate.

whose brother John was the ancestor of the earls Spencer of Althorp. It was not until 1817 that the 5th Duke applied for permission to add the name 'Churchill' to that of Spencer, in honour of his illustrious ancestor.

The 3rd Duke did not spend much time at Blenheim but his son George, 4th Duke of Marlborough, presided over its fortunes for nearly sixty years. He turned his attentions to the garden.

The 1st Duke of Marlborough's garden had been planned by Henry Wise with military precision. It covered seventy-seven acres and included a 250-yard parterre patterned in dwarf box, beyond which was a formal wilderness called the Woodwork with yews and hollies, bays and laurels planted to form symmetrical walks.

The 4th Duke employed 'Capability' Brown at Blenheim for a period of ten years between 1764 and 1774. Brown radically transformed what he found. He swept away Wise's garden and allowed the grass to grow up to the walls of the palace; he also landscaped the park and planted thousands of trees.

He then turned his attention to the problem of the bridge. The grand bridge was designed by Vanbrugh and constructed at vast expense to cross the marshland through which trickled the River Glyme. Vanbrugh had envisaged this marsh transformed into an ornamental expanse of water crossed by the finest bridge in Europe. After Marlborough's death, Sarah called in Colonel Armstrong to replan the waterworks in the park and the River Glyme was channelled into canals, with a cascade at the bridge and a formal pool on the western side. Brown dammed the river and created the lake, and thus gave meaning to Vanbrugh's great stone bridge at the same time as he half submerged it.

Brown created the perfect setting for Vanbrugh's architecture, although any tribute to his genius is tinged with melancholy at the thought of the garden he swept away. No one regretted the loss of the 1st Duke's garden more than Charles, 9th Duke of Marlborough, who succeeded his father in 1892 when he was twenty-one. He nursed a passion for Blenheim second only to that of his great ancestor. His melancholy face stares out of the great Sargent portrait which he commissioned of himself and his family in 1905. Dr Rowse has summed up the character of this singular man, 'an aesthete, with a cult of perfection, whether in riding or architecture, buildings, landscape, dress or women'.

First, he was forced by circumstances to set about repairing the Marlborough family fortunes. The 3rd Duke was fabulously extravagant, the 4th Duke spent £100,000 on the gardens and the 5th Duke wasted his inheritance and ended his life in virtual bankruptcy. The 7th Duke was a Lord Lieutenant of Ireland and a most worthy man, but he was hard-pressed for money and began the wholesale dispersal of the Blenheim treasures. First he sold the 1st Duke's fabulous collection of gems, and then the Sunderland library which had been formed between 1710 and 1728 by the 3rd Earl of Sunderland, the 1st Duke's son-in-law, and was one of the greatest collections of books in private hands. The 8th Duke, much to the bitter regret of his brother Lord Randolph Churchill, decided to disperse the whole of the Blenheim collection of paintings – eighteen paintings by Rubens, two Titians, two Rembrandts, eight Van Dycks, works by Claude, Poussin, Watteau and Lancret. The Rothschilds, the director of the Berlin Gallery and other great collectors snapped them up at the sale; and then the Duke began on the porcelain. The proceeds were not squandered; he spent the money on his favourite pursuits science and agriculture – hot-houses and farm buildings; he also put in the organ in the long library and his American second wife installed central heating and electricity. But the paintings had gone for ever.

There was only one way in which the young 9th Duke could establish himself at Blenheim and that was by marriage with an heiress. At the same time, on the other side of the Atlantic Mrs W.K. Vanderbilt, who was a very ambitious woman indeed, decided to bring her daughter Consuelo to Europe for her début. There was a strong American element in London society at that time and in the Prince of Wales's set alone this included Lady Paget, Lady Randolph Churchill and Consuelo, Duchess of Manchester, among others. At Lady Paget's, Consuelo Vanderbilt met the Duke of Marlborough for the first time; she was seventeen, and she noticed and remembered his beautiful hands. She was invited to Blenheim. Consuelo did not realize when she returned to America that her wedding dress had been ordered in Paris, so certain was her mother of the success of her carefully laid plans. The Duke visited America and caused a sensation wherever he went. He proposed to Consuelo in the Gothic room of the W. K. Vanderbilt mansion Marble House, Newport, Rhode Island, 'whose atmosphere,' Consuelo wrote in retrospect, 'was so propitious to sacrifice.'

Her introduction to the Spencer-Churchill family was nerve-racking, the Dowager Duchess was formidable, her mother-in-law Lady Bland-ford was friendly, but her eccentricities were disconcerting, for she was fond of playing practical jokes on her guests such as putting small pieces of soap among the cheese. Lady Randolph and her son Winston were utterly charming.

Consuelo found that in the whole of Blenheim there was not one pleasant room to live in; and each morning she was greeted by the sight of a motto which had been placed on the chimney-piece in her bedroom by the 8th Duke: 'Dust. Ashes. Nothing.'

Consuelo and the Duke parted in 1906 and were later divorced. She married Jacques Balsan and went to live in France; the memoirs she wrote, *The Glitter and the Gold*, give a vivid account of her life at Blenheim and the domestic arrangements common to great country houses at that time.

The household staff on the male side was ruled by the butler and consisted of the groom of the chambers, the under butler, three to four footmen and the odd men. Two electricians as men of science were considered the butler's equals. The rule of the housekeeper on the female side was absolute. Six housemaids, a barely adequate

The 9th Duke and Duchess of Marlborough and their two sons, by John Singer Sargent. The Blenheim standard, as the French royal standard captured at the battle had become known, hangs above them near a bust of the 1st Duke. The Duke wears his robes of the Order of the Garter but for aesthetic reasons Sargent refused to paint the Duchess with pearls, much to the horror of one of her sisters-in-law, who remarked that she should not appear in public without them. Blenheim spaniels have been bred here since the early eighteenth century.

contingent for a palace, lived in a tower which was known as Housemaids' Heights; there were also five laundresses and a still-room maid who cooked the breakfasts and the cakes and scones for tea. A French chef presided over a staff of four and there was constant friction between him and the housekeeper over the breakfast trays because meat dishes were provided by the kitchen, and the kitchen and the still-room were separated by yards of passages. Consuelo's personal maid, Rosalie, was a dour Swiss selected for her by her mother-in-law who remained with her for twenty years until she died; Rosalie was utterly devoted to Consuelo; she disliked men, the Duke in particular, and groaned at the idea of going away for a weekend party for she knew she would have to share a room with other maids and fight with them to secure the bathroom for her lady. Consuelo gives a vignette of life in the old-fashioned country house ill-equipped with bathrooms when she describes going up to dress for dinner and coming across a queue of maids standing with sponges, towels and underwear, waiting 'in sulky enmity' for possession of the bathroom for their ladies. At Blenheim there were very few bathrooms and a round bathtub was placed in each guest's bedroom before the fire with hot and cold water-jugs, soap and sponge bowls, towels and mats.

At the weekend house-parties, twenty-five or thirty guests arrived in the late afternoon on Saturday. Tea was laid out in the Italian garden, with scones, cakes, bowls of Devonshire cream, and mountains of strawberries and raspberries to eat, and tea or iced coffee to drink.

The Duke and Duchess were strict about the length of dinner – one hour for the eight courses – and woe betide anyone who enjoyed their food and lingered over it! Two soups, one hot and one

The Bernini fountain on the second of the water-terraces to the west of Blenheim, designed by Achille Duchêne and the 9th Duke in the 1920s.

The 10th Duke of
Marlborough and his cousin
Sir Winston Churchill who
was born at Blenheim in
1874.

cold, were served simultaneously, followed by a choice of hot or cold fish, an entrée, a meat dish, and sometimes a sorbet which preceded the game. In the summer when there was no game, quails from Egypt fattened in Europe or ortolans from France were served instead; they cost a fortune. Dinner ended with a sweet, a savoury and pyramids of fruit. The Duchess would rise as soon as the hour was up and lead the ladies into the long library where Mr Perkins, the organist, played Bach or Wagner. The men sat for half an hour over coffee and liqueurs.

These dinners required a superhuman effort on the part of the staff if they were to serve and remove the eight courses in the prescribed hour. Above all this meant close co-operation between the butler and the chef for the kitchen was a considerable distance away from the dining-room.

When the chef felt overworked, he would show his displeasure by serving ortolans for breakfast. The Duchess considered this *nouveau riche* as they cost even more than the quails which were expensive enough at 5s each.

In the dining-room, a basket full of tins was placed on a side-table on which the butler left the remains of lunch. The Duchess was expected to scrape the food off the plates into the tins which were carried to the neighbouring villages for distribution to the needy. Consuelo remarks that before she arrived at Blenheim, it had never occurred to anyone to separate the meat, vegetables and sweets into different tins.

The 9th Duke of Marlborough made an outstanding contribution to Blenheim for he gave back to the palace the formal setting which 'Capability' Brown had swept away. The Duke found a French architect, Achille Duchêne, with whom he worked for years. He began in 1910 by paving the grand north entrance court which Brown had grassed over; this was laborious because it covers three acres, but was not difficult to plan because there were early engravings to follow. The other work needed much more thought, and below the windows of the private apartments on the east side, Duchêne made a sunken Italian garden, with patterned beds of dwarf box, an echo of Henry Wise's work.

Between 1893 and 1919 the Duke planted nearly 250,000 trees on the Blenheim estate, and in 1896 he began to replant the great avenue of elms to the north of the palace.

In 1925 after the war he tackled the garden to the west where difficulties presented themselves because the land sloped away towards the lake. Together with Duchêne he conceived a series of water-terraces – two were constructed in the end – which covered most of the slope. The Duke lavished care and thought on the designs and was delighted with the results. Mr David Green quotes in his history of Blenheim a letter the Duke wrote. 'Pray tell M. Duchêne that the ensemble of the Terraces is magnificent ... The proportion of the house, the Terrace and the Lake is perfect.'

The Duke never turned his attention to the south front: by the time the water-terraces were finished, his second marriage had failed and he was a sick man.

Inside the house, he tampered with the decoration of three of the state rooms, but he was young at the time, and he lived to regret what he had done. He stripped the house of its Victorian accretions, and in the long library he reinstalled the book-cases which had been ripped out after the Sunderland collection had been sold, and bought some fine books to fill the shelves.

One of the more frequent visitors to Blenheim was his cousin Winston Churchill. Consuelo describes him as the life and soul of every party. It was at Blenheim in 1908 in the Temple of Diana that he proposed to Miss Clementine Hozier and was accepted. 'At Blenheim, I took two very important decisions,' Sir Winston wrote, 'to be born and to marry. I am happily content with the decisions I took on both those occasions.'

Blenheim is full of memories of Sir Winston and at Bladon Church he is buried with the other Spencer-Churchills. Blenheim Palace stands at the centre of an axis which extends from the church tower through the park and garden, the saloon and the great hall, across the forecourt and Vanbrugh's bridge to the Column of Victory, and along the avenue to the other horizon. On top of the column stands John, Duke of Marlborough, holding aloft a winged Victory, and gazing into the far distance over and beyond the grave where his most illustrious descendant lies buried.

116

Sir John Carew Pole inherited Antony from his father in 1924. He was a professional soldier for much of his life, retiring from his regiment, the Coldstream Guards, just before the outbreak of war in 1939, and serving with the county territorials through World War II. He was a Gentleman of HM Bodyguard of the Honourable Corps of Gentlemen-at-Arms and was appointed their Standard Bearer in 1968. He has been active in Cornish county affairs since the war. He served as High Sheriff in 1947–8, as Chairman of the County Council from 1952 to 1963 and was Lord Lieutenant of the County from 1962 to 1977.

He gave Antony to the National Trust in 1961 and lives there today with his second wife.

The staircase, lit with the original bubble globes. The delightful double portrait of Sir John Pole and his wife is by Thomas Hudson. Sir John Carew Pole inherited his baronetcy from the Pole family, together with many treasures.

'How long have your ancestors lived at Antony?'

'For ever. The Carews, of course, have only been here since the middle of the fourteenth century. But Alexander Carew inherited the house from his mother, Joan Courtenay. She married Sir Nicholas Carew, and divided her lands between her sons. Alexander was the fourth. We go back for centuries in the female line. How far we don't know, for beyond a certain point the documents just don't exist.'

'Will you explain why you began life as John Pole-Carew and are now John Carew Pole?'

'Antony is a Carew house but the baronetcy is Pole. I inherited this in 1926 from a distant cousin, Pole of Shute Barton in Devon; it's an ancient baronetcy – early seventeenth-century. I brought many Pole portraits, books and other possessions to Antony.'

'You inherited when you were a very young man. Who looked after the estate when you were with your regiment?'

'My mother. She had been brought up in Ireland; she was a daughter of the Marquess of Ormonde and she coped very well, with the help of an agent, of course. Exactly the same happened in the previous generation.'

'And your father?'

'He was a lieutenant-general. He had been Lord Roberts's ADC and had taken part in the march from Kabul to Kandahar. He commanded in the Boer War. He married late in life. They were a wonderful looking pair; he had grand, extravagant tastes and she rather simple ones, though she loved a party. My mother had great charm.'

'When were you first able to spend some time at Antony?'

'In the 1930s. My first wife was a daughter of Walter Burns, J. Pierpont Morgan's nephew. Her parents' house at North Mymms was full of treasures and she used to travel with her mother collecting furniture. We restored Antony together. I made the decisions about the paintings, and she had the last word on the furniture. We stripped the white paint from the panelling in the library, and brought down all kinds of things from the attic which my parents had banished. They did not much care for the furniture they found at Antony.'

'What happened to Antony during the war? It is so near Plymouth; did the house suffer?'

'We could not have been luckier. The Admiralty requisitioned the house in 1940, and we had two hundred Wrens living here for six years. The front staircase, the banisters and the panelling were boarded up. We stored some of the paintings in the wings, and the best ones were sent to Lanhydrock. The Wrens were model tenants. When the Germans came up the river to bomb Plymouth, the Wrens went on to the roof and pushed the fire-bombs over the edge; they were very brave. Later the Admiralty sent a naval patrol to watch at night.'

'Was there any war damage?'

'We lost the best palm-tree and quite a few windows.'

'When did you decide to offer Antony to the National Trust?'

'After the war. Lord Esher came down with Lady Esher and she fell in love with the place. It was accepted immediately. We endowed it with land primarily and kept the contents. In those days one could compromise with the Trust. We agreed that the family would live in the house, and that it would not be open during the weekends. I know that visitors appreciate the fact that the house is lived in by the family, they tell me so.'

'And the next generation?'

'My son Richard farms with me and is involved in lots of county organizations. And he and his wife have two sons.'

Life at Antony does not change much over the centuries.

Antony House

TORPOINT, CORNWALL

The National Trust:
Colonel Sir John Carew Pole Bt., DSO, TD

Antony House as it stands today was built between 1711 and 1721 by Sir William Carew, the 5th Baronet.

Sir William had time on his hands. As an ardent supporter of the Stuarts, he was out of sympathy with the government of the day and was prudent enough to remain at Antony at a good distance from the Hanoverian court.

He was not idle. He built and decorated a fine house, he intrigued with fellow Jacobites, and he met, wooed and married an heiress.

The Government worried enough about his activities to lock him up for a while in 1715. But, although he vowed to raise Devon and Cornwall in the Stuart cause, he did not make much progress beyond the exchange of his own portrait for that of a fellow conspirator who had pledged to raise Wales.

Sir William's political activities were neither successful nor disastrous and he died two years before the Jacobite rising in 1745. He is remembered by posterity as the builder of Antony.

The name of his architect is unknown which is surprising, for the serene dignified building is the work of an accomplished hand. He used Pentewan stone which came from the cliffs near Mevagissey and weathers a clear, silvery grey not unlike marble and as sensitive to the effects of light and shade.

The style of the house derives from the work of Sir Christopher Wren and was a conservative choice on Sir William's part.

The austerity of the main block makes a striking contrast with the warm red brick of the arcaded buildings, ranged round the forecourt and decorated at the four corners with lead cupolas of a light-hearted design.

The large, square hall on the south front is panelled in Dutch oak as are the smaller rooms, the dining-room, the saloon, and the Tapestry Room, which lie to the south. Rising from the hall is a magnificent oak staircase with the original glass globes for lighting. The library which faces north is panelled in pickled deal.

The hall is a handsome room, but the effect which Sir William and his architect planned was destroyed in the nineteenth century by the removal of the original stone flags and the addition of the porch which make the room darker today than was intended.

Sir William must have taken the decision to build before his marriage but he was no doubt encouraged in his ambitions by the arrival of his wife, Anne, the only child of the 4th Earl of Coventry, her money, and some pretty objects from Croome Court, her Worcestershire home. She was not quite a foreigner as far as her Cornish neighbours were concerned, for her grandmother

was an Edgcumbe of Mount Edgcumbe.

Little is known of the Tudor house Sir William replaced, nor even its exact position. Richard Carew, Sir William's great-great-grandfather, mentions it in his delightful volume *The Survey of Cornwall* published in 1602. But unfortunately Carew is reticent, and whereas he describes neighbouring houses such as Mount Edgcumbe, Antony he refers to as 'the poor home of mine ancestors'.

John Norden found the house 'profitablye and pleasantly seated' but he evidently decided that readers of his *Description of Cornwall* would be more interested in Richard Carew's fishpond than his house, for he gives details of the one but not the other.

Richard Carew, poet and antiquary, was Antony's most distinguished owner and the fifth member of the Carew family to inherit the estate. He was born in 1555.

Dr A. L. Rowse gives a vivid account in *Tudor Cornwall* of the manner in which the county was transformed in the course of the sixteenth century from the last outpost of the known world into a position of international significance. Exploration, the war with Spain, and the growing importance of Plymouth, all contributed to this dramatic change.

Richard Carew lived through this exciting and alarming period when armadas were sighted off the coast of Cornwall and Spanish raiding parties terrorized the countryside. But he was never distracted from the pursuit of knowledge, and the observation of his fellow men. His curiosity was boundless.

His *Survey* gives us a glimpse of life among the Cornish gentry in the late sixteenth century, for when he wrote, there were no noblemen living in that remote land, divided from England by the River Tamar as surely as any national boundary. They were intricately related ('all Cornish gentlemen are cousins', Carew wrote), not rich, but generally with the means to live pleasantly and to send their eldest sons to Oxford.

The families which appear and reappear in Carew's book: Arundell, Buller, Edgcumbe, Rashleigh, Rous, were his neighbours just as many of *their* descendants are of *his* descendants. 'They converse familiarly together', he wrote, 'and often visit one another. A gentleman and his wife will ride to make merry with his neighbour, and after a day or twain those two couples go to a third, in which progress they increase like snowballs, till through their burdensome weight they break again.'

Richard Carew was eight years old when he succeeded his father. He went up to Oxford at the age of eleven where he became a gentleman-commoner of Christ Church. With great pride,

Richard Carew by an unknown painter, shown at the age of thirty-two in 1586 wearing his chain of office as High Sheriff of Cornwall.

Carew described how at the age of fourteen he was called upon 'to dispute *extempore* with the matchless Sir Philip Sidney' in the presence of Sidney's uncles the earls of Leicester and Warwick.

He was admitted to the Middle Temple as his father before him, but instead of travelling abroad after his legal studies were finished, he returned to Antony to assume the responsibilities which would have been his father's had he survived.

Richard Carew became the foremost Cornish gentleman of his time, a Justice of the Peace, and Sheriff of Cornwall at the age of twenty-seven. He was twice elected a Member of Parliament, and was appointed a Deputy Lieutenant with special responsibility for the defence of Cawsand Bay and the neighbouring coast. He was elected a member of the College of Antiquaries in 1598 and joined the company of his friends William Camden and Sir Robert Cotton. He both wrote and translated poetry. In 1577 he married Juliana Arundell of Trerice, a member of the richest and most powerful family in Cornwall.

The hall. The painting in the centre is of the 1st Earl of Hardwicke, the great eighteenth-century Lord Chancellor. The original stone flags were removed in the nineteenth century.

Antony House: the south front.

He loved his books and his fish-pond. His son described how 'he ever delighted so much in reading ... for if he had none other hindrance, going or riding he would ever have a book and be reading'.

John Norden wrote of the fish-pond which played so important a role in Carew's life: 'Below his howse, upon the Creeke of the Sea, he hathe verie arteficially contryued a ponde of Salte water, and that stored with muche and greate varietye of good Sea-fishe'. The remains are still visible, but the banqueting house he planned to build on his island for 'fishing feasts' never materialized.

The pilchard cellars and pier at Portwrinkle are the only building works which survive from Richard Carew's reign at Antony.

Richard Carew died one afternoon in 1620 when he was saying his prayers in his study, and

The tapestry room. The chimney-piece, contemporary
with the building of the house, retains its original glass.
The Soho tapestry depicts a scene from the life of
Diogenes, and was given, with the Aubusson carpet, to
Sir John and Lady Carew Pole by her mother who was a
niece of J. Pierpont Morgan.

was buried in the church at Antony.

His son Richard was created a baronet just before the Civil War which he entered on the Parliamentary side. He died in 1643. A year later his eldest son and successor at Antony, Sir Alexander, was beheaded for treachery.

The Cornish families were fairly evenly divided between the two parties in the Civil War. Sir Alexander and his half-brother John followed their father into the Parliamentary camp.

Sir Alexander was not certain he had made the right choice. When the war broke out he was sent by Parliament to raise the Cornish militia against the King. Later he was appointed Governor of the Island of St Nicholas in Plymouth Sound, a fortress of considerable strategic importance. Sir Alexander wavered. After the fall of Bristol and other reverses on the Parliamentarian side, he appears to have made up his mind he was in the losing camp and he attempted to hand over the island to the Royalists. His treachery was soon discovered and he was arrested. He barely escaped death at the hands of the women of Plymouth (a Parliamentary stronghold) and he was taken to London, condemned to death by a council of war and taken to the scaffold on Tower Hill. He died with a troubled mind. His portrait which Royalist members of the Carew family had slashed when he had first declared for Parliament, was brought from the cellars, repaired and reinstated in its frame. It hangs in the library at Antony and the crude stitches with which it was tacked together are still visible.

John Carew, unlike Sir Alexander, was passionate in his beliefs; he was a staunch republican. He was appointed one of the King's judges, sat every day in court and signed the death warrant. At the Restoration he made no attempt to escape,

View of the hall from the inner hall. The portrait over the chimney-piece is of Charles I at his trial by the West Country painter, Edward Bower. John Carew was one of the judges at the trial, in the course of which the King's beard turned white.

but travelled to London as requested by Parliament to give himself up. He was tried as a regicide and found guilty. He was drawn on a hurdle from Newgate to Charing Cross where his body was quartered. He did not flinch from the pain or the insults of the mob. After his death, the King allowed his brother 'by a great favour' to remove his quarters before they were exposed as was customary on the city gates and that same night they were 'obscurely buried'.

Sir Alexander Carew was the father of Sir John Carew who actively promoted the Restoration, and the grandfather of Sir William Carew, the builder of Antony. Sir William's line died out and the estate devolved upon Sir John's great-great-grandson, Reginald Pole, who became the first Pole-Carew.

The Rt Hon Reginald Pole-Carew MP was full of ideas for the house and garden at Antony. He inherited the house in 1799 and immediately sought the advice of Humphry Repton who drew up one of his celebrated Red Books containing many suggestions for 'improvements'. It is not known how closely Repton's ideas were followed in the grounds surrounding the house but some of the landscaping to the south is almost certainly attributable to him. Regarding the house, Repton and his patron agreed to disagree. Repton's plan to face the brick forecourt with Pentewan stone, for instance, was firmly resisted.

Reginald Pole-Carew presided over the fortunes of Antony for thirty-five years, his son William Henry for fifty years. Father and son sat as Members of Parliament for Cornish constituencies, they preserved the house, tended their estates and were good landlords. William Henry added a billiards-room and the porch to Antony but had no further ambitions for the house. His son Reginald, on the other hand, had very grand ideas. He was a distinguished soldier who took part in the march from Kabul to Kandahar, he was a famous commander in the South African War and retired as a lieutenant-general.

He built on to Antony in about 1902 a wing of red brick, gabled in the Dutch style. It was known locally as Pont Street. He is said to have been away when the building was put up, returned to find it complete and confessed, 'I have ruined Antony.' The wing contained a billiards-room, a dining-room which converted into a ballroom for two hundred people, and a vast bedroom and dressing-room above. It is just visible behind the cedar in a photograph taken for *Country Life* in 1933; Christopher Hussey forced himself to mention 'this excrescence' in his article on the house. It is now no more than a memory.

A Red Indian gilt mask on a George I side-table in the tapestry room.

Sir Alexander Carew, the 2nd Baronet, by an unknown painter. He was arrested for treachery by the Parliamentarians and executed on Tower Hill in 1644. The portrait was hacked out of its frame by Royalist members of his family and the stitches where it has been repaired along the lower edge are clearly visible.

Mr Thomas Cottrell-Dormer receives his visitors in the painted parlour, and speaks of his ancestors as if they were the companions of his youth. In a sense they were, for the history of Rousham and its owners has been a passionate interest of his since childhood. He is by inclination a bookish man.

'Many members of your family have held the office of Master of Ceremonies at court. Was this an hereditary appointment?'

'No, but a son tended to be asked to succeed his father. Five generations of the family held this office, until Sir Clement Cottrell-Dormer, who was a hot-tempered man, lost it in 1797 by calling George III a silly old fool. By the way, it is his otter-hound which is commemorated in the garden.'

'It is not an appointment which would have suited you?'

'No, I have always preferred country life. Most of my ancestors did too, and they had difficulty getting away from their responsibilities in London. I feel closest to my great-grandfather Charles Cottrell-Dormer, who travelled extensively as a young man, returned to his library at Rousham, and read through the works of Alexander Pope once a year. An agreeable life.'

'Were you born in the house?'

'No. But my parents returned here when I was about three. My father had been in the army in India, and the house was let after my grandfather's death in 1880. I have a vague recollection of the bunting and the fireworks of Queen Victoria's Diamond Jubilee in 1897, but I remember quite clearly the huge bonfire we had in the walled garden for Mafeking Night, it was crowned by the figure of President Kruger in a top-hat.'

'And your parents?'

'My father was a very keen agriculturist. He bred cattle and started the first Rousham herd of longhorns here in 1910. Both my parents hunted, but they kept separate hunting establishments; he hunted with the Heythrop and she with the Bicester. They had eight grooms between them. My mother also had an aviary of exotic birds, and kept Italian greyhounds.'

'And your childhood at Rousham?'

'Paradise. My two brothers and I spent our time boating on the Cherwell, and bathing. My father and I used to go for long bicycle rides, and we were all great walkers. My father bought his first car about 1907.'

'What happened after 1914?'

'I had gone up to Oxford in 1913 and went to learn German in the summer holidays. I was in Eastern Germany when war was declared and I was interned. My father planted the avenue outside the house to mark the coming-of-age of my elder brother Clement in 1912. Both my brothers were killed in the war.'

'When did you return?'

'In 1918. My parents' marriage had not survived the war and shortly afterwards my mother left. I stayed with my father for a while and then in the early 1930s he went to live in the south of France and let Rousham.'

'And what did you do?'

'I travelled. An aunt left me Newbottle Manor, near Banbury, and I lived there after my marriage in 1936. It was a very pleasant house. In 1945 the Dutch tenants left Rousham, and we had the chance to move back. I jumped at it. Friends were amazed at the thought of our leaving the comforts of Newbottle, but I was determined to live at Rousham. I love the house.'

'And its history?'

'Yes, I had begun to take a serious interest in this in the early 1920s. I managed to reassemble the paintings and bronzes in the painted parlour which had been scattered all over the house. The brackets, for instance, were in the attic. The original windows had been removed from the south front of the house by my grandfather and replaced by plate glass. Fortunately I found the windows from the painted parlour in the local school, and was able to replace them in the 1950s.'

'When did you open the house to the public?'

'About twenty years ago after we had received a grant to repair the roof.'

'How do you manage today?'

'The house and the estate now belong to my son Charles who lives with his family in the Dower House. He is a farmer and has built up a champion herd of longhorns. We manage here at Rousham with a housekeeper and two gardeners. One gardener has been with us for many years, the other is a young man. He told me the other day he hopes to stay gardening here for the rest of his life.'

'Rousham inspires great devotion.'

'Yes, Rousham inspires great devotion.'

Rousham Park

STEEPLE ASTON, OXFORDSHIRE

Mr Thomas Cottrell-Dormer

Rousham from the gardens.

The portrait set into the overmantel in the great parlour at Rousham is of Lieutenant-General James Dormer and was painted in 1738 by Vanloo. It is difficult not to sympathize with the General. It is true that he presides over a drawing-room of great beauty, but it is not *his* drawing-room. The difference between the sturdy giltwood frame of his portrait and the elaborate rococo plasterwork surrounding the other portraits hanging on the walls, provides a clue to the history of the room. It was originally the General's library but, within twenty-five years of his death, Sir Charles and Lady Cottrell-Dormer, his successor's son and daughter-in-law, sold his books and redecorated the room in a style more suited to entertainment than to scholarship. They left intact the General's portrait, the chimney-piece, the vaulted ceiling and the bow-window; the bookcases and other decorations were taken down and have since disappeared.

Lady Cottrell-Dormer, whom no doubt the General would have considered a vandal, is depicted wearing an exotic sable-edged dress and turban in the full-length portrait by Benjamin West which hangs to his right. Sadly, she preferred London to Rousham and came to the conclusion soon after marriage that her Oxfordshire neighbours were too boorish to be entertained in her pretty new drawing-room. Unfortunately, no sketches have survived to give an idea of the appearance of the General's lost library. We gather from Mrs Delany's description that it was 'a most magnificent room, and finished with the highest expense'. But the sale catalogue shows precisely what was on his shelves. The books were auctioned in 1764 at a series of sales which continued for twenty successive evenings. The collection was rich in English, French, Italian and Spanish literature, in European history and, as might be expected, voyages and travels.

A statue by Jan van Nost of Bacchus in the garden designed by William Kent.

We learn from this catalogue that the General was a deeply cultivated man and a student of art and architecture. He collected sixteenth- and seventeenth-century books on Italian and French architecture and he bought the principal architectural texts published in his own day, such as Colen Campbell's *Vitruvius Britannicus* and the editions of Palladio by Leoni and Ware.

He also possessed a book of great contemporary significance: William Kent's edition of the designs of Inigo Jones published in two folio volumes at the instigation of Lord Burlington in 1727, a most important architectural source book of the early Georgian period.

When General Dormer decided that the house his grandfather had built just before the Civil War needed bringing up to date and enlarging to house his growing collection of books and works of art, he chose William Kent as his architect.

The Dormers were long established members of the Oxfordshire and Buckinghamshire gentry when Sir Robert Dormer bought the manor of Rousham in the mid 1630s. He set to work at once putting up a house in the Jacobean style using Oxfordshire stone. The hall survived the eighteenth- and nineteenth-century alterations to the house and remains today, as in the past, the core of the house. At first, the family dined in the hall. An inventory of 1650 shows that it contained three long tables and five benches. The pantry was at the east end separated from the hall by a screen which has since disappeared, and the drawing-room was upstairs.

The outbreak of the Civil War put an end to any further building activities. The Oxfordshire countryside bristled with troops; Sir Robert Dormer was a Royalist and the lead-lined holes through which the muskets were aimed at Cromwell's men are still visible in the great oak door in the hall. But Sir Robert did not enjoy his freedom or his house for long. He was imprisoned for a time in Oxford and died a few years later in 1649. Young Robert Dormer, his son, does not appear to have made any alterations to the house but he replaced the lead which the troops had stripped from the roof and put the house in order after the years of warfare. He married two heiresses in succession; his second wife, Anne, was a daughter of Sir Charles Cottrell, Master of the Ceremonies at court.

General Dormer, Robert Dormer's son, was born in 1679. He served with distinction in Marlborough's campaigns and in Spain, where he was a prisoner of war for two years. He was wounded at Blenheim and again in action against the Jacobites at Preston. His brief diplomatic career came to a sudden end through an incident when ambassador to the King of Portugal. In Lisbon he was unable to endure the sight of the British consul's house illuminated for parties to which he was never invited. He bitterly resented this insulting behaviour and relations between the two men deteriorated. The ambassador decided to punish the consul for his impudence; he sent his servants to give him a good hiding, dragging the poor man from his coach and beating him in public. George II was not amused by this display of undiplomatic behaviour and General Dormer was recalled.

In London, he resumed his book collecting. His interest in books dated from an early age. We know that he left behind £200 worth of French books (including novels) in the Spanish convent where he had been imprisoned and treated with civility by the nuns. Hearne described him in 1718 as 'well skill'd in Books'. He was a Whig and moved in literary circles. His brother Colonel Robert Dormer shared his tastes; he was a

Praeneste terrace by Kent.

member of the exclusive Whig Kit-Cat Club, a dining club composed of grandees and literary men. Both brothers were on friendly terms with Alexander Pope.

It was Colonel Robert Dormer who began the transformation of the garden at Rousham some years after he succeeded in 1719. His younger brother, the General, appears to have spent much time with him and was no doubt consulted at all stages. The Colonel commissioned Charles Bridgeman, the royal gardener, to draw up plans and work was nearing completion when the Colonel died in 1737. It is evidently Bridgeman's work that Pope describes so enthusiastically in a letter of 1728. 'Rousham,' he wrote, 'is the prettiest place for water-falls, jetts, ponds inclosed with beautiful scenes of green and hanging wood, that ever I saw.'

Right: The painted parlour, decorated by William Kent for General Dormer. It is used by the present owner Mr Thomas Cottrell-Dormer as a sitting-room.

Above: Jane, wife of Sir Charles Cottrell-Dormer, by Benjamin West. Her maiden name was Caesar, and her ancestor was an Italian who came to London and became physician to Queen Elizabeth.

When William Kent was called in by the General in 1738, he left intact Bridgeman's work but amplified it, applying as it were broad brush strokes over Bridgeman's canvas. General Dormer was the sixth son of his parents so that for much of his life the chances of succeeding to Rousham must have seemed remote. When he finally did so in December 1737, he was nearly sixty. The late Clough Williams-Ellis was fond of saying that a gardener should start young and live to be absurdly old. General Dormer was not deterred by age or ill-health and in the four years he owned Rousham, Kent created for him a garden of great beauty. We can be grateful to him, for his garden is one of the earliest landscape gardens in England and the only one of its period to survive untouched.

Kent also made alterations to the house. He castellated the roof and added two shallow wings which provided the General with a library and a sitting-room, the painted parlour, which Kent designed and decorated in the grand manner but on a miniature scale. This exquisite room is intact. It contains some of Kent's furniture, his ceiling painting, the wall brackets he designed to display the General's collection of Italian bronzes, and the paintings he chose for the walls. The original white-and-gold colour scheme was obliterated in Regency times when the walls were grained to imitate oak. The present Mr Cottrell-Dormer's father used the room as a smoking-room and the green paint is a survival of the redecoration carried out by Lenygon and Morant about 1910.

William Kent brought to garden design a practical knowledge of painting and first-hand impressions of the Italian landscape. He used the devices of landscape-painting and theatrical design to evoke in the fields and woods of England visions of the Roman countryside and the classical world. He was inspired by the paintings of Claude

Left: The great parlour. This was originally General Dormer's library. His portrait by Jean Baptiste Vanloo hangs over the chimney-piece which was designed by William Kent. The room was remodelled in 1764 by Thomas Roberts of Oxford who made the plasterwork frames for the portraits.

and Gaspard Poussin which were eagerly sought after by English collectors at the time. General Dormer was susceptible to the novel ideas introduced by Kent, for these had been nurtured by the great connoisseur Lord Burlington and were firmly rooted in the literary and political circles he frequented. 'A spacious Horison is an Image of Liberty,' Addison wrote in *The Spectator* in 1712, and, to Whig eyes, the formal garden enclosed within walls or hedges with rectangular beds and clipped hedges became a symbol of oppression and tyranny. This outlook had a decisive effect on the English countryside. Vanbrugh demolished the boundary wall and threw open the landscape to view, Bridgeman invented the ha-ha to make the invisible but essential division between garden and pasture, and Kent banished the straight line and replaced it with the serpentine. Kent, wrote Walpole, 'leaped the fence, and saw all nature was a garden'.

Far left: Marble group of a horse and a lion modelled by Peter Scheemakers in 1743 on a version of an antique group at the Villa d'Este in Tivoli.

Right: This drawing of
Venus's Vale by William
Kent shows the cascades he
designed at Rousham with
some of the visitors who
flocked to see this garden in
the eighteenth century. The
present-day view from the
same point is remarkably
similar although the
fountains have not worked
since Sir Charles Cottrell-
Dormer's time in the late
eighteenth century. The
gardener complained that he
would lose £60 a year in tips
from tourists when Sir
Charles refused to allow him
to switch on the fountains.

Far right: The temple of
Echo by Kent and William
Townesend.

Kent was fortunate in what he found at
Rousham. The garden to the north of the house
consisted of a bowling-green and terraces which
descended steeply to the River Cherwell; beyond,
there was an uninterrupted view of fields. By
extending the ha-ha, Kent was able to blend the
garden visually with the landscape. He retained an
old mill beyond the river which he transformed in
the picturesque style, incorporated the mediaeval
bridge, and put up a sham ruin, an 'eye-catcher',
which did all its name implies on the sky-line. He
smoothed the terraces into a concave slope, and in
the woodland garden, he contrived a series of
classical scenes set with buildings, cascades,
statuary and seats, composed like paintings and
designed to be viewed in sequence from a winding
path.

He achieved great variations and contrasts in
colour and mood in these scenes. John McClary,
the head-gardener, refers to a small opening in the
woods above Venus's Vale as 'made up with yew
and other evergreens as dark and Melancholy as it
was possible to make it'.

Kent's visits to Rousham during the construction of the garden were few and far between
and the task of interpreting his design in practical
terms fell to the General's Clerk of the Works,
William White, and to McClary. The General
supervised his men, but he was frequently in
London and White was often called upon to take
vital decisions such as where to place a statue.
There is no doubt from the surviving correspondence that the General was prepared to listen
to and to accept suggestions from both men. There

was also a small army of labourers to direct; in the
spring of 1738, seventy men were employed laying
turf and clearing the river.

After the feverish activity of the preceding years,
the General's death at Bath in December 1741
must have come as a bitter blow to White and
McClary. The transformation of the garden was
almost complete, work came to a halt and
labourers were dismissed. The atmosphere at
Rousham that winter must have been as melancholy as the glade of yews above Venus's Vale.

The General was the last of the Rousham
Dormers. He left his estates in Buckinghamshire
and Oxfordshire to his first cousin, Sir Clement
Cottrell, a man in his mid-forties who assumed the

Far left: Inside a yew hedge at Rousham.

Left: Charles Walter Cottrell-Dormer with his wife and three sons at Rousham in about 1900. The present owner, Thomas, is shown on the left; his two brothers Clement and Charles were killed in World War I.

additional name of Dormer. He was Master of Ceremonies at court as his father and grandfather had been before him. He was also a scholar, a Vice-President of the Society of Antiquaries, 'a very bookish man', and admirably suited to take over from the General. Mrs Delany visited Rousham in 1743 and was delighted with Sir Clement and his family. She found the house full of antiques 'enough to make one wild'. Sir Clement loved Rousham, but his court duties kept him in London and it was often late in the year before he could leave. The garden was kept up and McClary was allowed the ten gardeners he considered the minimum necessary to do so. But there is no doubt that McClary himself felt neglected. In 1750 he wrote a poignant letter to Sir Clement's wife: 'Madam, I'm Afraid my Master and all of you have forgot what sort of A place Rousham is, so I have sent you a description of it that it may not quite creep out of Your memorys.'

Perhaps McClary found some comfort in the increasing number of visitors to the garden, for Rousham soon became a popular tourist attraction. Kent had designed a gateway which allowed the public to enter from the road without going near the house and visitors were supervised by the gardeners. Unfortunately for McClary, Sir Clement's son, Charles, to whom the estate was made over in the 1750s, refused to allow him to switch on the fountains, which he reckoned lost him £60 a year in tips from visitors.

Sir Charles Cottrell-Dormer was a noted agriculturist and made many improvements to the estate. He also succeeded his father as Master of

Ceremonies at court. In 1760 Horace Walpole visited Rousham and described the place in a letter to his friend George Montagu, 'the garden is Daphne in little; the sweetest little groves, streams, glades, porticoes, cascades and river, imaginable; all the scenes are perfectly classic. Well, if I had such a house, such a library, so pretty a place, and so pretty a wife, I think I should let King George send to Herenhausen for a Master of Ceremonies.'

The pretty wife so admired by Walpole was the lady we have already met who destroyed the General's library and preferred her house in London's Chesterfield Street to Rousham's groves. The Rousham Walpole admired in 1760 was a bachelor house and had been so for many years. Jane Cottrell-Dormer's decision to remodel the library as a drawing-room in which to receive her Oxfordshire neighbours is understandable. Had she realized before she started how little she would find in common with them, it is just possible that she would have spared the General's library.

In the late 1870s Clement Upton-Cottrell-Dormer commissioned the architect J.P. St Aubyn to double the central part of Rousham to provide room for his large family of eight sons and six daughters. The garden was left untouched and has been lovingly cared for by subsequent generations. One single addition has been made to the garden in the two hundred years since it was created: Sir Clement Cottrell-Dormer – who died in 1808 – placed on the upper cascade a plaque to commemorate the life of his dog Ringwood, 'an OTTER-HOUND of extraordinary Sagacity'.

Henry, 10th Duke of Beaufort succeeded his father nearly sixty years ago, that is, to the dukedom, the house, the mastership of the family pack of fox-hounds and the great sporting traditions of his family. He is universally known as 'Master', a name he acquired at the age of eleven when his father gave him a pack of harriers for his birthday. Life at Badminton revolves round the horses, hounds and family dogs – the dogs as often as not rescued by the Duke and Duchess from the Dogs' Home at Battersea of which he has been President for many years. The Duke's great regret in life is that he has never seen active service in the field for, although he was at Sandhurst in 1918, the war ended before he joined his regiment, the Blues (the Royal Horse Guards). He was Master of the Horse from 1936 until 1977.

'You have described your affection for Badminton, the house, the estate and all it stands for, as "a permanent love affair". Does this feeling date from childhood?'

'Yes, I am never really happy when I am away from here, when I was a child I longed to be home.'

'What were your duties as Master of the Horse? Is it an ancient office?'

'Yes, it dates from the fourteenth century, and I was the seventy-sixth Master – five were executed – and I held the office longer than anyone else, just over forty years. When the Queen is mounted or in a horse-drawn carriage the Master of the Horse takes precedence over both the Lord Chamberlain and the Lord Steward and rides next to the Queen. It's one of the great offices of the Royal Household. I was in charge of the royal stable and state processions and I frequently represented the King and later the Queen on official occasions. My ancestor the 4th Earl of Worcester was Master of the Horse to Queen Elizabeth I.'

'Badminton is full of Somerset family portraits; have you been painted?'

'Yes, by Oswald Birley in 1945. The picture hangs in my study. The painting was given to me as a present by Queen Mary as thanks for her stay at Badminton during the war. I'm in my Garter robes. And then this is by Terence Cuneo. I'm mounted on the grey in my uniform as Master of the Horse. The Queen gave it to me to mark my retirement in 1977, but when she suggested it to me I asked if she and Prince Philip could be in the picture too. I can see the Cuneo from my desk and the portrait of the 1st Duke from my chair in the dining-room. I am always grateful to him for what he did to establish us here at Badminton.'

'Does it worry you to see the house full of visitors?'

'No, not at all. We open on Wednesday afternoons in the summer. We are happy to share the house. The Duchess shows visitors round the house herself, and this gives her great pleasure. And the kennels are open too.'

Badminton: the north front.

Badminton House

AVON

The Duke of Beaufort KG, GCVO, PC

One of William Kent's baroque pavilions, which terminate the north front.

The five great sporting paintings which dominate the hall at Badminton provide an appropriate starting-point for the history of the house. They were painted about 1730 by John Wootton for Henry, 3rd Duke of Beaufort, a patron of taste and learning who combined, as many civilized Englishmen have done over the centuries, discernment in the arts with a passion for sport. He brought to the portrayal of his horse, a grey Barb, who hangs in the place of honour above the chimney-piece, as much care as he did to the portrait of himself which he commissioned from Francesco Trevisani in Rome when he was on his Grand Tour. The other paintings in the hall depict hare-hunting and hawking on Salisbury Plain, racing at Newmarket, and stag-hunting at Badminton.

The history of the sporting tradition at Badminton in the 250 years since Wootton painted these scenes, is the history of hunting in England, and the kennel-books which date from 1728 demonstrate the gradual application over the years of scientific principles to the breeding and training of hounds.

The 3rd Duke kept two packs at Badminton, one for hare-hunting and one for the pursuit of the stag. In 1734 the kennel-books show that the pack consisted of thirty couple of harriers and only six of deer-hounds. In the early 1740s, the Duke's growing interest in stag-hunting is apparent, for the deer-hound pack has been much enlarged, and the two packs were more or less of equal strength. At about the same time he dropped hare-hunting in favour of fox-hunting; in the next generation, stag-hunting was also abandoned. The reasons for this change are partly a matter of fashion, and partly of practicality, for the increase in enclosures led to a decline in good stag-hunting country. The story is told in the family at Badminton of how in the 1760s the young 5th Duke was returning from an unsatisfactory day's stag-hunting, only to end it by complete chance with a hunt after a fox which was so fast, and so exciting an experience, that he was enslaved for life. In the latter part of the eighteenth century, the shortage of foxes was acute. For this reason, the 5th, 6th and 7th Dukes of Beaufort hunted the Badminton country and what is now the Heythrop country in alternate months, and removed the entire household backwards and forwards throughout the season. The fox was encouraged to breed over this period, and the migration to Oxfordshire ceased.

Henry, 8th Duke of Beaufort, was the best-known sporting figure of his day. He presided at Badminton in a golden age, for he succeeded in 1853 and died in 1899. He had been brought up under the legendary huntsman, Will Long, of whom Nimrod wrote, 'he rides without jealousy and takes the country as it comes.' From Long, the Duke acquired his first ideas of hunting and of hound lore, and in the 1855–6 season, the first in which he hunted his hounds himself, in 102 days, 123 foxes were killed (this includes 60 in cub-hunting), and 28 were run to ground. The lawn meets in his day were immense affairs, for there were sometimes over 2000 horsemen, and the Duke thought nothing of giving breakfast to 1000 people and lunch to 400–500. On a hunting morning the coach, laden with guests and friends, would be driven to the meet by the Duke or his son. When the day's sport was over, a change of clothing and lunch would be laid on at some convenient inn, and the party would then return in comfort to Badminton.

The Duke was enormously popular, for he was good-natured and generous. When his brown and

yellow coach appeared in the streets of Bristol, word would go round, 'the Duke, the Duke', and people would pour from their houses and cheer him. On his 27,000 acres in Wales, the tenants called him 'Uncle'. At Badminton, he and his wife used the great hall as a dining-room after the patriarchal fashion of his ancestors; he was notoriously unpunctual – dinner was at 8.30, 9.00, or even 10.00 if it suited him – and summer and winter, Beaufort Hunt coats and white waistcoats were the rule.

The Duke had prodigious energy. As a young man he would sit up half the night playing cribbage at Pratt's and catch a couple of hours' sleep in his brougham at Paddington; he would take a train at the crack of dawn to Chippenham, drive for the last ten miles to Badminton, hunt all day and frequently return to London again at night.

He was devoted to his children. From the

Left: The entrance hall. This was redecorated by Kent to accommodate the five great sporting paintings commissioned by the 3rd Duke from John Wootton. The Duke's horse, a grey Barb, is portrayed above the chimney-piece. The game of badminton was invented in this room by the great-aunts of the present Duke in the middle of the nineteenth century who rigged up a string from the front door-handle to the fireplace. The dimensions of the badminton court are derived from this entrance hall.

Above: Nixon, the house steward at Badminton, by Sir Edwin Landseer.

earliest possible moment, they were taught to ride. 'We are not allowed to hunt more than three times a week till we are five years old,' one of them told a visitor.

When the Duke was too old to hunt, he undertook the editorship, with the help of a writer named Alfred Watson, of a series of books on sport called the Badminton Library. The Duke took a most active part, for he researched tirelessly, and was most meticulous about checking the details; between them they turned out twenty-eight volumes.

The Duke was Master of the Horse in Lord Derby's second and third administrations of 1858–9 and 1866–8. This was a political appointment at that time, and a welcome change for the Tory Dukes of Beaufort who had been excluded from offices of state by the Whig oligarchy for so many generations. From the time of the 1st Duke, loyalty to Tory ideals removed them from court

and government, but what they lost in political power they gained in local influence and this was, and still is, immense. The present, and 10th, Duke of Beaufort is Lord Lieutenant of Bristol and Gloucestershire, High Steward of Bristol, Gloucester and Tewkesbury, Hereditary Keeper of Raglan Castle, and Chancellor of Bristol University.

The present Duke was born in Queen Victoria's reign and his childhood spanned the Edwardian era. In his memoirs, he describes with great affection his father who hunted his hounds from 1869 until 1914, six days a week, until he gave up at the age of sixty-seven, and his mother who presided over the great establishment at Badminton. For years when he was a child the kitchen was ruled by the French chef, Grand-Jean, who would be summoned by the bell each morning to discuss menus and plans with the Duchess. He was followed by the housekeeper who would await her

The dining-room, used as such by the present Duke and Duchess. The portrait shows the 1st Duke of Beaufort.

turn in the linen-room, and by the head butler who would be given information on guests who were expected for luncheon or dinner or for the night, all of whose names he would enter into his little book with notes on their idiosyncrasies. He would then know how much champagne to bring up from the cellar, for in the 9th Duke's day champagne was the only drink served at table. A bottle was placed in front of each man at dinner, and if there was any left over, the Duke would progress round the table, empty the remains of each bottle into his glass, and drink it. After dinner, the men were offered Madeira.

In those days, the under butler was in charge of the valets and the eight footmen who were powdered and liveried each evening – blue coats and blue-and-buff striped waistcoats. There was a platoon of odd-job men about the house such as the lampmen, the window-cleaners and the men who carried the coal; and the housekeeper presided over a mass of scullery maids, housemaids, parlour maids and ladies' maids. The housemaids, the Duke recalls, were so well trained to be neither seen nor heard that when the occasional fire-practice took place in the house, they would throw their skirts over their heads and display their beribboned drawers rather than allow anyone to see their blushes. The eighteen gardeners worked under a head gardener who was responsible to the Clerk of the Works, and the stables were under the authority of the stud-groom with a staff of forty-five. If the Duchess intended to drive out during the day, she would inform the head butler in the morning and he would arrange for the brougham to appear at the appointed time. He would then send page-boys to warn the gate-keepers. The gate-keepers, dressed in the green plush coats of the Badminton outdoor servants, would watch for the brougham and open the gates, doffing their top-hats as the Duchess passed.

The great drawing-room was redecorated in about 1800. It contains the two Canalettos of Badminton commissioned by the 4th Duke in 1748–50. One can be seen on the stand in the corner.

The Clerk of the Works was responsible for the sanitation at Badminton which was of the most primitive variety. The majority of country houses had water-closets by this date; Joseph Bramah had patented an efficient model as far back as 1797, and the 1st Duke of Wellington had installed some in cupboards at Stratfield Saye. At Badminton, the lack of water forced the household to rely on commodes for the women, and earth-closets for the men which were dug to the east of the house and screened by bushes. This state of affairs lasted until just before the outbreak of World War I. In fact the water shortage was so acute that the entire household was forced to migrate each summer to their Welsh home, Llangattock.

Apart from this summer exodus, the present Duke hardly ever left Badminton as a child until he went away to school at the age of nine. He was awakened each morning by the sound of the baying of his father's hounds, Nanny putting out his clothes for the day, and Toghill, the house-maid, preparing to lay and light the nursery fire. At eight o'clock the nursery footman brought up breakfast – bacon and egg, sometimes sausage, with toast, honey and marmalade. The Badminton children joined their parents for lunch and tea, and returned to the nursery for supper. The present Duke believes that the children in his family have always played a considerable part in their parents' lives and were never banished for long.

In fact, Badminton has a remarkably happy history, and this is due in large measure to the love of animals and sport, which has united one generation with another.

Badminton was bought in 1608 by the present Duke's ancestor, the 4th Earl of Worcester, as a half-way house between his Welsh estates and London. The family was founded by Charles Somerset, the illegitimate son of Henry Beaufort, Duke of Somerset, a gallant Lancastrian leader in

Right: The oak staircase, built by the 1st Duke. He bought thirty paintings at random to decorate the walls. He said to the Duchess that they were 'indifferent good in the judgement of those who understood these things'.

Far right: The east room: detail of the fireplace.

Below right: This wax figure of the fourteen-year-old dwarf Bébé, in the dress given to him by King Stanislaus of Poland, stands in a cabinet in the east room. He was born about 1740 and as a child became the favourite of the King who built a house for him complete with tiny pieces of furniture. It amused the King to serve up Bébé at dinner in a pie-dish, for Bébé would surprise the King's guests by dancing up and down the table. He died at the age of twenty-three.

the Wars of the Roses, who was executed at Hexham in 1464, and whose great-great-grandfather, John of Gaunt, was a son of Edward III. Charles Somerset married in 1508 a great Welsh heiress, and became the most considerable figure in South Wales. His bride's name was Elizabeth Herbert, and she was the only child of William, Earl of Huntingdon and Baron Herbert of Raglan, Chepstow and Gower. (The Herbert titles pass through the female line, and are borne by the present Duke.) Elizabeth brought with her both vast estates centred on Raglan Castle in Monmouthshire, and the Welsh roots which have been so greatly prized by subsequent generations of the family. Charles Somerset was created 1st Earl of Worcester in 1514, and lived in great state in the castle at Raglan. His descendant Henry, Lord Herbert of Raglan (later to become 1st Duke of Beaufort), caught as a child a tantalizing glimpse of this way of life which was swept away by the Civil War, for Raglan was destroyed by the Parliamentary army, and the family exiled. Miraculously, he was able to create at Badminton years later a life of almost regal splendour which was closer to the old-fashioned world of pre-war Raglan than to the lives of his contemporaries.

The Somersets were staunch Royalists. Henry, 5th Earl of Worcester, Lord Herbert's grandfather, sacrificed most of his worldly possessions in the service of the King, and was forced to surrender Raglan after a siege of seventy-seven days in 1646; his estates were confiscated, and he died shortly afterwards as a prisoner. He had been created Marquess of Worcester in 1642, but the promised Order of the Garter on which he had set his heart never materialized. His son, Edward, the 2nd Marquess, was not suited to political intrigue

or military life, for he was a scientist, and when he was forced into exile after his attempt to raise an army for the King in Ireland had failed, he resumed his investigations into the matters which interested him such as the potential of steam power. His son, Lord Herbert, was not content to kick his heels abroad, and, in 1650, returned to England. He arrived with certain disadvantages: he was penniless, he was nominally a Catholic, and he bore a name and a title associated with the Royalist cause; he was, on the other hand, only twenty-one years old, ambitious, level-headed, and determined to win back what his family had lost. His first move was to become a Protestant, regardless of the feelings of his father, who had suffered deeply for his loyalty to the Catholic Church; his second, to secure the support of Oliver Cromwell. He then successfully petitioned Parliament for the return of some of the family estates which secured him an income of £1700 a year.

The 1st Duke and Duchess of Beaufort with their children, by Stephen Browne.

Fortune smiled on the young Herbert. Five years after he returned to England, he was left the Badminton estate by a cousin, Elizabeth Somerset, and, in 1657, he married a young widow, Mary, Lady Beauchamp, who was beautiful, intelligent and rich, and with whom he lived happily ever after.

After Cromwell's death, Herbert worked and intrigued for the restoration of the King and, in response to an appeal by the local gentry, he was appointed Lord Lieutenant of Gloucestershire, Herefordshire and Monmouthshire.

In 1663, Lord and Lady Herbert entertained Charles II and Queen Catherine at Badminton. Sadly, the dukedom he hoped for, and indeed felt his family deserved, was not forthcoming on this occasion, but the royal visit had unexpected repercussions, for it almost certainly prompted Lord Herbert to examine the 'fayre stone house' which the Botelers had built, and his great-

grandfather had bought just over fifty years before, and decide that the house as it stood was neither grand nor large enough. Had he thought of making improvements before? It is possible, but we know for certain that from this time, building became one of the major pleasures of his life.

Lord Herbert, who became 3rd Marquess of Worcester on the death of his father in 1667, was well rewarded for his loyalty – and his patience. In 1672 he was made Lord President of the Council of Wales and of the Marches, a Knight of the Garter and a Privy Councillor; and in 1682, he was created a duke. The painting by Stephen Browne shows him, in 1685, in his Garter robes surrounded by his family – his wife, his sons Lord Worcester and Lord Arthur Somerset, and three daughters Mary, Henrietta and Anne.

Badminton grew in splendour with its master. There is a plan of 1699 which gives an idea of the scale of the Duke's improvements to the house and

The present Duke of Beaufort in his study. The portrait of him on horseback to the left was painted by Terence Cuneo and given to him by the Queen and the Duke of Edinburgh, who are also in the picture, when he retired as Master of the Horse in 1977.

garden. He added state rooms, and extensive accommodation for himself, his family, and his large household. He built new stables, kennels for greyhounds and other dogs, an aviary, and a banqueting house in the garden. He laid out formal gardens, which included a labyrinth, and extensive orchards and kitchen gardens. And he planted thousands of trees. A painting of the north front of about 1700 shows the avenues which radiate from the house, and when Celia Fiennes visited the house about this time, she commented on the magnificent views from the roof of the house along the twelve great avenues.

The gardens did not reflect the taste of the Duke alone, for the Duchess was one of the foremost gardeners of her day. Gardening was in her blood: she was a daughter of Arthur, 1st Baron Capel, and she appears as a child with her parents and brothers and sisters in a painting by Cornelius Johnson which depicts in the background her father's celebrated garden at Hadham. The Duchess was renowned as a collector of rare specimens, and a propagator of great skill. She was in correspondence with the principal botanists of the time; she obtained seeds and plants from all over the world – the East and West Indies, the Canaries, the Cape, Malabar, Ceylon, China and Virginia – and introduced many new varieties into England. She contributed numerous examples of dried plants to Sir Hans Sloane's 'Herbarium' and asked to be forgiven for labelling them with their familiar names, as neither she nor her gardener understood Latin.

Sloane described the exquisite care the Duchess gave her plants at Badminton: 'Her Grace having what she called an Infirmary or small green house, to which she removed sickly or unthriving plants, and with proper culture by the care of an old woman under her Grace's direction brought them to greater perfection than at Hampton court or any where.'

When the Duchess sought a tutor for her son,

Worcester Lodge which terminates the great axial avenue, three miles long, of the park to which it forms the north entrance. It is one of the most delightful buildings designed by Kent and contains the 'grand room where the Duke dines in summer'.

she asked Sloane's advice. He sent her the great botanist William Sherard, which delighted her, 'hee loveinge my diversion so well', and Sherard in turn was overwhelmed by the chance to work at Badminton, and introduce new plants to a garden which he reckoned would shortly 'out-do any yet in Europe'.

The Duchess commissioned a florilegium in water-colours of plants growing under her direction at Badminton, and in her Chelsea garden: one volume is drawn by a professional illustrator of plants, Everard Kickius, and the other is signed by Daniel Frankcom who is described on the title-page as 'A servant of My Lady Dutchess of Beaufort's'. Sir Oliver Millar has referred to them – together with another set of flower drawings at Windsor – as perhaps the most important set of botanical drawings of this kind to be executed in England in the seventeenth century.

The Duke showed great loyalty to James II; he defended Bristol when the city was threatened by the Duke of Monmouth, and the King visited Badminton in 1686 to thank the Duke personally for his support. The house was then at the height of its splendour. Francis North, the Chief Justice, spent a week at Badminton about this time and described the establishment, which recalls in its magnificence that of the Duke's grandfather at Raglan forty years before. North believed that the Beauforts lived in a style rivalled only by European crowned heads. The household numbered 200, but North was impressed by the smooth way in which it ran, and the lack of ostentation. The efficiency was due to the Duchess who made a tour of inspection of every department of the house each morning. Members of the household sat at nine long tables in the hall; the women had their own dining-room. The Duchess breakfasted with her guests at an oval table in a room which looked on to her garden; she was attended not by servants but by gentlemen – another old-fashioned custom which had virtually died out in England. North enjoyed his stay at Badminton. The Duke, he said, 'had always some new project of building, walling or planting, which he would show, and ask his friends about; and nothing was forced, or strained, but easy and familiar'.

After James II's flight, the Duke kept aloof from the court. He reluctantly accepted King William, and went so far as to invite him to Badminton in 1690 – it was noticed that during prayers the domestic chaplain prayed for the King, but did not mention his Christian name.

The Duke died in 1700. John Evelyn admired him as 'a person of great honour, prudence & estate'. The Duchess survived into her mid-

Right: Bell-pulls in the
kitchen quarters.

Below: Henry, 3rd Duke of
Beaufort, by Francesco
Trevisani (finished by John
Wootton). He is shown here
in Rome, where he built up
his collection of works of
art, with the Colosseum in
the background. He sent
Wootton to study in Italy
and commissioned from him
the sporting paintings in the
hall.

eighties; she retired to their house in Chelsea
where she tended her garden, and communed with
her neighbour, Sir Hans Sloane.

Henry, 3rd Duke of Beaufort, who inherited
Badminton at the age of seven in 1714, had an
influence on the house second only to his great-
grandfather, the 1st Duke.

He was a highly educated man who went on a
Grand Tour after he came down from Oxford.
Whereas the 1st Duke had ordered a load of
paintings at random to decorate the staircase at
Badminton, the 3rd Duke sought the advice of
connoisseurs in Rome, including Cardinal
Alberoni. He bought paintings, vases, cabinets,
intaglios and table-tops which he shipped in large
quantity to Bristol. When he returned from Italy,
he commissioned William Kent to transform
Badminton. Kent altered all but the south front,
which remains much as it was in the 1st Duke's
time. On the north front he added the pediment
flanked by twin cupolas, the curved gables, the
front door, and the long low wings which end in

massive pavilions. Kent also remodelled the hall to provide a setting for the five great sporting paintings which were painted by the Duke's protégé John Wootton. And Kent designed for him the delightful building known as Worcester Lodge which served as an entrance to the park and as a focal point visible from the house at the end of a three-mile avenue. On the first floor of the lodge is a summer dining-room which has been the setting for many parties over the years.

The Duke also turned his attention to the park; he acted on the advice of 'Capability' Brown and swept away his great-grandparents' formal gardens, creating a landscape which is visible in the painting by Canaletto commissioned by his brother, the 4th Duke, and is still intact today.

The 3rd Duke established at Badminton the great sporting tradition which thrived under his successors, and flourishes today under Henry, 10th Duke of Beaufort, the senior Master in the land.

Above: The servants' hall, hung with copper pans and antlers.

Left: Henry, 8th Duke of Beaufort, by Sir Francis Grant. The Duke was one of the greatest sportsmen of his age and is shown mounted on a dapple grey, with two of his favourite hounds, and the Duchess on an Andalusian mare, Mazagan, which he bought for her in Gibraltar.

George Iain, 10th Duke of Atholl, Chief of all the Murrays, has the last remaining private army in Europe, the Atholl Highlanders. One of his ancestors, the brilliant Jacobite general, Lord George Murray, fought with the Athollmen for Prince Charles Edward, but his dukedom is due to the loyalty of another ancestor to Queen Anne and although the Atholl Highlanders have received permission within the last few years to march through Edinburgh with fixed bayonets, it is safe to say that the present Duke has no military ambitions. He lives in a wing of Blair Castle in the midst of his great 148,000-acre highland estate and also has a home in London.

'Who were your immediate predecessors at Blair Castle?'

'My immediate predecessor, the 9th Duke, was a prisoner in Poland in the first war and spoke Polish – and eight other languages – like a native. He was passionately interested in the fate of the Poles and spent his life after the last war helping displaced Poles in Scotland. But he never owned Blair. Bardie – as the 8th Duke was always known – inherited a bankrupt estate in 1971, and the financial crises became worse and worse. The estate was saved by my grandmother, my mother's mother, Lady Cowdray. She financed a company which took over the castle and estate in 1932. So it passed from Bardie's ownership. You can read about Bardie in his wife's book *Working Partnership*. She was a musician, and a local MP. She later became Under Secretary of Education but resigned over Munich. She was known as the Red Duchess – not what we would think of as "Red" – but she took up the cause of the communists in Spain during the Civil War when her party supported Franco. She lived until 1968.'

'When did you decide to open Blair Castle to the public?'

'I didn't make the decision. We've been open since 1937. In fact, we were among the first in Scotland to open on a regular basis; we've now thirty-two rooms on view.'

'The presentation and labelling of the paintings and other treasures at Blair Castle are excellent. Did you organize this yourself?'

'No, Rupert Gunnis, thanks to him. I asked him to help me soon after I took over and he reorganized the rooms and the displays.'

'And the visitors have poured in ever since?'

'We have had just over 100,000 this year; our best was 1977 with 131,000 but numbers have fallen back since then. We are in the middle of a very popular tourist area and we have a caravan site of thirty-one acres within walking distance of the castle. With an estate the size of Atholl we've always regarded it as an obligation to make land available for tourism and it is an important source of employment. The gift shop, the restaurant and the caravan site are all run by local people.'

'Was your childhood spent in Scotland?'

'No, my father was a banker at Lazards. But I visited the house.'

'Do you spend most of your time at Blair Castle?'

'Yes. But I am for instance chairman of the Westminster Press and the Royal National Lifeboat Institution so I am frequently in London.'

'How many men do you have in your private army and how often do you summon them together? Do you enjoy military life?'

'We have two parades a year but our activities are entirely ceremonial – guards of honour. There are about twenty officers – about six appear regularly – and eighty Highlanders; the majority are estate employees and tenants. I never did National Service and there are many times that I have to look at the photograph of the 7th Duke and his three sons in their Atholl Highlander uniforms to make certain I am dressed correctly!'

Blair Castle: the west front.

Blair Castle

BLAIR ATHOLL, PERTHSHIRE

The Duke of Atholl

When John, Ist Duke of Atholl, died in 1724, he was succeeded not by his eldest son William, Marquess of Tullibardine, but by his second surviving son, Lord James Murray, for Lord Tullibardine was attainted for his part in the Jacobite Rising of 1715 and exiled. The Ist Duke was a loyal supporter of Queen Anne as his father, the Ist Marquess, had been of William of Orange, and for this reason the Athollmen who supported Montrose in 1644 were not at the battle of Killiecrankie in 1689 when Lord Dundee made his last stand for James II. There is no doubt, however, that most of them were there in spirit, for in the '15 some 1400 Athollmen served under the Jacobite Lord Tullibardine and his brothers Lord Charles and Lord George Murray, and in the '45 they were in action again.

Their ancestor Sir John Stewart was a half-brother of James II of Scotland and in 1457 the earldom of Atholl was conferred on him with almost regal powers over the ancient province; indeed Atholl resembled a principality until the overthrow of the clans in 1746. The male line of the Stewarts, earls of Atholl, came to an end in 1595, but the heiress of the 5th Earl, Lady Dorothea Stewart, married the 2nd Earl of Tullibardine, and their son John Murray, Master of Tullibardine, was created Earl of Atholl in 1629. He was also chief of all the Murrays, for the Murrays of Tullibardine in Strathearn had assumed the leadership by the sixteenth century.

James, 2nd Duke of Atholl, was dissatisfied with the fortified castle he inherited from his father. The main tower of Blair Castle on the extreme right of the entrance front is known as Cumming's Tower and we know that its foundations date from the thirteenth century, for in 1269 the Earl of Atholl complained to Alexander III that during his absence in England John Comyn or

A corridor in the oldest part of the castle, Cumming's Tower. The antlers belonged to the four stags which were kept in the park in the mid-nineteenth century. They were collected each year when cast, and mounted on the skulls of other stags. The favourite, Tilt, who died in 1850 aged thirteen, was stuffed after his death and is to be seen in the hall.

Cumming of Badenoch had begun to build a castle at Blair without permission. The hall range which is visible only from the west is said to have been built by the 3rd Earl in 1530.

James, Duke of Atholl, stripped the house of all the battlements and fortifications and remodelled the house in the style of a Georgian country house. He had thought of doing this before the '45 but the Rising interrupted his plans. However, work was far advanced in the park and thousands of trees had been planted before hostilities began.

When Prince Charles Edward landed in Scotland in July 1745, he was accompanied by the 'Seven Men of Moidart', chief of whom was William, Marquess of Tullibardine, Duke James's elder brother, who raised the Jacobite standard at Glenfinnan. As soon as he set foot on Scottish soil he assumed the title Duke of Atholl and in August sent word to a cousin to prepare Blair Castle for a visit from the Prince. Thus Duke William re-

turned, in the company of the Prince, to the house which he had not seen for twenty-nine years and, but for the attainder, would have been his on the death of his father in 1724. Duke William entertained the Prince at Blair, and made efforts to raise the Athollmen in the cause. After a few days, the Prince moved on to Perth where he was joined by Duke William's brother, Lord George Murray. Lord George had not wanted to take part in the '45 Rising. He had spent ten years in exile and was pardoned by the Government only after his brother Duke James had interceded on his behalf. But Prince Charles Edward is believed to have brought him a personal letter from his father, King James, the 'King over the Water', which Lord George could not fail to obey. He wrote to his brother Duke James: 'I was not a little dificulted when you left this place . . . for, to spake the truth, I was at that time resolv'd to take a step which I was certain you would disprove off as much when you

The drawing-room. This is one of the state rooms created by the 2nd Duke when he remodelled the castle in the style of a Georgian house after the 1745 Jacobite Rising. The painting by Johann Zoffany set in the over-mantel shows the 3rd Duke and Duchess with their seven children. One of the children is sitting in a tree with Tom, a pet racoon, who was brought from the West Indies by their uncle Major-General James Murray.

The entrance front.

knew it, as it would surprise you to hear it. I never did say to any person in Life that I would not ingage in the cause I always in my heart thought just & right ... My Life, my Fortune, my expectations, the Happyness of my wife & children, are all at stake (& the chances are against me), & yet a principle of (what seems to me) Honour, & my Duty to King & Country, outweighs every thing.'

Lord George was the effective leader of the Jacobite army. He marched on foot in highland dress at the head of his men, he defeated Sir John Cope at Prestonpans, besieged Carlisle, and during the retreat from Derby he attacked the Duke of Cumberland's dragoons and checked his pursuit of the Prince. He led the right wing at Falkirk, but was unable to avert the encounter at Culloden in April 1746 when he fought with conspicuous gallantry. Sir Walter Scott wrote that Lord George had 'that intuitive acquaintance with the art of war, which no tactics can teach'.

One month before the battle of Culloden, Lord George gathered together a force of Athollmen in an attempt to drive the Hanoverian troops from that part of Scotland. This was the last occasion, according to Sir Iain Moncreiffe, when the Fiery Cross was used to call the clansmen to war. This ancient Scottish custom was in use all over the country as late as the sixteenth century. The cross itself was made up of two sticks, fastened together and charred at the upper ends with a bloody rag attached to it. This cross was sent, as a symbol of Fire and the Sword, in relays throughout the countryside and each successive bearer shouted one word: the name of the Gathering Place. In this instance, the Gathering Place was Blair Castle, which was occupied by 300 Hanoverian troops under the command of an English officer, Sir Andrew Agnew. Lord George and his Athollmen laid siege to his old home. His weaponry was not of the first order – the Minister at Blair reported to

Duke James that 'One of their cannon could not be made to keep in due position, which obliged them to call the smith of Blair several times to work at it' – and, all things considered, Lord George decided to starve them out, for he knew supplies in the castle were low. The Hanoverian soldiers shouted from the windows, 'come forward, you cowards.' But Lord George bided his time. He did think twice about attacking his home for he wrote to his brother Duke William, during the siege: 'If we get the Castle, I hope you will excuse our demolishing it.' And his brother, the staunch Jacobite, told him to get on with the job. 'Our great-great-grandfather, grandfather, and father's pictures,' he wrote, 'will be an irreparable loss on blowing up the house, but there is no comparison to be made with these faint images of our forefathers and the more necessary Publick Service, which requires we should sacrifice every thing.' Whatever else the brothers were called upon to sacrifice,

their ancestors were spared. A large Hanoverian force under the Prince of Hesse began to move north from Perth and, just as the news reached Blair, Lord George was called to join the other Highlanders in Inverness. He had no option but to abandon the siege. On 16 April the battle of Culloden was fought and lost.

Lord George escaped to France and died in Holland in 1760; Duke William gave himself up after the defeat and died in the Tower of London.

Duke James returned to Blair Castle and to his house at Dunkeld. His beautiful grounds and his trees were ruined. 'What do you think of 3000 Hessiens, 70 Hussars, 240 Dragoons, besides all the Army horses, being within the inclosiers here,' he wailed to Captain James Murray, 'where I would hardly trust a single stranger to have a key, for fear of Mischeif; this is after the Rebells haveing done all manner of damages for six months befor ... The poor trees are no more that I have taken so much pains to propagate ... I am cured of all manner of fondness for either place ... I had brought them to some perfection, and amused myself in the mean time ... I am now too old to begin again.'

Duke James was in his mid fifties when he wrote this letter in 1746. He soon recovered from the shock and spent much of the remaining eighteen years of his life happily employed on the embellishment of Blair Castle and its surroundings. The exterior of the castle as it was in his time, shorn of its fortifications, can be seen in the background of David Allan's painting of the 4th Duke of Atholl and his family; Blair was remodelled by the 7th Duke in the nineteenth century and the baronial character was restored. Duke James's interior decoration – on the picture staircase, in the small drawing-room, the tea-room, and the magnificent dining-room and drawing-room – is untouched. Most of it dates from between 1747 and 1758. The dining-room contains fine stucco decoration by Thomas Clayton and a marble chimney-piece made in 1751 by Thomas Carter of London. The five wall-paintings were commissioned from the Scottish landscape painter Charles Steuart and depict local scenes including the Falls of Bruar, Black Lynn Fall on Bran and Dunkeld Cathedral. They were painted between 1766 and 1777. The 2nd Duke also collected furniture, paintings and works of art.

Although the 4th Duke is known as the Planting Duke in the family – some 20,000,000 trees were planted on the estates in his time – the 2nd Duke introduced the larch to Scotland. Sir Iain Moncreiffe has told the story of how Menzies of Culdares brought back from the Tyrol in 1737 three larches which he presented to Lord George Murray. Lord George passed them on to his brother, the Duke, who at first treated them as hot-house plants. As soon as he realized his mistake and planted them out, they thrived and somehow escaped the boots of the Hanoverian soldiers and the hooves of their horses. In 1883 the 7th Duke returned to Blair with some seedlings of the Japanese larch; these were accidentally cross-pollinated with the European larch and produced the hybrid larch, which has become the standard tree for Scottish forestry and replaced the deciduous forests of oak and alder which used to cover the Highlands.

At the foot of the front staircase at Blair, there is a life-size model of a knight in armour mounted on a horse. The armour was worn by George, 2nd Lord Glenlyon, the 5th Duke's nephew, at the Eglinton Tournament in August 1839. This event was more than a romantic revival – and a magnificent folly – for it was also the last real tournament ever held in the British Isles; the knights fought in armour according to the ancient rules and some of them were wounded.

The Earl of Eglinton had announced in 1838 that he proposed to hold a tournament in the grounds of his castle in Ayrshire. Mark Girouard has described the electrifying effect this news had on the young men of fashion in the Tory ranks raised on Sir Walter Scott's stirring account of the tournament in *Ivanhoe*. They were bored by the endless talk of reform, and outraged that the banquet after Queen Victoria's coronation with all its mediaeval ceremonial had been cancelled by the Whigs on the grounds of economy. The staging of the tournament was seen as a gesture of defiance and no one can have been more surprised than Lord Eglinton himself at the hullabaloo which ensued; the world appeared to divide into two camps, one was wild with enthusiasm, the other seethed with indignation.

Initially, 149 potential knights gathered to discuss the proposed tournament in Samuel Pratt's new arms and armour showroom in London. Dates were fixed for the rehearsals in June and July and the tournament in August. The ranks of knights shrank over the next few months; thirty-five came to the rehearsals, nineteen took part in the dress rehearsal and thirteen fought on the day. The young Lord Glenlyon laid his plans carefully. He entered himself under the style of 'The Knight of the Gael' and ordered his armour and dress from Pratt who was the official outfitter to the tournament. When the plan had first been mooted, the expenses were reckoned at about £40 for each participant, but this figure grew and grew and had reached £400 by the early summer of 1839. Ian Anstruther published Lord Glenlyon's accounts with Pratt in his book on the tournament, *The Knight and the Umbrella*. These show that Lord

Glenlyon bought a suit of knight's polished steel *cap-à-pie* tilting armour, horse caparisons, horse armour and a tilting saddle, a buff leather dress to wear under the armour, a helmet, a coronet for the helmet, gilt spurs, a sword and fifteen lances; he also hired a large tent and two pavilions painted in his own colours. For the ball after the tournament, Pratt made up a rich evening costume out of tartan velvet supplied by Lord Glenlyon with cap and plume, two pairs of 'superior' scarlet silk hose pantaloons, embroidered ankle boots and a rich velvet cloak. The bill came to £346 9s 6d; but as Lord Glenlyon spent an additional £1000 on the uniform and equipment of the seventy-four officers and men who escorted him to the tournament, it comes as no surprise to hear that Pratt's bill was left unpaid for two years.

During the spring Lord Glenlyon called for volunteers from among his Athollmen and selec-ted five officers and sixty-nine men to attend him as a highland bodyguard or 'tail'. Each man was given a specially made uniform for the occasion which was much the same as that worn by the body of Athollmen who prepared to attend the 4th Duke at the time of the historic visit of George IV to Edinburgh in 1822. At that time, the 4th Duke had grave misgivings about the plan to fill the capital with armed men of many different clans,

Left: James, 2nd Duke of Atholl, by Jeremiah Davison in 1738. He remained loyal to the Hanoverians in the Jacobite Risings and after the '45 remodelled Blair Castle.

Opposite above: The over-mantel in the dining-room depicts trophies of arms in stucco by Thomas Clayton.

Opposite below: Detail of the dining-room showing the thickness of the walls of the old castle.

The dining-room. This was formerly the banqueting hall and
is another of the state rooms created by the 2nd Duke.
The landscapes are by the Scottish painter, Charles Steuart,
and were commissioned in the 1760s by the 3rd Duke.

The picture staircase. The large portrait shows the 1st Marquess of Atholl by Jacob de Witt. He is wearing classical dress with the Battle of Bothwell Brig raging in the background.

and in the end the Athollmen stayed at home. Lord Glenlyon did not share his grandfather's fears, for the '45 Rising was that much further away, and he was a romantic soul who loved pageantry. The uniform he had made for his Athollmen consisted of 'a blue jacket ... kilt and plaid of hard Athole tartan, red and white hose, brogues, Glengarry bonnet and crest, white goatskin sporran and crest ... broadsword and target'. The men caused a sensation when they arrived at Eglinton.

As the day drew nearer, Lord Eglinton announced that anyone who wished to attend the tournament must apply for a ticket. He had envisaged a crowd of about a thousand: his guests in a covered grandstand which Pratt had undertaken to build, members of the public in open stands, and others on the surrounding slopes who could look down upon the tilt-yard. Eglinton Castle was about twenty miles from Glasgow and reasonably easily reached by public transport.

Applications for tickets began to pour in and the estate office at Eglinton was swamped with letters from all over the world; people who were anxious to attend stressed their Tory affiliations as it was known that neither Whigs nor Radicals were likely to be admitted.

The rehearsals were a great success although it was apparent that many of the knights needed more practice: Lord Glenlyon was unable to control his horse which continually swerved away from the barrier.

Towards the end of August, the knights began to assemble at Eglinton. They had all taken mediaeval names such as the Knight of the Red Lion and the Knight of the Burning Tower. The oldest knight was forty, but the majority were in the twenties or thirties. Lord Glenlyon himself was twenty-five.

On 28 August the sun shone. From dawn people poured in from the surrounding countryside; by

Lord George Murray, younger brother of the 2nd Duke, a 'brilliant Highland guerrilla leader and Jacobite general'. He is wearing his campaigning dress with sword, dirk and target, and a white cockade in his bonnet.

noon every road or lane was packed with coaches and pedestrians and traffic was brought to a standstill. It was estimated that 100,000 people converged on Eglinton Castle that day. The great procession, half a mile in length, of knights and their attendants, esquires, heralds, the Queen of Beauty, the King of the Tournament (Lord Eglinton in gilt armour), ladies in gorgeous mediaeval dresses, pages and musicians failed to set off in time; one hour passed, then two, then three, and finally this unwieldy body began to move slowly towards the lists. And then there was a clap of thunder, the heavens opened, and torrential rain fell for the rest of the day. The ground was transformed into a sea of mud, the grandstand flooded, the dresses were ruined; people likened the scene to the retreat of a vanquished army. The Athollmen raised the spirits of Lord Eglinton's house-party with pipes and reels, and it was announced that the jousting would resume in the morning. Two days later the procession to the lists set out in sunshine. Lord Glenlyon opposed the Knight of the Black Lion (Lord Alford) in the lists and was declared the victor. After the tilting, a mêlée with swords took place between eight knights and Lord Glenlyon received a severe blow from the Knight of the White Rose which smashed his gauntlet. On the same evening a banquet and ball were given at the castle.

After the festivities were over, the Athollmen marched back to Blair. Lord Glenlyon and his officers spent one night at Blair Drummond where Miss Home Drummond was anxiously awaiting news, for it was her tiny glove which was tied to his tilting-lance. When the Athollmen approached Dunkeld, crowds of people turned out with flaming torches to escort them for the last few miles, and the cathedral bells rang out in welcome. A few years later Lord Glenlyon gave each of the

men who had attended him a medal, struck to commemorate the tournament, which was worn with an Atholl Murray tartan ribbon. These men were always known as 'the Tournament Men' in Atholl and the last one, according to Sir Iain Moncreiffe, lived on until 1906. And thus Lord Glenlyon constituted the Atholl (or Athole as he preferred to spell it) Highlanders as a ceremonial bodyguard. From this time he began to recruit men for his army and he gave back to the Highlands

some of the colourful pageantry and ceremonial which had disappeared when local warfare died out. He played a considerable part in the revival of the armed gatherings and travelled far and wide to attend them, escorted by his men as on the first expedition to Eglinton. In 1846 he was painted wearing his Eglinton Tournament armour, and both this and the costume he wore to the ball were carefully preserved at Blair, together with other evidence of his fondness for romantic revivals such

The Tullibardine room. The tent bed is covered with tartan over 200 years old which is said to have been on an older bed in which slept the seventeen sons of Sir David Murray of Tullibardine. The portrait is of the great Jacobite general, Lord George Murray, son of the 1st Duke.

Detail of the bed in the
tapestry room with hangings
of Spitalfields silk and
ostrich-feather plumes,
formerly in the 1st Duke's
suite at the Palace of
Holyrood in Edinburgh. It
was brought to Blair in 1709.

as the red and white robes of the Order of the Temple.

A few weeks after the tournament, Lord Glenlyon married Miss Home Drummond. The ceremony took place at her father's house at Blair Drummond and afterwards Lord and Lady Glenlyon set out to drive the sixty odd miles to Blair. The Blair tenantry and the Tournament Men had been entertained that afternoon to a large dinner in a wooden pavilion put up for the occasion; later bonfires were lit on all the hill-tops between Dunkeld and Blair Atholl, and the Tournament Men assembled at the Bridge of Tilt and kept themselves warm dancing reels to await the approach of the carriage. When it arrived, the men removed the horses from the shafts; some drew the Glenlyons up the grass avenue, and others ran beside the carriage brandishing their flaming torches. They passed under a wooden arch decorated with evergreens to the sound of cannon fire and stopped at the front door of the castle. The Tournament Men carried Lady Glenlyon over the threshold of her new home and Jean the dairy maid pulled a string at the appropriate moment to break an oatcake over the bride's head. 'The only light,' Lady Glenlyon recalled years later, 'was afforded by a pair of candles in the tallest plated candlesticks, borne by the Dowager Lady Glenlyon's maid, Alsey, dressed in white.'

For a time, Lord Glenlyon returned to his regiment, the Scots Greys, but reluctantly he had to retire in the following year. On 6 August 1840, Lady Glenlyon gave birth to a son at Blair Castle; Lord Glenlyon went out on the same day and killed five harts in the forest and on his return home 'blooded' the infant. The child was christened John James Hugh Henry a few months later, and the ceremony was followed by a ball for 1200 tenants in the wooden pavilion put up for the wedding. The child grew up and later succeeded his father as 7th Duke of Atholl.

Two years later, in the autumn of 1842, the news reached Blair that the Queen and Prince Albert intended to visit Scotland for the first time.

John, 4th Duke of Atholl, and his family, by David Allan. The Duke is proudly wearing highland dress which had been banned after the '45 by the hated Dress Act which was not repealed until 1782. The house in the background is Blair Castle as remodelled by the 2nd Duke. The head gamekeeper, Alexander Crerar, was fowler to the 2nd and 3rd Dukes. The Duke raised a regiment in 1777 to help the British Army overseas. This was called the 77th Atholl Highlanders, but it was disbanded after three years.

This was the first visit to Scotland by the reigning monarch since George IV's visit twenty years before and excited enormous interest. The royal party travelled by sea to avoid Chartist unrest, and on their way from Scone Palace to Taymouth the Queen accepted an invitation to lunch at Dunkeld with the Glenlyons. Lord Glenlyon was at this time almost totally blind after a hunting accident and what is described as 'over-exertion' on the hill (he later recovered the sight of one eye), but he was determined to put on a memorable show, for no sovereign had visited Atholl for over two hundred years. He increased the strength of the Atholl Highlanders by another five officers and one hundred men and added white facings to their Tournament coats. A marquee 100 feet long was provided by Edgington's, with other tents put up for the guests including one for the royal party, and the catering arrangements were in the hands of Gunter's. Lord Glenlyon was taken in a carriage to Dunkeld because of his blindness and mounted on his charger at the last possible moment. The

Atholl Highlanders marched from Blair to Dunkeld; each of the two companies comprised sixty men, one armed with Lochaber axes and the other with broadswords and targets, and not one of the contingent was under 5 foot 9 inches in stocking feet.

As they marched they were joined by the other lairds in the district with their attendants and the tenantry; when Lord Glenlyon entered Dunkeld he rode at the head of a body of men 870 strong. The Queen and Prince Albert feasted with the Glenlyons and their guests in the marquee, and after lunch the Queen asked to see some Highland dancing. The Duchess of Atholl's footman, Charles Christie, performed a sword-dance, and Pipe-Major Macpherson provided the music. The visit was a great success and when the Queen had gone, Lady Glenlyon presented to the Tournament Men the medals already referred to. In the following year, Lord Glenlyon increased the strength of the Atholl Highlanders to four companies and when the Queen made a second

Right: 'Death of a Hart in Glen Tilt' by Sir Edwin Landseer who painted this picture after his visits to Blair in the mid 1820s. The painting shows the 4th Duke of Atholl with his grandson, later 6th Duke, with John Crerar, head forester and gamekeeper, Donald MacIntyre, head hillman and Charles Crerar, hillman.

Far right: A collection of Scottish arms on the landing of the entrance hall: targets, swords and rifles.

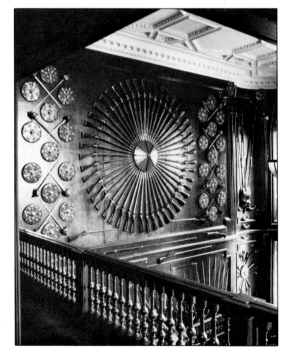

visit in 1844, the welcome was even more impressive, for he had added two three-pounder mountain guns to fire salutes.

The royal visit to Scotland in 1842 was the beginning of the great love affair between Queen Victoria and the Highlands. Prince Albert and she had caught a glimpse of the countryside around Dunkeld and resolved to return. Lord Glenlyon was approached in 1844 and asked to lend Blair Castle to the royal party as Queen Victoria had been unwell and wished to recuperate in Scotland. The Glenlyons had one month in which to prepare the castle which they felt was woefully underfurnished for their royal visitors, and to provide accommodation for the suite of seventy-five. Lord and Lady Glenlyon moved into the factor's house at Old Blair and left the Castle to their guests but they and their little boy were at the front door to receive the Queen and Prince Albert and their children at the start of their three-week visit.

The Queen and Prince Albert went for long walks together; he drove her in the pony phaeton along Glen Tilt, Lord Glenlyon took her to see the Falls of Bruar and Prince Albert drove the ladies on an expedition to the Pass of Killiecrankie. Prince Albert went deer-stalking and the Queen sketched and they went into the hills on ponies attended only by Sandy McAra in the Highland dress which the Queen comments upon with such evident delight. She found at Blair 'a quiet, a retirement, a wilderness, a liberty and a solitude that had such a charm for us'. Each morning a groom was sent up Glen Tilt to fill a bottle of water for her at the small spring now known as the Queen's Well. Prince Albert loved the severity and grandeur of the countryside, the naturalness of the people and the wealth of historical associations which he recognized through his reading of the novels of Sir Walter Scott. 'We ... live a somewhat primitive, yet romantic life,' he wrote from Blair, 'mountain life, that acts as a tonic to the nerves, and gladdens the heart of a lover like myself of

Far left: A chair made of antlers with ivory mounts.

Left: John, 7th Duke of Atholl, and his three sons in their Atholl Highlander uniforms photographed at Blair in about 1900. The Atholl Highlanders are the Duke's private bodyguard and form the last remaining private army in Europe.

field sports and of Nature.' Four years later, in 1848, he took over the lease of the Balmoral estate.

The royal guests were attended by the Atholl Highlanders throughout their visit and when the Queen left they escorted her to the Atholl border. Lord Glenlyon accompanied the Queen on horseback as far as Dundee. The party had left Blair at 9.30 a.m.; Lord Glenlyon bade her farewell at Dundee, turned his horse and rode straight back to Blair which he reached at 5.00 on the following morning, a distance in all of 120 miles.

In the following year, Queen Victoria presented Colours to the Atholl Highlanders and thus placed them in a unique position in the realm. She sent Prince George of Cambridge and Prince Edward of Saxe-Weimar to take part in the presentation ceremony on 4 September, exactly a century to the day since Lord George Murray joined the Jacobite forces in the '45 Rising. Lady Glenlyon acted on behalf of the Queen and presented the Queen's Colour and the Regimental Colour to the Athollmen. 'I am convinced,' she said in her address, 'that the same devoted loyalty which caused the Athollmen to rally round the banner of their sovereign in the last '45 will induce you now to preserve these colours with untarnished honour.'

In 1846, the 5th Duke died and Lord Glenlyon succeeded him. The Duchess became a lady-in-waiting to the Queen, and Blair Castle was the scene of great festivities as the Duke and Duchess received a steady stream of royal and noble visitors from all over Europe. Queen Victoria visited Blair Castle in 1861 and again in 1863 to see the Duke who was suffering from an incurable disease and whom she found much altered. He died in 1864 at the age of forty-nine and his widow later became Queen Victoria's Mistress of the Robes.

The 7th Duke of Atholl was married in the year before his father died to Louisa Moncreiffe, daughter of Sir Thomas Moncreiffe of Moncreiffe. The 7th Duke restored Blair Castle and gave it back its old fortified appearance. The 'large plain white building' which Queen Victoria described in her diary was transformed by the architects David and John Bryce between 1869 and 1872. The attic floors were heightened, battlemented and re-roofed, two storeys were added to Cumming's Tower and a new entrance hall was constructed two storeys high with two floors of bedrooms above. In 1876–7 the Duke added a ballroom to the north of the castle; the great ball which the Duke and Duchess gave for 700 of their tenants in the spring of 1872 to celebrate the birth of their son, John George (later 8th Duke), took place in the riding school behind the stables.

During the South African War, the 7th Duke and his son, Lord Tullibardine, raised two regiments of Scottish Horse. The present Duke's father, Lieutenant-Colonel Anthony Murray, was a descendant of both the 2nd Duke and Lord George Murray; he was killed in Italy in 1945 commanding the Scottish Horse. The present Duke succeeded his kinsman, the 9th Duke, in 1957.

Mr Humphrey FitzRoy Newdegate has owned Arbury since 1950 when the house and estate were made over to him by his mother, the Honourable Mrs L. C. S. FitzRoy Newdegate OBE, who still lives in the house. Mr FitzRoy Newdegate lives with his wife and sons in a house on the estate.

'Have you spent all your life at Arbury?'

'Yes, apart from the time I was in the army. It was, you know, my mother's family house.'

'And she remembers it before World War I?'

'She moved to Arbury with her parents when she was six in 1902 but they spent some years abroad for her father, Sir Francis Newdegate was the Governor of Tasmania and, later, Western Australia.'

'Arbury must have been a very agreeable place to live in.'

'With a staff, and all the fires going, yes. Sir Roger did not allow for curtains when he designed the drawing-room and saloon. I remember in my grandparents' day a footman bringing in the curtains at tea-time and hoisting them with a long pole on to hooks.'

'How extensive is the Arbury estate now? Has its size altered very much in the past fifty years or so?'

'When my grandfather died in 1936 the estate was about six or seven thousand acres; we are down to about four and a half now. Up to 1902 we had a deer park but this was taken over as farmland in 1950, and I now farm about 1600 acres.'

'When did you open Arbury to the public?'

'In 1953, with help from Rupert Gunnis who advised us on how to go about it.'

'And you don't mind people wandering through the house?'

'It doesn't worry my mother who lives in the library which is not open to the public. We are only open on Sunday afternoons after all. Arbury is a remarkable house. I feel – we all do – that it should be open.'

'You are so near Coventry, did the house suffer during the war?'

'We had 10,000 German prisoners of war living in the park! The house was taken over at the very beginning of the war but most of the time my mother lived on her own in one corner. I was with my regiment, but she of course heard the planes coming over the house on their way to bomb Coventry. The lake was the signal to the pilots to change course; there was talk of dredging it.'

'And Arbury miraculously survived, only to be threatened in the 1950s by the National Coal Board. It was one of the early conservation battles; what precisely happened?'

'The Board applied for permission to mine fifty acres *under* the house and there is no doubt this would have threatened the structure and the decorations. The conservation groups, the County Council and the Nuneaton Borough Council fought with us. To everyone's surprise Harold Macmillan, who was then Minister of Housing and Local Government, supported the objections.'

'A landmark in the history of the conservation movement. But how ironical, considering that the house was rebuilt out of the profits of a coal-mine!'

Detail of the plasterwork in the saloon.

Arbury Hall

NUNEATON, WARWICKSHIRE

Mr Humphrey FitzRoy Newdegate

R oger Newdigate was a schoolboy at Westminster when he inherited the family baronetcy and estates from his brother in 1734. This was unexpected, for he was only a few years younger, but at the time of his birth the likelihood that this would come about was even more remote since he was his parents' seventh son. All the strength and energy which passed by the first six brothers was concentrated in the tall, stately figure of Sir Roger whose many interests – architecture, classical literature, politics, the University of Oxford, and much else – kept him happily occupied into his eighty-seventh year.

After Westminster, Sir Roger's education continued at University College, Oxford, and in France and Italy, for in common with many others of his rank and fortune at that time, he made a Grand Tour. He visited the principal architectural sights and galleries and made numerous sketches of what he saw; he also acquired some works of art.

When he returned to England, Sir Roger took steps to establish himself in life; he became Member of Parliament for Middlesex in 1741, and two years later married Sophia Conyers. In his father's time Harefield Place, near Uxbridge, was the principal family home. Harefield had been acquired by the Newdigates through marriage with an heiress in the fourteenth century, but John Newdegate (as he spelt his name) exchanged the house in 1586 for Arbury in Warwickshire; Sir Richard Newdigate, the first baronet, made a fortune at the Bar and bought Harefield back into the family. His grandson, Sir Roger, inherited both properties, but it was clear from an early stage in his life that he preferred Arbury.

Sir Roger was an old-fashioned Tory who was said to have barely concealed his Jacobite sympathies. He represented Middlesex in the House of Commons until 1747 and then, for thirty years between 1750 and 1780, the University of Oxford. He was devoted to the University and always retained his links with classical scholarship; he was also a benefactor – at the very end of his life he founded the Newdigate Prize for English Verse – and he helped to build the hall of University College. He spent three months in London each spring to attend Parliament, the summer and autumn in Warwickshire, and November would see him in London again. The greater part of his life was passed on the Arbury estate, which included not only farmland and woods but also the Bedworth colliery. Sir Roger was one of the foremost promoters of road and

The north front showing the main entrance with *porte cochère*.

canal building in the Midlands, and he tried to impress upon local landowners and his fellow members of the House of Commons the importance of a good system of transport. He cut many miles of canals himself, and made a link between his colliery and the Coventry Canal.

In his early years he appears to have mixed freely with the local families. He was a magistrate, and even held a commission for a time in the Warwickshire Militia. He loved walking, and made a daily tour on foot of his farm and garden. There are a few references to shooting in his diary, but it is evident that he did not care for hunting, and that in his time the hounds were not welcome on the Arbury estate. In later years, he became increasingly reluctant to leave his demesne, and his neighbours tired of his obsession with the decoration of Arbury which continued for so many years to the evident discomfort of his household.

When he began, Arbury was a quadrangular Elizabethan house built on the site of an Augustinian monastery. In the latter part of the seventeenth century, his grandfather added the handsome chapel with its rich plaster ceiling in the north-east corner of the house, and consulted his friend Sir Christopher Wren about a new stable block, but he made no alterations to the structure.

In the late 1740s Sir Roger decided to bring the old-fashioned house up to date. He began in a modest way, on his wife's dressing-room and his own library, and then proceeded to work round the house, room by room, so that by the time he finished fifty years later very little, apart from the chimney-piece in the long gallery, had escaped his attention. Sir Roger progressed slowly with his work. According to Mr Anthony Wood who has made a study of the copious diary Sir Roger kept, he never employed more than a few workmen at a time, and appears to have supervised the work himself, for he did not appoint a Clerk of the Works. Sir Roger was a careful man; the money for his building works was put aside from his farm rents and the profits from the colliery, and paid in cash.

He chose to build in the Gothic style which had enjoyed a great vogue in the ten years before he began, and he remained faithful to this to the end. Sir Roger's architectural taste had been formed in the 1740s, when the reaction to the classical style favoured by the previous generation had provoked all manner of fantasies which fall under the heading Rococo, and of which Gothic is one and chinoiserie another. Horace Walpole's house

Below left: Sir Roger Newdigate in his library at Arbury, painted by Arthur Devis in the late 1750s.

Below: The drawing-room, decorated by Henry Keene in the early 1760s.

The south front and the lake.

Strawberry Hill was the most influential example of the eighteenth-century Gothic, but Sir Roger's Arbury is the most complete and best preserved. We can only guess why he chose this style, but it is worth considering that as a schoolboy Sir Roger lived in the shadow of Westminster Abbey, a building which was to be plundered freely for designs and details, not least by his own architect for Arbury. And did Sir Roger return perhaps from the continent and decide, as Walpole did, that the buildings in England were as fine as any in the rest of Europe?

Before he began, Sir Roger sought the advice of a Warwickshire squire and amateur architect, Sanderson Miller, who was almost an exact contemporary, and had also inherited his family home and a fortune at an early age. In the mid-1740s Miller had built an octagonal tower in the Gothic style on the site of the battle of Edgehill, which attracted much attention, and Miller's friends were so enthralled by his Gothic alterations to his family house, Radway Grange, that they clamoured for designs from him for their own houses, and for sham-castles, ruins and summer-houses. Miller gave Sir Roger advice on his first plans, and may well have introduced him to the

architect Henry Keene who worked on Arbury from about 1761 until his death in 1776.

Keene held two surveyorships at Westminster Abbey during this time and some of the details of the work at Arbury reflect this close association. The chimney-piece in the drawing-room is derived from the tomb of Aymer de Valence in the Abbey, an exquisite work which recalls Walpole's comment that 'the great delicacy and richness of Gothic ornaments was exhausted on small chapels, oratories, and tombs'. And the fan vaulting in the dining-room is in turn based on that of Henry VII's chapel. Details were used for decorative purposes only; their structural role was ignored.

Some of the rooms at Arbury took years to complete. Work started on the library in the early 1750s, and Arthur Devis portrayed Sir Roger sitting in the finished room a few years later. Sir Roger was evidently dissatisfied with the ceiling; he found a design which pleased him in 1780, started work again, but for some reason – money, or availability perhaps – the plasterers did not finish until 1791.

Henry Keene drew up designs to convert the old great hall into a dining-room. Work began in 1769, and one day in the winter of 1773 Sir Roger noted in his diary that he had breakfasted, dined and supped in the room, which he described as the warmest in the house. He bought some plaster casts in Italy to decorate the room: Endymion was placed in his niche in 1777 and, at the same time, poor Cupid was smashed and had to be glued together. In 1787, however, we read that Sir Roger gave up the dining-room for over a year to the plasterers to finish their work.

How did his household cope? His wife, Sophia, apparently bore the upheavals with good humour and, as the first designs were for her dressing-room, it is reasonable to suppose that she was enthusiastic when Sir Roger began work. We know that she was untidy, and that Sir Roger teased her about the possessions she could never find, so she probably took the chaos at Arbury in her stride. Sadly, in 1774, she died, and just over a fortnight afterwards, her broken-hearted husband left in the company of two relations, Charles Parker and Mary Conyers, for an eighteen-month journey on the continent. We know more about Sir Roger's second visit to France and Italy than we do about his first. In Paris, we gather from his diary that he left to sightsee at nine in the morning and did not return to his hotel until ten at night. He studied some of the great Gothic cathedrals including Amiens, Rheims and Milan, and visited Sir Horace Mann in Florence, Sir William Hamilton in Naples, Piranesi in Rome, and was in Venice in July when the heat and stench were unbearable. He bought statues, casts, antique medals and other objects, but as far as paintings were concerned, he appears to have ordered copies rather than buy original works.

Sir Roger returned to Arbury on the last day of December 1775, and in the following year his architect Keene died. It is evident that throughout the remodelling of Arbury Sir Roger played a formative part, and provided the link between the various professional hands which worked on the house. Keene was replaced by a Warwick builder named Henry Couchman who set to work to complete the south front and to begin on the finest room at Arbury – the saloon – which may well reflect Keene's ideas. The saloon took twenty years to complete; the bow-window with its exquisite tracery was not installed until 1795. Under Couchman the cloisters were constructed out of the Elizabethan courtyard, and the east, west and north fronts were Gothicized.

In 1789 Sir Roger fell out with Couchman over a bill, and dismissed him. He then appears to have supervised all the work himself, for after he relinquished his seat in the House of Commons in 1780 Sir Roger spent most of his time at Arbury. His second wife, Hester Mundy, a Derbyshire

woman whom he married in 1776, gave up her attempts to persuade him to travel with her, although he would make occasional journeys to London and he sat to Romney for the portrait painted to hang in the saloon.

Hester Newdigate was a musician who played a curious hybrid instrument called a clavicello – a 'cello with a keyboard attached – which can be seen in the portrait Romney painted of her to hang alongside that of her husband. She attended music festivals all over the country and, where possible, combined these with visits to watering-places, for she suffered from rheumatism and headaches. We gain a vivid picture of her at Buxton from some letters she wrote to Sir Roger soon after they married. She chided him gently on one occasion for sending a love-letter to her in Latin (which she could not read): 'What a bold man you are to hazard your wife's character at such a Place as Buxton by sending a Lattin note open by a

The dining-room, designed by Henry Keene. This was originally the front hall of the old house.

Above: Detail of the fireplace in the drawing-room. The design is derived from the tomb of Aymer de Valence in Westminster Abbey.

Right: Lady Newdigate, wife of Sir Roger, painted for the saloon by George Romney and wearing the white dress which the painter insisted she wore. She was a musician and her clavicello is just visible on the left.

Postillion.' The waters and her opium pills (of which Sir Roger disapproved) eased her head-aches, and she and her companions amused themselves by day observing their fellow visitors, and in the evening by reading aloud from the *Sorrows of Werther*. At Arbury, 'our sweet Arbury', she kept an eye on the poultry-yard and her bees.

In the 1780s there entered into the lives of Sir Roger and Lady Newdigate, who were childless, a young girl named Sally Shilton, who is believed to have been the daughter of one of the miners at Bedworth colliery. Lady Newdigate heard her singing on a cottage doorstep and was captivated by her voice. She took Sally to Arbury, where she graduated from the housekeeper's room to the drawing-room, and eventually shared the Newdigates' lives. Years later, George Eliot, who was born and brought up on the Arbury estate, for her father was agent to one of Sir Roger's successors, took the story of Sally Shilton, her upbringing at Arbury, and her marriage to the local clergyman, and wove it into one of her *Scenes of Clerical Life*. 'Mr Gilfil's Love Story' was serialized in *Blackwood's Magazine* in 1857. There was intense speculation about the author-ship, for the story was unsigned, and there were many people in the neighbourhood of Arbury who recognized in her tale Sir Roger Newdigate, Sally Shilton and the Neapolitan music master, Motta, who came to live at Arbury to teach her, Lady Newdigate and the Arbury servants. George Eliot did not know any of them, for she was not born until 1819. But the stories she would have heard as a child in the housekeeper's room as she waited for her father of the transformation of Arbury over the years, and of its inhabitants, the sight of the Romney portraits in the saloon, the books in Sir Roger's library which she was allowed to read, enabled her to make an imaginative recreation which is so vivid that no reader of her tale is able to separate fact from fiction at Arbury again. George Eliot like all novelists was at pains to explain to John Blackwood that she had merely used the story of Arbury as a quarry. 'Certain vague traditions about Sir Roger Newdegate,' she told him, 'which I heard when I was a child are woven into the character of Sir Christoper Cheverel, and the house he improved into a charming Gothic place with beautiful ceilings, I know from actual vision – but the rest of "Mr Gilfil's Love Story" is spun out of the subtlest web of minute observation and inward experience, from my first childish recollections up to recent years.'

And yet, despite her warning, her intuitive rendering of the character of Sir Roger is unforgettable. She describes Cheverel Manor as 'growing from ugliness into beauty' under the

The saloon, designed by Henry Couchman and decorated between 1776 and 1786.

single-minded dedication of Sir Christopher, and she attributed 'that unswerving architectural purpose of his, conceived and carried out through long years of systematic personal exertion, to something of the fervour of genius, as well as inflexibility of will'. And Lady Cheverel? She did not share her husband's architectural enthusiasms, any more than his fox-hunting neighbours understood the financial sacrifice – the running down of cellar and stables – which were made to enable work on the house to continue. And the neighbours sympathized with Lady Cheverel, 'who had to live in no more than three rooms at once, and who must be distracted with noises and have her constitution undermined by unhealthy smells'.

Lady Newdigate tried to launch Sally Shilton as a professional singer, but the girl was too delicate to bear the strain. George Eliot envisaged the domestic scene at Cheverel Manor: Caterina sings songs from Paisiello and Gluck after dinner, promptly followed on the stroke of nine by Sir Christopher and Lady Cheverel's game of piquet, and then prayers in the chapel, with the domestics headed by the housekeeper kneeling on red-covered forms, and the baronet and his wife on red velvet cushions.

George Eliot does not picture Sir Roger as a county magnate, a benefactor of Oxford, or as a distinguished classical scholar, but as an honest, good-humoured, kindly English country squire.

Sir Roger survived his second wife. He was able to install the chandelier in the saloon in 1805, and in the same year to establish the Newdigate Prize for English Verse at Oxford. 'My morning walks are much abridged in length and time,' he wrote to a friend, 'but you will still find me, like old Laertes ... creeping about my farm and garden, and seldom going beyond the park pale.' And, in 1806, his architectural labours concluded, Sir Roger died: he had been master of Arbury for seventy-two years.

His successors have preserved Arbury almost exactly as he left it. He bequeathed the house to his cousin Francis Parker who took the name of Newdigate, and his great-great-grandson Sir Francis Newdigate Newdegate MP left it to his daughter, the Honourable Mrs L. C. S. FitzRoy Newdegate OBE who has lived at Arbury since she was six, and is devoted to the house and its history; she made over Arbury to her son Mr Humphrey FitzRoy Newdegate in 1950.

Hugh, 10th Duke of Northumberland is Lord Steward of the Royal Household. He lives at Alnwick Castle in Northumberland and at Syon, the last of the great patrician houses in the neighbourhood of London to remain in private hands.

'It is such a surprise to find an eighteenth-century nobleman's park only eight miles from Hyde Park Corner; how much land have you at Syon?'

'About 200 acres in all, and that figure breaks down into fifty-five acres of garden open to the public, sixty acres of tide meadows and eighty acres of outer parks let for grazing to a local farmer. It has gradually dwindled over the years. I can remember walking with my father through the park as far as the Great West Road.'

'How much time do you spend at Syon?'

'We are coming and going all the time. It is our London house, though of course it wasn't in the past. We had Northumberland House at Charing Cross until it was demolished in 1874, and Syon was then a country house. I spend most of my time at Alnwick. I am Lord-Lieutenant of Northumberland, and Syon is a summer house – it always was – there is no central heating and in the winter you need to wear a coat to walk from one room to the next. Living at Syon has its austere moments.'

'Do you have a large staff there?'

'No, a housekeeper, a houseman and a night watchman.'

'You have one of the most successful garden centres in the country at Syon. What proportion of people visiting the centre go on to look round the house?'

'You wouldn't believe the figures if I told you. It is something I have never been able to under-stand. I suppose there is too much competition in and round about London, too much else to amuse people. I'll look up the figures. The maximum number for the selling centre is 380,000 in a year and very few of those – who go to buy plants after all – go through the Syon gardens; the maximum figure is 120,000. And we have never had more than 30,000 in the house.'

'Which is why the house is always such a joy to visit, it is never crowded. And the state of the rooms and their contents is so superb. Have you carried out much restoration?'

'Oh yes! 160 bombs fell in the park during the last war but luckily only one fire bomb came through the roof. We were fortunate because the fire service kept their engines in the park. Syon was saved by one elm tree. A "doodle-bug" making straight for the house caught the tree and came down; it blasted every window – and the tree – and would have destroyed the house. After the West Middlesex Hospital nurses' home was bombed out they moved to Syon. We had dry rot and death-watch beetle – everything. The War Damage Insurance Scheme enabled us to make a start with urgent repairs in 1946 but it was not until the 1950s that the major restoration started.'

'Have you altered any of the furniture and paintings at Syon? The guide-book mentions furniture brought from Northumberland House.'

'Yes. We sold Albury, a house in Surrey where my mother lived. Some of the furniture from there came to Syon and some of the Syon books went to Alnwick. Oh yes and we brought down a bed from Alnwick and put it in the print room because so many visitors to the house wanted to see one of the bedrooms. I managed to acquire the Griffier view of Syon; I was telephoned by a friend – an art dealer – who thought he had discovered a painting of Syon in an auction. It was very dirty, but he took a chance and bought it.'

The dining-room. This was the first room completed by Adam.

Syon House

BRENTFORD, MIDDLESEX

The Duke of Northumberland KG, TD, PC

The Percy family came to Syon at the end of the sixteenth century, which by the standards of this ancient family is recent history. Henry de Percy, whose Norman ancestor came to England with William the Conqueror in 1066, acquired Alnwick Castle, in the wild Border country north of Newcastle-upon-Tyne, in 1309. His descendant, another Henry, was created Earl of Northumberland in 1377. For over two hundred and fifty years, the inhabitants of that county 'knew no other Prince but a Percy', and from their battle-scarred castle the Percys engaged in continuous warfare with the Scots. Their rivalry with the great Douglas family over the border was the inspiration of one of the oldest ballads in the English language 'The Ballad of Chevy Chase'; and the legendary exploits of the young Harry Hotspur, the 1st Earl's son, were immortalized by Shakespeare in *Henry IV, Part I*.

The immense power which the Percys built up in the north posed a threat to one king after another, but in the sixteenth century their support for the Catholic cause led them into the losing camp, and gradually eroded their strength. An attainder for high treason in 1537 was followed by the execution of the 7th Earl in 1572 after he had joined the Rising of the North in favour of Mary, Queen of Scots and, as a result, his brother, the 8th Earl, was required to live in the south of England. He made his home at Petworth in Sussex, which the Percys had owned since 1150. His son, Henry, began their long connexion with Syon.

Henry Percy was born in 1564. At the age of eighteen he was sent abroad to study, and was liberally supplied with money by his father who was living 'like a rustike' at Petworth. The 8th Earl was not left in peace for long, for he was dragged away from Petworth to begin a third term in the Tower of London in 1584.

Henry travelled for a time, and then settled in Paris where, after a hectic period of high living, he began to take an interest in mathematics and the occult sciences which were to become his principal concerns in life, and earn him the name by which he is generally known, 'the Wizard Earl'.

These studies were interrupted in 1585 by the sudden death of his father in mysterious circumstances in the Tower. Henry returned to England; he was twenty-one, and totally unacquainted with business affairs. The Percy estates which were spread across eight counties were in a chaotic state, his mother with whom he was on bad terms made some predatory swoops on his possessions, and some of his servants took advantage of his ignorance. He would recall this period in later years: 'I was not worth a fire shovel, or a pair of tongs.'

The young Lord Northumberland opened up Alnwick Castle, and lived there for a while to master the intricacies of estate management. At the same time he continued to develop his interests in science, and to lay the foundations of a library. He also spent a few months abroad as a soldier in the Low Countries.

Queen Elizabeth looked on the young man with favour, and was instrumental in finding him a wife around whom it was impossible for the Catholic faction to rally. Thus in 1594 he came to marry into the Devereux family, which was a sensible move, for his bride, Lady Dorothy, was a sister of the Queen's favourite, Robert, Earl of Essex. Although their marriage proved most unhappy and Northumberland warned his own son against making a marriage for worldly reasons, Lady Dorothy brought one possession to her husband which was to bring him great joy, for from her previous husband, she acquired a right to the lease of the Syon estate. And when this was confirmed by the Queen, Syon became their principal home.

As Queen Elizabeth's life drew to its close, Northumberland entered into a correspondence with James VI of Scotland. When the King entered London in triumph as James I of England, Northumberland rode at his right hand. In 1604 the King gave him Syon as a gift.

The history of Syon before 1594 is almost as turbulent in character as that of the Percy family. Syon, as its name implies, was originally a monastery, founded by Henry V in 1415. The monks and nuns belonged to the Order of St Bridget and under a succession of wise abbesses the community prospered until, at the accession of Henry VIII in 1509, it was one of the richest in the country. It was thus a ripe plum which fell after much resistance into the royal lap when Henry dissolved the monasteries in the late 1530s.

As soon as Edward VI came to the throne in 1547, his uncle, Edward, Duke of Somerset, the Lord Protector, acquired the estate. He loved Syon, he built the house and made the garden. But he did not enjoy himself there for very long, for he was executed in 1552. In the following year, Syon was granted to John (Dudley), Duke of Northumberland, who was father-in-law of Lady Jane Grey. It was at Syon that Lady Jane gave her consent to the fateful plan to make her Queen and as a result of her decision she and her family died on the scaffold. Syon then reverted to the Crown in the person of Queen Mary who recalled the nuns from the Low Countries. They returned only to find themselves expelled again as soon as Queen Elizabeth came to the throne. Syon then fell into Percy hands, and has remained so ever since.

When Lord Northumberland took over Syon in 1594, he found the house much as the Lord Protector had left it. Dr G. R. Batho, who has

carried out extensive researches into the history of the Percy family and their estates, discovered a drawing of Syon of about 1600 in the margin of a family pedigree. This shows a house remarkably similar to the one we see today, a three-storeyed, quadrangular building with angle-turrets, round a central, open courtyard, faced with stone, and battlemented. The courtyard presumably bears some relationship to the cloister of the monastic building. Northumberland also found a remarkable garden, for the Lord Protector employed as his personal physician Dr William Turner, who founded at Syon one of the first botanical gardens in England. It is believed that he planted the mulberry trees which still flourish, and which had been introduced into England from Persia in the early sixteenth century. Turner's book *The names of herbes* was written at Syon, and dedicated to the Lord Protector. Lord Northumberland was also a gardener, and able to appreciate the legacy he acquired from Dr Turner in the way of rare plants.

Northumberland set about altering Syon in the last few years of the sixteenth century. Apart from the new stables, much of his work was renovation and the redecoration of the interior. We know, for instance, that he made the long gallery which is carried on a Renaissance arcade. Typically, he adopted a scholarly approach, he read architectural treatises and made a tour of country houses. It is evident that he wished to entertain on a grander scale than he had. This was largely due to his greatly improved financial position, for his efforts to put his estates in order had been successful. Virtually his entire income came from land. The only office of profit he ever held from the Crown was the captaincy of the Gentlemen Pensioners in 1603–04 at a fee of £280 per annum. Northumberland was a careful man, and his household at the beginning of the seventeenth century numbered about seventy servants which was a modest amount for a man of his rank at that time. He lived in some style, nevertheless, and sent the Syon chef to take lessons from his opposite number in the French Embassy. An unknown contemporary quoted by Dr Batho claimed that Northumberland kept one of the best tables in the kingdom: 'wherin I mean not only the diet of flesh and fish which answer to the stuff of our clothes; but I consider also the bread, wine, salads, oil, vinegar, fruit, sweetmeats, linen, plate, and lights

The garden front.

The great hall, with the
bronze of the 'Dying Gaul'.
This room is the first of the
great series of state rooms
designed by Robert Adam
for the 1st Duke and Duchess
of Northumberland.

The ante-room. The columns shown are
part of a set of twelve discovered in the bed of
the Tiber in Rome and brought to Syon in 1765.

Henry, 9th Earl of
Northumberland, after Sir
Anthony Van Dyck. He was
named 'the Wizard Earl'
after his interest in the occult
sciences.

Dorothy gave birth to two sons who died as infants, then daughters, and finally, in 1602, to a son and heir, Algernon.

When the great calamity of Northumberland's life occurred, Lady Dorothy proved a tower of strength. On 4 November 1605, a distant cousin, Thomas Percy, dined at Syon. He was the rapacious agent for the family's northern estates, and a committed Catholic. The story lingers in the Percy family of how a visitor called in the middle of dinner that night, and rode away with Percy. The visitor was supposed to have been Guy Fawkes and, on the following day, their plot to blow up the Houses of Parliament was discovered. Percy was killed, but the news that he had dined the previous night at Syon soon leaked out. It was a rotten stroke of luck. Northumberland was arrested; he protested to the council that his interests lay far from political conspiracy: 'Examine but my humours,' he said, 'in buildings, gardenings, and private expenses these two years past.' He was tried by the Court of Star Chamber and, despite his obvious innocence, was sentenced to a fine of £30,000 and imprisonment for life. He appealed in vain, for he was unable to raise the money and he spent the following sixteen years in the Tower.

Northumberland took with him into captivity a large number of books, 'retorts, crucibles, alembics, zodiacal charts and globes', also a selection of his favourite pipes. Food, good wine, and quantities of tobacco were sent to him regularly, and baskets of fruit were dispatched from his orchards at Syon. Sir Walter Raleigh and other kindred spirits were fellow-prisoners, there were always visitors, and he had living with him three wise men, scientists known as the 'Three Magi' who assisted him with his experiments. He played chess and draughts, and an early version of kriegspiel, for one item in his accounts is for 300 model soldiers and other necessary equipment.

Lady Dorothy behaved with great courage. She divined accurately that Lord Salisbury was at the root of her husband's downfall, and she proceeded in full sail to Whitehall 'to give the Ferrett a nipp'. But it was fruitless, for the terrified Salisbury merely gave orders that she was never to be admitted to his presence again, and Queen Anne's efforts to influence the King in Northumberland's favour came to nothing.

Northumberland continued to manage all his affairs from the Tower. Building continued at Syon under the able Clerk of the Works, Christopher Ingram. Ingram sent all the plans and accounts to his master and, when necessary, samples of stone were sent to the Tower for approval. The accounts for 1607–13 show that Northumberland spent £1903 15s 8d on the house,

which at the table account as the petty toys of our attire.'

We know much about the company he kept at Syon. Although he entertained King James on several occasions (one visit in 1603 cost Northumberland £364 in food and drink), he was not a courtier, and he quickly became disenchanted with the whims of that most capricious monarch.

Northumberland preferred his independence, his laboratory, his garden and his 'pypes of tobacco', for he was hopelessly addicted to the weed. He enjoyed the company of intelligent men. He was the 'favourer of all good learning, and Maecenas of learned men'. His accounts are full of payments to writers, geographers and scientists; he knew Shakespeare (and formed a collection of the early quartos), Francis Bacon, Ben Jonson, Edmund Spenser and the aged magus, Dr John Dee, who settled at nearby Mortlake.

His wife, Lady Dorothy, did not share his interests. She had adored her rash, handsome brother Essex who was executed; and she appears never to have cared greatly for the cautious, scholarly Northumberland. They both had violent tempers, and were formally separated no less than four times in the first five years of marriage. Lady

which included the cost of a new suite of rooms for Lady Dorothy with a bathroom. He groused about this particular expense in a letter to Lord Knollys in 1608, 'It costes me £400 this laste year paste in building of Bathing Houses, cabinettes, and other thinges Shee had a fancy to, which this 15 yeare before she neuer miste nor wanting.' Lady Dorothy appears to have been far in advance of most of her contemporaries, for bathrooms were rare in English houses at that time and John Aubrey thought that the two 'Bathing-roomes' which he saw at Francis Bacon's worthy of mention. There may have been at Syon the remains of a monastic water supply, for monasteries were generally well organized in this respect and there would have been no shortage of water.

The gardens at Syon were in the hands of Anthony Menvell who was a gardener there before the Northumberlands arrived, and head gardener for many years. The household accounts show that in the year 1590–91 his wages were £1 10s per annum, and had risen to £6 10s by 1606, at which figure they stuck until 1616.

However hard Northumberland tried to restrict his staff – and he cut the numbers to forty after his imprisonment – the household began to grow larger, until in the 1620s he employed eighty servants at a cost of £400–£500. The tendency, however, was for households to shrink, and by the middle of the seventeenth century most large establishments managed to run effectively with no more than thirty to fifty servants. Northumberland was ruthless where his tenants were concerned, but he appears to have treated his staff with consideration. He also had respect for them as he told his son, 'I have them more reasonable than either wife, brother or friend; you must not expect to find gods of them for knowledge, nor saints for life.' Some of them remained with him for years. Christopher Ingram, for instance, the Clerk of the Works, worked for him from 1599 until his death in 1628. John Vaughan was a groom for at least eighteen years. John Greyme or Grymes, who is first mentioned in the Syon household accounts as a porter in 1607, was still with him in 1628 but by then as a waiter earning £5 a year. Andrew Barton, on the other hand, the mole-catcher, who earned £2 13s 4d, drops out of sight after two years.

As soon as Algernon was old enough, he went to live with his father in the Tower, so that his education could be supervised by the 'Three Magi'. At the same time, Northumberland took up a book he had begun to compile for his eldest son and then abandoned when the child died. This is full of the worldly wisdom Northumberland had acquired over the years, with hints on how to handle subjects as varied as servants, women and

Algernon, 10th Earl of Northumberland, as Lord High Admiral, by Sir Anthony Van Dyck. This painting hangs at Alnwick, the family seat in Northumberland.

foreign travel. He did not mince his words about the female sex. 'Wives are commonly great scratchers after their husband's deaths, if things be loose,' he wrote with feeling, and thoughts no doubt of his own mother; whereas it is his wife he had in mind when he grumbled, 'And the cry is always not what is modest for them to doe, but "sutche and sutche doeth this", not what is fitt for them and their Children to weare . . . but "sutche and sutche weare this and that".' Lord Northumberland himself preferred the eternal quest for the philosophers' stone.

In a vain attempt to secure his release, Northumberland went so far as to offer his beloved Syon to the King in part payment of the fine, but the King predictably refused to take back what had been, after all, his gift.

Finally, in 1621, Northumberland was released. He went from the Tower to Syon for ten days, and then on to Penshurst to see his favourite daughter Dorothy. He was at first required to stay at Petworth, but this restriction was lifted and he chose to remain there and make the occasional visit to Syon. His wife died in 1619. He spent the summer of 1632 with Dorothy at Penshurst and with his Sidney grandchildren, Philip, Algernon,

The red drawing-room. The walls are hung with Spitalfields silk which was restored in 1965 by Lady Meade-Featherstonhaugh and her assistants at Uppark, using a soap made from the herb saponaria grown on her estate. The carpet was designed by Adam for the room and was made by Thomas Moore who has woven his name and the date, 1769, into one end. The paintings are all Stuart portraits.

little Dorothy ('Sacharissa'), and the others. He returned to Petworth in the autumn, and in November he died. His only son Algernon had committed an unforgivable sin and married the daughter of his old enemy Lord Salisbury, but the enormous marriage portion Lord Salisbury had to pay—£12,000, the equivalent of one and a half years of gross landed income—must have given him some satisfaction.

Algernon, 10th Earl of Northumberland, refused to side with the King during the Civil War, and remained aloof from party intrigue. He had found favour with King Charles who had bestowed on him the Garter and the high ranks of Lord High Admiral and Captain General and Governor of the Army. (It is as Lord High Admiral that he is portrayed by Van Dyck in the magnificent portrait at Alnwick.) Although he was stripped of his ranks, he remained active in public life, for he believed to the last in the power of

negotiation. For a time, the Royal children, the Duke of Gloucester and the Princess Elizabeth, were lodged with him at Syon and were near enough to Hampton Court for visits from their father. The painting of Charles I and his son by Sir Peter Lely which hangs in the red drawing-room at Syon was commissioned by Northumberland and painted there. After the death of the King, he dispatched the Royal children to his sister Dorothy at Penshurst and withdrew from public life.

The 10th Earl loved Syon and enriched the gardens, for he had a passion for rare and exotic plants. He also made alterations and repairs to the house. He was a discriminating collector of works of art and he purchased many paintings which surfaced during the years of civil war; the great painting by Titian of the Vendramin family now in the National Gallery was once in his collection. Through his second wife, he was able to acquire a mansion near Charing Cross which was renamed

The long gallery. This was originally a Jacobean gallery and was transformed by Adam in a style 'to afford variety and amusement' for the ladies. It was 136 feet long. Most of the furniture was designed for the room by Adam.

Northumberland House and became the town house of the earls and dukes of Northumberland until the late nineteenth century. He died in 1668.

His son Joceline survived by a mere two years, and with his death the direct male line of the great Percy family died out. The 11th Earl's widow married Ralph Montagu of Boughton, and his daughter, Lady Elizabeth Percy, became at the age of three the most considerable heiress in England.

Lady Elizabeth's grandmother set about to look for a suitable husband. Her eye lit on the sickly Lord Ogle who was married to Elizabeth when she was only twelve. He died shortly afterwards, and the profligate Thomas Thynne of Longleat was produced, but he was murdered in his coach in Pall Mall shortly after their marriage by a disappointed suitor, Count Königsmark. Lady Elizabeth's third and final marriage was to Charles, 6th Duke of Somerset. The 'Proud Duke' of Somerset, as he was called, made some alterations to Syon, and

planted the avenue of lime trees which frame the main approach to the house, but his principal efforts were directed towards the embellishment of Petworth House. Lady Elizabeth never cared for Syon; she described it as a 'hobble-de-hoy place, neither town nor country'.

The Duke's eldest son and his wife, Lord and Lady Hertford (he had assumed the name Percy) had two children, Lord Beauchamp and Lady Elizabeth Percy. Lady Elizabeth was given Syon by her father in 1748, and she and her husband, Sir Hugh Smithson, commissioned Robert Adam to transform the interior of the house into the neo-classical palace we know today.

When Sir Hugh Smithson married Lady Elizabeth – Lady Betty as she was always known – in 1740, she was not an heiress, for her brother was still alive. Sir Hugh was a Yorkshire baronet of great charm and ability, who was interested from an early age in the arts. Her parents, who were

Elizabeth, 1st Duchess of
Northumberland, by Sir
Joshua Reynolds. She and
her husband commissioned
Adam to remodel the interior
of Syon.

devoted to her, agreed to the match, though Sir
Hugh's antecedents did not satisfy her grandfather
the 'Proud Duke'. Sir Hugh was the 4th Baronet.
His family had been haberdashers in the City of
London who had migrated to Yorkshire with their
money, bought the estate of Stanwick in 1638, and
proceeded to marry with the northern Catholic
aristocracy. After her marriage with Sir Hugh,
Lady Betty settled down to life among the
Yorkshire gentry. The sudden death of her brother
Lord Beauchamp in 1744 from smallpox on his
Grand Tour, transformed Lady Betty into a great
heiress, although her crafty grandfather made
certain that the Percy estates in Sussex, Yorkshire
and Cumberland should go to his Wyndham
grandchildren and not to the Smithsons.

Sir Hugh Smithson was the ideal person to
revivify the Percy estates. He was most astute –
Gainsborough captured this quality on canvas
with great skill – and he managed to make
improvements with the result that their revenues
rose from £8000 in 1749 to £25,000 in 1765 and
£50,000 in 1778. The 'Wizard Earl' had tried to
exploit the coal resources on his estates in
Northumberland without much success, but Sir
Hugh succeeded where his predecessor had failed
with a dramatic impact on the family fortunes.

One of the earliest glimpses we have of Sir Hugh
is just after his marriage when he set out with Lady
Betty to visit an ancient Smithson cousin in
Tottenham (of whom he had great expectations).
Sir Hugh we are told wore 'a lead colour and silver
stuff Coat embroidered with silver, and Waistcoat
and Parements of white silk, embroidered with
silver and colours'. He was later a glorious figure
about court, and reckoned to be the handsomest
man of his time. George III liked him, he became
Lord Chamberlain to Queen Charlotte, and Lady
Betty was not only a Lady of the Bedchamber to
the Queen but also a great personal friend. Their
success was a source of great envy at court. Sir
Hugh's adoption of the name 'Percy' had been
ridiculed, but he could not be ignored. He received
the Order of the Garter and in 1763 was appointed
Lord Lieutenant of Ireland where he astonished
the Irish with the magnificence of his establishment. In 1766 he was created Duke of Northumberland which was an extraordinary advance
in life, for no dukedom had been created in
England for half a century. His dress and his style
of living became steadily more ostentatious.
George Selwyn described him at a dinner as
'nothing but fur and diamonds ... he looked as if
he was to represent the Bear Star'.

He and Lady Betty were devoted to each other.
She sails through the drawing-rooms of the period.
Horace Walpole described her as 'a jovial heap of
contradictions ... her person was more vulgar
than anything but her conversation, which was
larded indiscriminately with stories of her ancestors and her footmen ... She was mischievous
under the appearance of frankness: generous and
friendly without delicacy or sentiment.'

The Duke entrusted the transformation of the
three great Percy houses Alnwick, Northumberland House and Syon to Robert Adam. The Duke
was aided and abetted in all his artistic plans by
Lady Betty whose knowledge of country houses
and craftsmen in England and on the continent
was considerable.

Adam began work at Syon in 1762 and finished
about seven years later. He did not have a free
hand. His brief was to remodel and redecorate the
interiors, not to rebuild. Thus he had to grapple
with the problems of varying floor levels (between
the great hall and the ante-room for instance) and
the decoration of the ancient long-gallery 136 feet
in length. Adam conjured out of old Syon House a
great hall, the ante-room, and a suite of three
magnificent state rooms, the dining-room, red
drawing-room and long gallery and created in
each radical contrasts in mood and colour. In the
long gallery he avoided a tunnel-like effect by
means of a complicated pattern on the ceiling and
also a series of decorative devices on the walls

opposite the windows – classical columns, book-cases, chimney-pieces, and a series of portrait medallions. The richness of the decoration is enhanced by furniture, much of which was designed by Adam, and by paintings and works of art.

Thomas Percy, Bishop of Dromore, wrote: 'Syon House, which was old, ruinous, and inconvenient, His Grace hath finely improved; and fitting it up, and finishing it, after the most perfect models of Greece and Rome, hath formed a Villa, which for taste and elegance is scarce to be paralleled in Europe.'

The parties which the Duke and Duchess gave at Syon were sumptuous. Mrs Delany described one given in 1768 for the King of Denmark. Guests thronged the state rooms, and a large marquee was put up in the courtyard and illuminated by 4000 lamps of varying shapes. When the King asked the Duke if it was not difficult to light 4000 lamps in time, the Duke replied airily, according to Mrs Delany, 'No, for he had two hundred lamp-lighters for that purpose.'

The Duke was also a botanical expert, and turned his attention to the garden at Syon. He commissioned 'Capability' Brown to sweep away the old garden and to landscape the grounds. The view from the windows in the state rooms is now of grass stretching down to the water-meadows, through which the River Thames meanders. Beyond are the gardens of Kew.

James Smithson, who was an illegitimate son of the Duke, left over £100,000 in his will to the United States of America to found in Washington the Smithsonian Institution 'for the increase and diffusion of knowledge'.

Lady Betty died in 1776, followed by the Duke in 1786. Syon was inherited by their son, Hugh, who was a soldier after whom the famous regiment, the Northumberland Fusiliers, is named. Walpole said that he was 'totally devoid of ostentation, most simple and retiring in his habits', although his life expanded after he succeeded. His second wife had a menagerie at Syon which included gazelles, a collection of gold and silver pheasants and black swans, later joined by some grey Barbary monkeys given to her by her son. The 2nd Duke is said to have built the Pavilion Boat House as a surprise for his duchess.

The 3rd Duke succeeded in 1817. He made many alterations to Syon; he recased all the exterior walls with Bath stone and put in sash windows throughout the house. He built the conservatory after designs by Charles Fowler and filled it with a celebrated collection of tropical trees and flowers. When Prince Pückler-Muskau visited Syon in the 3rd Duke's time, he noted that 'In the vast pleasure-ground twelve men are daily mowing from five till nine o'clock'.

The 3rd Duke attended the coronation of Charles X of France as George IV's ambassador extraordinary and bore the cost himself of the whole undertaking; he is said to have placed even the Czar's ministers in the shadow by the magnificence of his display.

His parties at Syon were legendary. He would entertain 700–1000 people at a time. To accommodate them Edgingtons made him a vast marquee large enough to hold 600 diners which was placed near the kitchens. The Duke had a dinner service specially made as he had previously had to make do with hired sets of many patterns. After the dinner, the marquee was cleared and made ready for dancing. The river played a part in the festivities. Displays of fireworks on the south and east lawns were answered by rockets from the steamboats, and from the opposite bank of the Thames. The displays were designed by Mr Darby the pyrotechnist of Vauxhall at an average cost of £120.

The 3rd Duke was Lord Lieutenant of Ireland in 1829–30 and died in 1847. He was succeeded by his brother who spent most of his time at Alnwick. After the demolition of Northumberland House in 1874, Syon became the family's London house. But for over 150 years the principal residence of the Percys has been at Alnwick.

Helen, Duchess of Northumberland, with her family in their coronation robes, 1937: Lady Elizabeth Percy (now Dowager Duchess of Hamilton), the 9th Duke, killed in 1940, the present and 10th Duke, Lord Richard and Lord Geoffrey Percy, photographed by Yvonde.

180

The Honourable David Lytton Cobbold, a great-great grandson of Edward Bulwer Lytton, moved into Knebworth House with his wife and children in 1971. They left behind a warm, comfortable, medium-sized house in the village to face the rigours of life in a mansion then in an advanced state of decay.

'Would you make the same decision today?'

'Almost certainly not. It is the sort of decision one makes in one's thirties and regrets in one's forties. The sacrifices are very great. At the time I would have done anything to save the house.'

'Why did the house deteriorate to the extent that it did?'

'During the last war, the Froebel Institute moved into the house and the state drawing-room was used as a store-room. My grandfather died in 1947. Throughout my parents' tenure there was a question mark over the house's future. In the 1950s and 1960s they made efforts to establish a viable future for the house as an institution of some sort. They approached American universities and, as a result of the Robbins report, a University of Hertfordshire was nearly set up here. But the project was killed by local politics; no one could agree where the new university should be built. The Open University considered Knebworth as a headquarters too. In the end, we moved in, I took two three-month sabbaticals from my bank in 1970 and 1971 and started the repairs.'

'Which were extensive.'

'The structural restoration programme on the house itself has cost £121,000 to the end of 1980 but this has been supported by grants from the Historic Buildings Council of £53,000. We have a long way to go.'

'And what about the park and the rest of the estate?'

'We have restored the gardens and replanted the chestnut avenue. And we spent a further £366,000 on capital improvements and equipment for the park. The Countryside Commission gave us a grant of £25,000 towards the cost of the road system. But the rest was borrowed.'

'And Knebworth has been a great success with the public?'

'Yes, in the ten years 1971–81 since we moved to the house, 2,250,000 people have visited the house and park. The figures jumped from 8000 visitors in 1970 before we took over, to 120,000 in 1971. Our maximum was 1976 – 350,000 – but the Rolling Stones gave a concert that year which accounts for a large proportion of that figure.'

'Have the pop concerts had a great effect on the Knebworth figures?'

'They have enabled us to survive.'

'How large is the estate?'

'It is now 2500 acres of which 1500 acres is tenanted farm, 600 is woodland and 250 parkland. I think the maximum figure was probably 9000 acres – that was in 1707. Quite a chunk disappeared in 1947 under a compulsory purchase order for Stevenage New Town.'

'But after all your hard work and your improvements which have made such a difference you can't abandon the house?'

'No, of course not, but it's an uphill struggle. Bulwer's stucco was not made to last!'

The west front from the park.

Knebworth House

HERTFORDSHIRE

The Honourable David Lytton Cobbold

Edward Bulwer Lytton was his mother's favourite son, and Knebworth House was her family home. When he was born in 1803 the house was let, and had been for many years for his maternal grandfather, Richard Warburton Lytton, was an eccentric scholar who preferred to devote himself to his studies in a small modern house in Ramsgate rather than live at Knebworth and manage his estate. Richard Warburton Lytton muddled away his great inheritance but Knebworth was entailed, so that this alone of all the properties which he had inherited passed to his daughter, Elizabeth Bulwer Lytton, on his death in 1810. Three years before, her husband, General Bulwer, had died and thus within a short space of time Mrs Bulwer Lytton was freed from pecuniary cares on the one hand, and from the misery of an unhappy marriage on the other. Her eldest son inherited his father's estates in Norfolk and her second son had expectations from his grandmother; Mrs Bulwer Lytton was thus able to enter upon her inheritance of Knebworth in complete freedom in the company of her beloved youngest son, Edward.

Mrs Bulwer Lytton was an intelligent woman, a painter and a poet, unconventional in dress, and with an accent so old-fashioned that the younger generation were sometimes tempted to mimic her. She had had a singular upbringing, for her father had read Rousseau and taught her to curtsey to the gardener's boy. She enjoyed the company of blue-stockings, and was a frequent visitor to gatherings in upper rooms where single women of small means and independent views gave tea-parties. Her own house in London was run on more prosperous lines, and villagers at Knebworth remembered how she would walk the short distance between house and church followed by two footmen in knee-breeches and silk stockings, one of whom carried her Bible and the other her Prayer Book.

Mrs Bulwer Lytton visited Knebworth with Edward when he was very young. 'How vividly I still remember the day,' he wrote years later, 'when we drove, towards evening, along the melancholy, neglected park and the old house rose for the first time upon my view . . . uncouth, heavy, sombre, dismantled, half decayed.'

Knebworth House at that time was a quadrangular brick building two storeys high, fashioned by Sir Robert Lytton from the old fortress he had bought in 1492. Mrs Bulwer Lytton was forced to take drastic action, for she did not have the means to repair the entire structure and live in it in any degree of comfort. She therefore decided to demolish three sides of the quadrangle, and to make a more manageable house out of the fourth. She commissioned John Biagio Rebecca to encase this in stucco, to Gothicize some of the windows, and to add battlements and turrets.

While this work was in progress, Mrs Bulwer Lytton divided her time between her house in

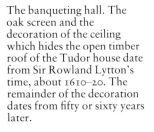

The banqueting hall. The oak screen and the decoration of the ceiling which hides the open timber roof of the Tudor house date from Sir Rowland Lytton's time, about 1610–20. The remainder of the decoration dates from fifty or sixty years later.

London, and the Manor House in Knebworth village which was five minutes' walk through the woods from the main house. For months before the ancient galleries were demolished, Edward roamed through them at will. This playground – with its tapestries, portraits and secret room beneath the trap-door in the gatehouse – was a powerful influence on his imagination. 'How could I help writing romances?' he said, in retrospect.

Mrs Bulwer Lytton's Knebworth, shorn of its old atmosphere, was finished in 1816. When Edward inherited the house from her in 1843, he set to work at once to recapture the character which Rebecca had successfully obliterated. He never criticized his mother for what she had done to the house, for in his eyes she could do no wrong, but from time to time he did express more than a hint of regret for what had been lost.

Mrs Bulwer Lytton died on 19 December 1843. Her son watched her life ebb away, and was shattered by her death, for he could not envisage an existence without her. Bulwer (as he was known to his friends) was forty, and had reached a plateau in his life. He had received a baronetcy in Queen Victoria's Coronation Honours List for services to literature; he was a best-selling novelist, with a string of successful novels to his name: *Pelham, Eugene Aram, The Last Days of Pompeii* and *Rienzi*, and had written several plays for Macready. He was a ceaseless experimenter with different literary forms, and in the February before his mother's death he published *The Last of the Barons* and announced that it would be his last work of fiction. He was a great dandy, he rouged, smoked exotic tobacco in a long pipe which reached to the ground, and was a most agreeable companion. His political career had prospered, and then fizzled out. He represented the City of Lincoln as a reformer from 1832, and joined the motley gang of Radicals in the House of Commons in their uneasy alliance with the Whigs. He had been offered a minor position in the Government by Lord Melbourne which he refused, and in 1841 lost his seat at Lincoln, and was ousted as a candidate by the Whigs. He was in the wilderness. Throughout his career, Bulwer was torn between his political and his literary life. When he was in the House of Commons, he longed for the peace of his study; in his study he longed for the challenge of politics. He never reconciled the two interests or learnt to assuage his restlessness. When he was in London he pined for Knebworth, and at Knebworth unless he had friends staying, his loneliness drove him back to London after a few days, or to Margate or Brighton or further afield to Nice or Rome, where he could see and watch human life about him. As a very young man, he made a

disastrous marriage with an Irish girl, Rosina Wheeler, which ended in bitter tears. His two children Emily and Robert spent much time with him as they grew older, and were frequently at Knebworth with their grandmother. After Mrs Bulwer Lytton's death, he would take them for special occasions such as Christmas or Easter to stay with one of his closest friends, Charles Tennyson d'Eyncourt MP, who lived at Bayons Manor in Lincolnshire. Bulwer and Tennyson d'Eyncourt (he was an uncle of the poet), had much in common; they shared political views,

antiquarian researches and a passionate interest in family and pedigree. They met when Bulwer became MP for Lincoln, and would sit together at dinners with the city merchants under banners bearing slogans such as, 'Victoria, and may she ever remember that Monarchy is dependent on the freedom of the People'; but, although their political learnings may have been radical, they both believed passionately in the role of a benevolent aristocracy.

Charles Tennyson d'Eyncourt was the son of a prosperous Grimsby solicitor, George Tennyson. When the old man died in 1835 at Bayons, the son had assumed the name of an ancient family called d'Eyncourt who owned the estate in mediaeval times and from whom he descended through his grandmother. He then proceeded to transform his father's modest Regency house into a vast fortified castle with a drawbridge and moat, a great hall which would seat 200, and a ruined keep.

Bulwer stayed with his friend at Bayons from time to time during the rebuilding. Charles Tennyson d'Eyncourt was a distinguished amateur architect with a good knowledge of buildings of different styles and periods. Bulwer shared this interest: throughout his life he

Left: The banqueting hall from the minstrels' gallery.

Above: Edward Bulwer Lytton, later 1st Lord Lytton of Knebworth, by Daniel Maclise in 1850.

Knebworth House from the garden.

sketched in his notebooks, on his manuscripts, and on the backs of bills and receipts, details of real and imaginary buildings, battlements, turrets, gargoyles, doorways, windows and bookcases. Thus when his mother died in 1843, he was steeped in the atmosphere of Bayons.

For some time after his mother's death, Bulwer was unable to write a word of poetry or prose, but he sought refuge from his great sorrow in plans to transform Knebworth into a baronial mansion in a style which would do more justice to his proud ancestral claims than his mother's tame Regency Gothic. He was encouraged by Tennyson d'Eyncourt and by another friend, Thomas Baylis.

Baylis was an antiquary who bought a small house called Vine Cottage on the banks of the Thames in Fulham and proceeded to rebuild it in the Gothic style and call it Pryor's bank. This he filled with wood and stone carving, panelling of all sorts including some from the chapel of Magdalen College, Oxford, and unfashionable sixteenth- and seventeenth-century furniture including carved oak bedsteads and high-backed chairs. Bulwer knew this house well, for he rented for a few years before he inherited Knebworth a cottage a short distance upstream called Craven Cottage. This had been converted by Thomas Hopper for Walsh Porter, and contained a central vaulted apartment in the Egyptian taste and a large Gothic dining-room. Bulwer gave memorable parties at Craven Cottage for his friends including Disraeli, Prince Louis Napoleon, Lady Blessington, Count D'Orsay, Leigh Hunt and many others. He loved Craven Cottage, it was a short ride from Hyde Park Corner, and he kept a dog there; he was sad to give it up. Bulwer may well have been present at the sale of the contents of Pryor'sbank in May 1841; Baylis remained a close friend, and was a

frequent visitor to Knebworth staying at times for weeks on end. If he did not advise Bulwer on the first stage of his alterations at Knebworth, he exercised a great influence on them, and when Bulwer made additions to the house in the late 1850s Baylis helped him, for Bulwer told his son in 1859 that he was 'writhing in the agony of paying Bills for the improvements suggested by his taste'.

We know positively that Bulwer sought the advice of three people: an architect, a decorator and a genealogist. The architect, H. E. Kendall Junior, was at work within weeks of Mrs Bulwer Lytton's death, and the specification for the exterior was drawn up within three months. John G. Crace, the decorator, set to work, but as the theme of his decoration was largely heraldic, he had to wait until Mr Courthope had done his researches.

Bulwer had always possessed a fierce pride in his ancestors – his mother's ancestors – but it was not until this period that he began to take a technical as opposed to a romantic interest. He knew that he had not a drop of Lytton blood in him for though the name and tradition had survived, the last Lytton, Sir William, had died in 1705 and left the estate to a great-nephew, Lytton Strode. He in turn left it to his cousin William Robinson, a Welsh-man who assumed the name Lytton and was the ancestor of the later family at Knebworth.

Mr William Courthope was Rouge Croix Pursuivant at the College of Arms, and through-out the early part of 1844 he delved into Bulwer's maternal ancestry. He was lucky enough to find exactly what his client wanted. 'You will see that there are some splendid descents in this Pedigree,' he wrote to Bulwer, 'Anne, the wife of Sir William Norreys was great aunt to King Henry VII & directly descended thro' the Welsh Chieftains

KNEBWORTH HOUSE 185

from Coel Godeby, King of Britain.' Bulwer was delighted, for Courthope provided him with ninety-nine quarterings, the majority of which were of Welsh origin, and Crace was able to create a decorative scheme for the state drawing-room which incorporated these discoveries.

The forty-four coats of arms on the ceiling are the armorial bearings of Mrs Bulwer Lytton's ancestors, and those on the frieze depict the arms of the families through whom she derived her descent from Edward III and Cadwallader, the last British king; Crace used the Tudor rose as a motif on the panelling, and placed a full-length portrait of Henry VII in stained-glass in the great window at the end of the room.

Kendall's estimate was £1725 and for this sum he remodelled the house and created what Bulwer described as 'two wings of the purest Tudor architecture, flanked by highly ornamental turrets,

surmounted with cupolas and gilded vanes'. On the entrance front above the porch is a tall square tower. The whole building was covered in stucco decoration: battlements, coats-of-arms and heraldic beasts, and the majority of the mullioned windows contained stained glass.

Crace's bill amounted to £1480 10s 1d. He supervised the work carefully, for his account shows that he visited the house on twenty-five occasions in 1844. He decorated a library in the Gothic style and a drawing-room which was painted to imitate oak, but both of these rooms are known only from photographs, also a staircase, bedrooms to sleep seven, and – the *pièce de résistance* – the state drawing-room, which survives and is, as Crace decided it should be, 'very Gothic'. The accounts show that the stained-glass window panel of Henry VII cost £35, and that Crace charged £43 15s for painting the forty-four

The state drawing-room, decorated by John G. Crace for Edward Bulwer Lytton in the mid 1840s.

Victor, 2nd Earl of Lytton, with his family in the garden at Knebworth. His wife, Pamela Plowden, was one of the great beauties of her day. The young Winston Churchill wished to marry her, but she refused him and married Lord Lytton. Antony, Viscount Knebworth, on the right, was killed in 1933 and his father compiled *Antony: a Record of Youth* in his memory. John, Viscount Knebworth, on the left, was killed at El Alamein. Lady Hermione seated on the left, is married to Lord Cobbold, and Lady Davina to Mr C. M. Woodhouse.

panels on the ceiling. The curtains (the pelmets alone remain) were of crimson cotton velvet (1s 9d a yard) lined with tammy and interlined with canvas, and cost £9 2s 3d a pair. Crace also put in heating, supplied gilt leather for some of the walls, and covered the stone-flagged floor in the banqueting hall with 'stout carpet canvas'. The banqueting hall with its fine original early seventeenth-century screen was the core of the house; and Bulwer painted the old panelling with dark paint to resemble oak, and filled it with suits of armour and military banners. It was used by him as a dining-room whenever he had guests.

Bulwer had always haunted the sale-rooms and he filled the house with paintings, carvings, sculpture, appropriate furniture – an antique Spanish bed, chair and a sofa from James I's state bedroom at Wanstead, Venetian cabinets – and armour. To supplement the family paintings he bought portraits of Sir Philip Sidney, Cardinal Wolsey, Andrew Marvell, Sir Francis Drake and Shakespeare, and he hung on the staircase a copy of the vast painting by Titian of the Emperor Charles V mounted on his charger crossing the battle-field of Mühlberg.

In 1847 the 'new' Knebworth appeared in S.C. Hall's *The Baronial Halls and Picturesque Edifices of England* with illustrations and a lengthy account of the antiquity of the house and family;

and in 1850 Bulwer printed a guide-book for visitors.

He continued to add furniture and works of art to the collection. He bought an 'Elizabethan' bed from Mr Pratt of Bond Street, a notorious purveyor of stage-properties to the baronial halls of his day, and his son Robert Lytton bought furniture for his father when he served as a diplomat in Italy, Spain and Austria. Sadly, the major part of Bulwer's collection of ancient furniture, armour and decorative items was packed up by the 2nd Earl of Lytton and shipped to New York, where it was sold at the Anderson Galleries in 1927. The catalogue makes melancholy reading.

Bulwer also laid out the gardens – with a Jacobean arrangement immediately below the house, and a series of less formal gardens including one dedicated to Horace further afield.

Bulwer spent very little time at Knebworth in the late 1840s for his health broke down; he haunted the water-cure at Malvern and spent some time in Italy and the South of France. He began to write novels again and, at Bayons, he completed *Harold, the Last of the Saxon Kings* and dedicated it to his old friend, Tennyson d'Eyncourt. His daughter Emily died in 1848 and he was loath to return to the house without her. The 1850s on the other hand were the heyday of Knebworth. Bulwer was anxious to become Member of Parliament for the County of Hertfordshire, and with this in mind he entertained lavishly. He invited his friend Charles Dickens to bring his group of amateur actors to Knebworth in November 1850 for a series of performances of Ben Jonson's *Every Man in His Humour* and Mrs Inchbald's *Animal Magnetism*. A portable stage was put up in the banqueting hall, and the cast which included Dickens himself, Douglas Jerrold, Mark Lemon, John Leech and Augustus Egg performed for three nights to audiences of friends, local gentry and other assorted bigwigs. 'Everything,' wrote Dickens, 'has gone off in a whirl of triumph, and fired the whole length and breadth of the county of Hertfordshire.'

Bulwer was duly elected MP for Hertfordshire in 1852 – as a Conservative – and held the seat until he was elevated to the House of Lords in 1866 as Baron Lytton of Knebworth; he held office under Lord Derby as Secretary of State for the Colonies in 1858–9. Bulwer's publisher, John Blackwood, told Robert Lytton: 'I remember him saying what a pleasure he took in planning at things whether it was a Garden, a Novel or a Colony.'

Bulwer filled the house with friends: politicians, writers, actors, journalists and clairvoyants. When his guests departed, the house seemed large and lonely and, for much of the year, very cold. In the late 1850s, and with the help of Thomas Baylis, he made on the east side of the house overlooking the gardens, a small study for himself with a bedroom above, and retreated into these rooms to read and write, looked after by his faithful housekeeper Sophy Tate, who was a survival from his mother's day and would do anything for her master. Tate ruled the household at Knebworth and in London with a rod of iron and terrorized the other servants. She was eventually pensioned off by Bulwer's son and the entire household breathed a sigh of relief.

In the 1860s, Bulwer's visits to Knebworth began to decrease, he bought a house in Torquay in which to spend the winter months, and at one stage thought of letting Knebworth since the expense of keeping it up was so great and, as he told his son, 'the place had ceased to agree with me for any long time at a stretch'. He still entertained there: the young Leslie Ward, later well known as the cartoonist 'Spy', remembered going to Knebworth with his parents to stay with Bulwer, and reminisced: 'I can see him now standing on the hearthrug awaiting the announcement of dinner – dressed up "to the eyes", and listening with bent, attentive head to his guests.' And he was still an enchanting companion. The young Swinburne was invited to Knebworth after some particularly wounding reviews. He described the drive back to London in the carriage with Bulwer, who told a long ghost story as they ate their picnic lunch.

Two years before he died, Bulwer quite suddenly burst into renewed activity at Knebworth. He commissioned plans for extensive additions to the house from the architect T. H. Watson in 1871. The estimates for a grand new library, more bedrooms and a servants' wing began at £1500, grew to £2000, then to £2500 and reached £3000 by the end of the year, but most of the ideas remained on the drawing-board. After Bulwer's death in 1873, his son Robert commissioned John Lee to complete the bedroom floor his father had planned and George Devey to add the servants' wing. The library was never built.

Robert, 1st Earl of Lytton, was a diplomat. He became Viceroy of India and later Ambassador in Paris. He and his wife Edith loved Knebworth, but their commitments abroad prevented them from spending long periods of time at the house, and it was frequently let. Just at the moment that Robert envisaged returning to Knebworth in 1891, he died in harness at the early age of sixty. His son, Victor, was only fifteen. Knebworth deteriorated in the years of his father's absence abroad, and during his own minority. He married in 1902 the beautiful Pamela Chichele-Plowden, who had a little while before refused Winston Churchill's proposal of

marriage. The tenant at Knebworth invited them to spend part of their honeymoon at the house, and later they attempted to make Knebworth habitable again. One of Lord Lytton's sisters, Lady Emily, had married the architect Edwin Lutyens, and under his direction Knebworth was restored between 1908 and 1910. Most of Bulwer's interior decoration was swept away, with the exception of the state drawing-room which was hardly touched. His library and drawing-room, his small sitting-room and bedroom were dismantled, and the rooms recreated by Lutyens in different styles. The panelling in the banqueting hall was stripped of its brown paint by Keebles, and the upholstery and curtains were renewed by Morants. The house was rewired, the heating overhauled and the furniture, paintings and clocks restored.

Knebworth was once again a family home, which it had not been for any length of time for generations, and the house was greatly loved by the Lyttons and their children, Antony and John, Hermione and Davina. But in the 1920s history repeated itself, for Knebworth was again deserted by the family during the period that Lord Lytton was Governor of Bengal and, for a short period, acting Viceroy of India. Lord Lytton was a man of independent views and great integrity: his ideals crystallized in the concept of the League of Nations, of which he was a fervent supporter. Their son Antony became MP for Hitchin in 1931. He was a pilot officer in the Auxiliary Air Force and was killed tragically two years later at Hendon in a Hawker-Hart aeroplane which crashed when practising for a display. Lord Lytton's tribute to his son, whom he saw as a youthful personification of the spirit of chivalry, was published as *Antony: A Record of Youth* with a preface by J. M. Barrie. This book struck a chord of sympathy throughout the English-speaking world, and brought the name of Lytton and Knebworth to the knowledge of hundreds of thousands of readers.

John, Antony's younger brother, was killed at El Alamein in 1942, and the house passed on Lord Lytton's death in 1946 to his eldest daughter Lady Hermione Cobbold. Lady Hermione and her husband, Mr C. F. Cobbold (who became 1st Lord Cobbold of Knebworth KG, GCVO), once more attempted to alter Knebworth to suit the requirements of another generation. They demolished Devey's wing in 1950, and commissioned Philip Tilden to design a new façade for the east front, and to make convenient living quarters. Their efforts to find an appropriate institutional role for Knebworth failed, and in 1971 they moved to a house on the estate and handed over to their eldest son, David Lytton Cobbold, and his wife who live there today with their family.

Sophy Tate, Bulwer Lytton's fractious housekeeper, at Knebworth. She worked for the Lyttons for over forty years and terrorized the other servants.

Lady Janet Douglas Pennant is the daughter of the 6th Earl of Yarborough of Brocklesby Park, Lincolnshire. She inherited Penrhyn Castle from her uncle, the 4th Lord Penrhyn, in 1949. The year before she had married Mr John Harper who subsequently assumed the name Douglas Pennant, the Penrhyn family name. Today, Mr John and Lady Janet Douglas Pennant live in a house on the Penrhyn estate a short distance from the castle.

'Had you any idea of your uncle's intention to leave Penrhyn to you?'

'No. It was a great surprise. In fact, it was overwhelming and I was only twenty-four at the time. But my mother was my uncle's favourite sister and he knew my brother would inherit the Yarborough estates.'

'How was the news broken to you?'

'My mother telephoned to tell me that my uncle had died, and that I ought to come down to the funeral. She told me to find a black dress, which was rather difficult with shortages after the war.'

'But she didn't break the news of the bequest to you over the telephone?'

'No, she waited until I had arrived at Bangor.'

'Did you know Penrhyn well before you inherited it?'

'No, I visited the castle for the first time when I was ten. I remember the Lent lilies on the lawn but the rest was rather intimidating. I came up on leave several times during the war to see my uncle. He had a sitting-room in the keep and still used the small dining-room. He kept a butler throughout the war. The castle was the headquarters of the Daimler car company which had been evacuated and he was able to share a footman with their senior men.'

'Was the estate in good order after the war?'

'Yes, my uncle was very interested in farming and his wife had loved the garden.'

'What did you feel about the prospect of living at Penrhyn?'

'I had just married and together John and I visited and revisited the keep to try and decide whether we could live there, and perhaps let the rest, or open it to the public. But any alterations would have meant blasting through the walls. The two circular staircases were quite impracticable, yet there was nothing we could do to adapt them. We decided that it was impossible, but we were anxious to keep the tradition going; many of the old retainers were still on the estate. Tudor the lampman, for instance, who must have been born about 1860, was then the keeper of Grand Lodge.'

'Turning to the history of the castle, does family tradition throw any light on why George Dawkins Pennant built Penrhyn? We have the contemporary account of a visitor who called it "a plaything".'

'Yes, as far as I know it was for fun, but Penrhyn's best days were in the time of my great-great-grandfather, the 1st Lord Penrhyn. He must have been a delightful man.'

'Penrhyn was hardly an obvious candidate for adoption by the National Trust. Was there much opposition?'

'Some members of the committee resisted at first, but James Lees-Milne took away the series of lithographs of the interiors made in the 1840s.'

'Full of atmosphere and romance.'

'Yes, they won over the waverers on the committee.'

Penrhyn Castle from the south-east.

Penrhyn Castle

BANGOR, GWYNEDD

The National Trust:
Lady Janet Douglas Pennant

Edward Gordon Douglas was an impecunious young officer in the Grenadier Guards when he went to Penrhyn Castle in the early 1830s to ask George Hay Dawkins Pennant for the hand of his eldest daughter. Although he came from a distinguished Scottish family (his grandfather was the 14th Earl of Morton), he was the younger son of a younger son and he lacked financial prospects.

It must have been an intimidating experience, for Mr Dawkins Pennant's aspirations were clearly visible; he was in the midst of transforming the modest house his great-uncle had left him into a Norman castle of enormous proportions. And, as he had no sons, his dynastic ambitions were centred on his two daughters, Juliana Isabella Mary and Emma Elizabeth Alicia, whose family nicknames, 'Slate' and 'Sugar', were evidence that Mr Dawkins Pennant had already given thought to the eventual distribution of his fortune.

Edward Gordon Douglas had fallen in love with Juliana and was encouraged by the girls' stepmother to approach Mr Dawkins Pennant and ask for his consent to their marriage. After a stormy interview the young man packed his bags and left the castle. But he did not go far. He set up at the Penrhyn Arms Hotel just outside the lodge gates and did not have long to wait before he was recalled.

Mr Dawkins Pennant gave his blessing and extracted a promise from the young Douglas that he would add to the estate whenever opportunities presented themselves and would in time put together a collection of paintings to hang in the castle. Edward and Juliana were married in 1833. Edward was to be known for the greater part of his life as Colonel Douglas Pennant; he was later created 1st Baron Penrhyn of Llandegai.

George Hay Dawkins had inherited the Penrhyn estate in 1808 from his grandmother's brother,

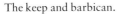

The keep and barbican.

Richard Pennant, and added the name Pennant to his own. The ancestors of Richard Pennant of Penryhn were Flintshire gentlemen who had migrated to Jamaica in the middle of the seventeenth century and acquired extensive sugar plantations. Richard Pennant was heir to three generations of his family and the entrepreneurial skills they had developed over a century in the West India trade.

His marriage in 1765 to Anne Susannah Warburton, the heiress of half the Penrhyn estate, brought him back to Wales. She was a descendant of Ednyfed Fychan, ancestor of the Tudor dynasty, who was granted the Penrhyn lands in the middle of the thirteenth century. Richard Pennant came from a distinguished Welsh family himself, but it was upon his wife's deep roots at Penrhyn that he chose to build.

A water-colour drawing on display in the library at Penrhyn Castle shows the crenellated building in Gothic Revival style which Samuel Wyatt designed for him in the last years of the eighteenth century. Wyatt did not demolish the early mediaeval house, but incorporated the remains, including the great hall, the watch-tower, and a spiral staircase, into the new building. The oubliette in what is now the ebony room of the castle is believed by the family to lead to a passage and an entrance on the shore and to have been put to good use in smuggling days.

Richard Pennant threw himself into the management and improvement of the Penrhyn estate. He took in hand the slate quarry at the entrance to the Nant Ffrancon valley and exploited the vast slate resources in a manner which revolutionized the North Wales slate industry. He placed the quarry on a sound commercial footing, using his trading contacts in Liverpool to find markets for his slates as far afield as the West Indies. He encouraged the construction of roads in North Wales and he built Port Penrhyn which he linked with the quarry by a horse-drawn railway. At the quayside he established a factory for writing slates and before long he had dented the monopoly of the continental manufacturers. As the Industrial Revolution gathered momentum so the number of houses and factories grew and the demand for roofing slates increased. The quarry became a tourist attraction visited by people who marvelled at the awe-inspiring sights.

Richard Pennant was a benevolent master: he laid out the model village of Llandegai with cottages for his estate staff and he formed a Benefit Club for his quarrymen as early as 1787.

He never achieved a Welsh seat in Parliament but represented Liverpool for many years. Presumably a combination of his own interests and pressure from local magnates in his constituency led him to oppose the abolition of the slave trade, although he took a kindly, if distant, interest in the welfare of the slaves on his own estate in Jamaica.

He was created Baron Penrhyn of Penrhyn, Co. Louth in the peerage of Ireland, and died in 1808 at the age of seventy. His tomb in Llandegai church is dominated by the life-size marble figure of a quarryman.

Sadly, he and his wife were childless and he chose as heir to all his endeavours his sister's grandson, George Hay Dawkins.

His widow survived him for eight years, delighting in the company of her pet animals. She dressed her dogs in bonnets and capes, set them on the seat of the carriage opposite her and drove to Ogwen Bank, her tea-house near the quarries, and when she died she left pensions of £45 each to her six horses.

George Hay Dawkins Pennant inherited on the

The keep. The family had their private apartments here with the nurseries on the top floor.

Detail of the ceiling decoration in the hall.

Detail of the staircase.

one hand an infant industrial concern of almost unlimited prospects and on the other a site between the mountains and the sea, with views, both rugged and placid, swept by sudden storms and startling contrasts of light and shade. The building itself was undistinguished but the foundations were as ancient and historic as any in North Wales. It is hardly surprising that this romantic setting fired the imagination of patron and architect. But it is unlikely that Dawkins Pennant would have allowed himself to be carried away in such a dramatic manner had he not succumbed with good humour to the persuasion and enthusiasm of Thomas Hopper. Dawkins Pennant had owned the Penrhyn property for many years and was nearly sixty when he began to think in terms of rebuilding his great-uncle's house in the early 1820s.

The slate industry had prospered in general, the workforce in the Penrhyn Quarry rose from 700–800 men in 1821 to 1200 in 1826, but the profits fluctuated widely. In the 1820s, a period of speculation, they ranged between fifteen and thirty-five thousand pounds. This financial uncertainty was felt most strongly by the quarrymen who complained that their wages varied between 17s a month and £5–£6. The work was exhausting and dangerous and many quarrymen walked miles across the mountains to work, returning home only at weekends. But it was employment, and the quarryman's wage was generally above that of the local agricultural worker. In 1826 there was a strike at the quarry in support of a demand for a minimum wage. Dawkins Pennant was conciliatory, he listened to the men's grievances and the outcome was a period of industrial peace which lasted until the 1860s.

We do not know when Dawkins Pennant

commissioned Thomas Hopper to design Penrhyn, but in the summer of 1828 a Silesian nobleman, Prince Pückler-Muskau, visited the castle and met both architect and patron. By that date work had been in progress for seven years and was expected to last another four. Dawkins Pennant was delighted at the Prince's interest and showed him the building and the plans; 'his enthusiasm,' the Prince comments, 'was agreeable and becoming in a man otherwise cold.' The Prince notes that the cost of building Penrhyn to that date was £20,000 According to the reminiscences of Adela, youngest daughter of Edward, 1st Lord Penrhyn, the total cost was in the region of £50,000.

Dawkins Pennant allowed Hopper a completely free hand; one assumes that he asked for a castle but that the style was left to the choice of the architect.

Part of Richard Pennant's house was encased within the walls. The present drawing-room and state bedroom were fashioned out of the great hall, and the old watch-tower was left and is still visible between the drawing-room and the ebony room. The southern wall of the house remains as the middle wall of the present library which accounts for the presence of the central fireplace.

The family lived initially in a house near Colwyn. This was such a modest establishment that Pückler-Muskau wondered whether Dawkins Pennant would ever bring himself to forsake his simple habits and move into the castle; 'he feasts once a week on the sight of his fairy castle,' the Prince wrote. But the Prince was wrong. Dawkins Pennant was quite prepared to transpose his fantasy into reality, and as work progressed he moved with his family into a corner of the unfinished building. Edward, 1st Lord Penrhyn, would laugh when he told his children how 'Hopper would come in after breakfast and ask leave to add another tower'. The castle grew and grew until it measured 600 feet in length. The vast keep was the last substantial building to be put up. It was said to be an afterthought on the architect's part but judging by its integral part in the design it was more likely an idea kept up his sleeve for the first few years.

According to Adela Douglas Pennant, Dawkins Pennant said one day to his brother-in-law, Captain Maude: 'They want to add a *keep* out there, Francis. I don't know what they mean.'

She describes how Hopper supervised local Welsh workmen who carried out the entire work, including the carved decoration in the hall and on the staircase. He designed the 'Norman' furniture which was made by the estate carpenters and chose other furniture for the castle including Dutch cupboards, ebony chairs and the Cellini

candelabra in the drawing-room.

Hopper designed in what he considered to be the Norman style. Every available surface is decorated and where there was no Norman prototype, which was frequently the case, he invented one. Even the bedside tables and wash-stands are in the 'Norman' manner.

The stone used for building was Anglesey 'marble' brought by sea from the quarries near Penmon. The decoration of the castle must have continued for some years after building ceased, for the stained glass in the hall with roundels depicting the signs of the Zodiac was not installed until about 1837.

It is possible that a stained-glass panel was put in place at the same time in the turret room off the library. This is of a knight in armour which judging by the Pennant arms on his shield portrays the Knight of Penrhyn. Dawkins Pennant had a sense of humour and could laugh at his preten-sions. Perhaps he felt that Hopper had gone too far, and banished this figment of his architect's imagination to an obscure corner of the castle.

A collection of lithographs by George Hawkins made about 1846 gives a good idea of the rooms soon after the castle was finished. A considerable proportion of the interiors and fittings has survived intact and much of the furniture has been replaced in the positions indicated in the litho-graphs. Hopper's taste was diluted by the addition of pieces in other styles by Dawkins Pennant's successors and in the late 1920s his furniture was hidden away, only to reappear from the attics after the National Trust took over.

Dawkins Pennant died in 1840 leaving the estate to his daughter 'Slate' and her husband, Edward Douglas, the young officer who had hesitated to ask for the hand of so great an heiress.

Colonel Douglas Pennant presided over the fortunes of castle and quarry for a period of forty-six years. This was the heyday of Penrhyn.

The castle and the family had become integral parts of the North Wales landscape. The Colonel was widely respected, he was a magistrate, he represented the local constituency in Parliament and became Lord Lieutenant of the county, he was full of charitable works, he built schools and churches, he gave money to hospitals and guided their fortunes. In 1859 Queen Victoria and Prince Albert spent two nights under his roof and in 1866 he was created 1st Baron Penrhyn of Llandegai.

He was also, in Charles Dickens's words, 'the arch magnate Colonel Slater'. The Colonel assumed control of the Penrhyn Quarry just as the slate industry entered the period of its greatest prosperity. The population of England and Wales trebled between 1801 and 1881: the demand for roofing slates was almost insatiable. In 1862 Penrhyn Quarry produced a record 130,000 tons of slate employing in that year approximately 3000 men. But there were always fluctuations. In the early 1840s trade was depressed and some workers were dismissed. The average weekly wage in 1845 was 15 shillings. The Pennants were considered good landlords, and the Colonel continued his predecessors' efforts to provide houses for the quarrymen. By the end of the century they occupied nearly 900 cottages on the estate, almost all with gardens.

Colonel Douglas Pennant's marriage with Juliana was singularly happy. They divided their time between Penrhyn and Wicken, a house near Stony Stratford in the heart of excellent hunting country. Wicken was also nearer Parliament than Penrhyn which was convenient after the Colonel became MP for Caernarvonshire in 1841.

Sadly, his marriage was brief. Juliana was always delicate. One day she joined some friends climbing Snowdon. A member of the party had failed to bring a cloak and she lent her own. A succession of coughs and colds followed which weakened her lungs. Her husband took her to the Mediterranean to recuperate but she died at Pisa in 1842 at the age of thirty-five. She left five children.

He was shattered by this blow and left Penrhyn to recover at Harewood House, his mother's family home. There he was painted by Eden Eddis who was staying in the house. A couple of years later he espied the lady who was to become his second wife, a daughter of the 5th Duke of Grafton, at a meet of the hounds at Wicken. They were married in 1846 and he took her home directly after the ceremony to find his five children lined up in the hall to receive their stepmother. He and his wife Maria Louisa subsequently had five daughters of their own.

The drawing-room, showing the candelabra copied from originals by Benvenuto Cellini. The sofa and side-table were designed for the room by Thomas Hopper.

Life at Penrhyn was agreeable. The Colonel very rarely entertained on a grand scale, but there were weekend visitors and frequent dinner parties. Lord and Lady George Cavendish were yearly visitors from Derbyshire in the coldest months, for the heating at Penrhyn was efficient. Apart from the wood or coal fires in each room, there was a system of steam-heating which worked so well that generations of Douglas Pennant children attempted to lure the unsuspecting visitor to the hot-air gratings and to watch as skirt and petticoats were wafted into the air.

The family sitting-rooms were in the keep, but for a large gathering before dinner or at weekends, the library was used. This contained no fewer than three open fires and also a small snuggery in the turret. The billiards-table was made for the house and has, apart from the usual slate bed under the baize, a frame and legs of slate.

Colonel Douglas Pennant spent most of the day in the library. He was well-read and collected books. He refused to employ a secretary to deal with his voluminous correspondence. Whenever a copy of an important letter was needed, he would summon one of his children from the school-room by a bell, a welcome interruption to their lesson.

The Colonel was most unpunctual. His youngest daughter Adela remembered the old servant Hume and the solemn procession he made across the hall each evening to her father's room, old Hume leading the way with a lighted candle and her father's dress clothes, while a footman followed with the hot-water can which old Hume could no longer carry. It was the signal to the rest of the household to dress for dinner, always held at uncertain hours.

His large family spent most of their time at Penrhyn. Life centred on school-room and stables. The head groom was a Yorkshireman named John Pickard. He was a good friend to the family from

The library, with the billiards table which is entirely made of slate.

the eldest to the youngest. Adela described his role thus: 'Every joy or sorrow, and every news, family, local or political was discussed, as we sat on the corn bin in the stables, with Pickard, whose opinion, though a man of few words, carried weight with every member of the household.'

Colonel Douglas Pennant was true to his word. He built up a collection of paintings for Penrhyn as Dawkins Pennant had wished. He bought Dutch, Flemish, Italian and Spanish paintings including a Rembrandt (now hanging in the National Gallery of Wales). Many of these were purchased from an old Belgian dealer named Nieuwenhuys who lived in Wimbledon and provided a favourite excursion for the Douglas Pennant children who would make frequent visits with their father to inspect new treasures.

He also bought furniture and tapestries. He had a fine London house, Mortimer House in Halkin Street, and a house in Scotland for shooting.

The highlight of this period at Penrhyn was the visit of Queen Victoria, Prince Albert and four of their children, in October 1859. Colonel Douglas Pennant was by this time a very important personage indeed in North Wales.

The royal party arrived by train from Glasgow a day late, which must have caused chaos in the Penrhyn kitchens. A large house-party of over twenty-five people stretched the accommodation in the castle to its limits and the Douglas Pennant children were lodged in the Penrhyn Arms Hotel. The Royal Family were given rooms in the keep.

A man was brought down from Millers, the London lamp shop, to see to the lighting in the castle during the royal visit. This was an arduous job at all times. Tudor, the lampman in the latter part of the century, collected the lamps in the morning and spent all day cleaning and trimming, finishing just in time to light them again in the early evening. Tudor's predecessor had the last

Edward, 1st Lord Penrhyn of Llandegai, by Eden Eddis in 1845. This was painted at Harewood but Eddis has included a view from Penrhyn. His daughter thought it a good likeness but 'the expression does not indicate sufficient strength of character'.

laugh during the royal visit. The grand lampman from London deserted his duties to watch the arrival of the royal party and failed to light the circular staircase in the keep. When Lady Louisa took the Queen to her room, she found the staircase in total darkness. She begged the Queen to wait while she ran upstairs for a light only to find that the Queen had, with great good humour, groped her way up the stairs.

Very grand dinners took place on both evenings. Prince Albert spent some time at the quarry and the Queen and Lady Louisa drove up but did not emerge from their carriage because of the rain. On Sunday evening four local choirs sang choruses from Handel's *Messiah* in the hall.

Colonel Douglas Pennant's last years were clouded by industrial problems at the quarry. As long as the slate industry prospered, labour relations were generally harmonious; when the decline set in, these deteriorated rapidly. Between 1865 and 1874, the Colonel refused to allow unions to recruit members in his quarry; he was horrified at the suggestion that anyone should intervene in his dealings with his men. Although class, religion and language divided master and men, there existed a bond between them which it is easy to overlook or disparage. The Colonel's paternalism was benevolent and the majority of the quarrymen responded with affection and

respect. Their work was highly skilled and competitive; this engendered pride in a great enterprise and its leader which survived until economic decline soured the atmosphere of prosperity and achievement. Quarries entered their products at international exhibitions all over the world; Penrhyn Quarry was foremost among the prize winners.

In 1874 the Colonel made substantial concessions after a strike during which the newly formed Penrhyn Lodge of what later became the North Wales Quarrymen's Union recruited 2200 members. He was seventy-four and felt unable to cope with these developments. He turned to his eldest son, George, who was then recovering from a serious illness at Bournemouth. The Colonel decided with his son that the union's demands must be resisted, but on his return to Wales he capitulated. A Quarry Committee was recognized and a minimum wage agreed which was reasonable at a time of prosperity but untenable in a decline. The committee was supposed to be independent of union interference, but this situation did not last; non-union members were terrorized and the quarry reduced to near bankruptcy by the time the Colonel handed over to his son in 1885.

He died in 1886. 'He is gone to a better castle,' was the comment of an old man who had worked for him all his life.

George, 2nd Lord Penrhyn, was twice married and had an enormous family of fourteen children. Apart from the dining-room, there never seemed enough space at Penrhyn for them all to sit down on chairs.

He was a passionate fisherman. As a child he agreed to sit to Eddis for his portrait if he was allowed to hold his fishing rod. Later in life he had a horse saddled for him when he came from the Bangor train still in his House of Lords clothes, all set to rush to the banks of the Ogwen where the water-bailiff awaited him with his fishing tackle.

He divided his year into three. He spent the spring at Wicken hunting (he was Master of the Grafton for some years), he was in London for four months during the season and the autumn found him at Penrhyn where the family always gathered for Christmas.

George Penrhyn hated ostentation and lived very simply. He gave his children one penny a week pocket money out of which they were expected to provide birthday and Christmas presents for relations and retainers. Their clothing was so plain that they were known as 'the charity children'. The school-room and nurseries at Penrhyn were at the top of the keep; nanny had to carry the children up and down the stone spiral staircase. The children were lonely at Penrhyn and pined for Wicken and London. As a special treat the head coachman, Robert, who had begun life as a pony boy at the Rectory at Hawarden (the home of George's wife), allowed them to take the reins of the wagonette on expeditions to Beaumaris. Lilian Douglas Pennant who was in her late teens when the South African War broke out remembered how her father, George, ordered his children to remove the festoons and garlands which hung in the Penrhyn hall at Christmas because her two brothers were serving officers. The war and the Quarrymen's Strike overshadowed life at Penrhyn.

George Penrhyn had brought to the management of his father's quarry a firm hand and a forthright tongue. He lacked his father's gentleness and charm. He set out to break the power of the union and to abolish the committee which had proved ineffective.

Economic factors worked against him and he felt unable to pay the minimum wage negotiated in 1874. After years of wrangling the men went on strike in 1897. George Penrhyn replied by closing the quarries and refusing any concessions. The men capitulated. In 1900 another strike took place; the quarries were again closed but were reopened for the 400 men who agreed to return. Bitter animosity followed and troops were sent in to restore order. The strike lasted three years. Before it began, the Penrhyn Quarry produced in the region of a quarter of the total output of Welsh slate. By the time the strike was broken and the men returned, many of the outlets had disappeared.

George Penrhyn died in 1907. His son Edward, who succeeded him as 3rd Baron Penrhyn, rarely visited Penrhyn. The castle staff was cut to a minimum and the castle itself became little more than a shooting-box. Edward Penrhyn's eldest son and two of his half-brothers were killed in World War I and he was eventually succeeded in 1927 by his second son, Hugh.

But Penrhyn came alive again in the late 1920s, for Sybil and Hugh Penrhyn made the castle once more the principal family home. They made many changes in the cause of comfort. There was much restoration to carry out; they put in electric light and banished the Hopper furniture. They found in the butler's bedroom the Romney portrait of Richard Pennant which was reinstated in a place of honour, and in an attic a series of twelve tapestries depicting scenes from the months of the year which they hung in the great hall. They entertained on a lavish scale. Throughout the 1930s, when Lord Penrhyn was Lord Lieutenant of Caernarvonshire, there were fourteen indoor servants including five housemaids. The gardens and greenhouses were enormous and were cared

for by forty gardeners. Lady Penrhyn was a keen gardener herself and grew many rare and delicate shrubs in the mild atmosphere near the Gulf Stream. The estate was well cared for.

But the good life could not and did not last. By the outbreak of war in 1939, Penrhyn's days as a family home were numbered; Dawkins Pennant's castle was just over one hundred years old. Lord Penrhyn remained there until his death in 1949. He left Penrhyn to his niece, Lady Janet Douglas Pennant, who decided after much consideration not to live there. She and her husband entered into negotiations with the National Trust, and the castle was conveyed to the Trust through the Treasury in 1951.

Nanny Rust (seated), photographed with her sister. She was nanny to the children of the 2nd Lord Penrhyn and carried his many children up and down the circular stone staircase to the nurseries at the top of the keep.

198

Victor, 6th Marquess of Bristol, has been Chancellor of the Monarchist League for a number of years. This is a world-wide organization founded about sixty years ago with the intention of supporting the institution, and upholding the concept of monarchy. The chancery is in Monte Carlo and the executive offices in Norwich, and the league consists of a distinguished Council of Honour, an executive Grand Council, and members drawn from all races and creeds. The league's journal appears twice a year and has a readership of over half a million.

Lord Bristol is Hereditary High Steward of the Liberty of St Edmund.

'How long did you live at Ickworth before you moved to Monte Carlo?'

'About sixteen years, but I lived there also as a child. My father was in the Foreign Office so I was brought up at Ickworth and went to school from there. I helped run the show for my uncle the 4th Marquess until his death in 1951, and then I had to leave while the estate was being sorted out. I insisted on moving back to Ickworth into the wing in which the family has always lived. The roundhouse, as we called it in the family, was used for entertaining and that was taken over by the Trust which now calls it the rotunda.'

'You made your wing very beautiful. Is this mostly family furniture?'

'Some of it is, but lots of the furniture went to the National Trust; the collection of silver which is one of the finest in England went to the Trust for a nominal sum as did for instance the fans. I suppose something like eighty-five per cent went to the Trust or elsewhere.'

'What about the estate?'

'The National Trust now owns the gardens, park and some woodland, amounting in all to about 1500 acres. Seven thousand acres were retained and I ran this estate professionally, replanting the woodland and replanning the agricultural land. I have now handed over to my eldest son.'

'What would have happened to Ickworth had the National Trust not taken over?'

'It would have remained a family house; it was a perfectly viable proposition, open to the public of course, and with further developments on the estate. I had made a start building houses at Horringer and other parts of the estate, which was most successful. Ickworth was acquired by the National Trust against my wishes, which was due to the unilateral action of the executrix, the wife of the 4th Marquess of Bristol.'

'Why do you think that the 1st Earl of Bristol never built a principal house at Ickworth?'

'You must remember that he had a large house in London in St James's Square—Number 6—a magnificent house. It had been in the family for nearly 300 years and was sold for £110,000 to pay death duties in 1952. It has now been demolished. No one had thought about the decorations, so at the very last moment I moved in with fifty workmen one weekend and carried away to Ickworth a chimney-piece by Canova, two free-standing Canova figures, magnificent mahogany doors and over-doors, and marble flooring. I was glad to have them for Ickworth.'

'Have any of the original Hotels Bristol survived from the Earl-Bishop's day?'

'The hotels in Vienna, Berlin and Paris were the last survivors. Berlin is gone, Paris is semi-genuine for the original hotel survives but not on the same site. Only Vienna remains intact. I have never seen this but a friend who visited it told me that the Bristol arms are over the entrance and that there are references to the Earl-Bishop inside, including a magnificent coach and horses in porcelain, made in the Capodimonte factory, presumably modelled after his principal coach.'

Ickworth: the entrance front.

Ickworth

BURY ST EDMUNDS, SUFFOLK

The National Trust:
The Marquess of Bristol GOStA, GCLJ

It is not surprising that one of the most eccentric Englishmen of the eighteenth century should build a house in an eccentric shape; but by the time Frederick, 4th Earl of Bristol and 48th Bishop of Derry, began work at Ickworth in 1795, his behaviour had alternately shocked and amused European society for so long that his contemporaries would have been more astonished by a conventional house. But since none of them saw Ickworth completed, we can only speculate on their reaction. The Earl-Bishop himself did not see his house at all, for the plan took shape in Rome where he lived and was brought into being in Suffolk by two architects whom he directed by letter. Eight years after work began the Earl-Bishop died, but the house is such a positive fragment of his genius it is hard to believe that he did not set foot in a single one of its rooms.

The Earl-Bishop began to build at Ickworth late in life because the Hervey ancestral acres did not come to him until two of his brothers had succeeded in turn and died without legitimate heirs. Even then he procrastinated for a number of years and built a house in Ireland before he started work at Ickworth. The 3rd Earl died in 1779; the Earl-Bishop visited Ickworth in the winter of 1781–2 for the first time since he inherited it and consulted 'Capability' Brown about plans. Nothing came of them. The Earl-Bishop was uninspired by the flat Suffolk landscape and considered it unsuitable for 'sublime' architecture; he also disliked the 'ferney' air of Ickworth and preferred the bracing atmosphere of his old home in the north of Ireland. Furthermore he quarrelled with his wife on that visit to Ickworth and left her behind in the old farmhouse in which the Hervey family lived from the time the old manor house was pulled down by the 1st Earl of Bristol until the Earl-Bishop's house was habitable.

The Earl-Bishop was anxious to create a worthy setting for the great collection of works of art he had amassed in Italy. He was not so much concerned with domestic arrangements; he was in his own words a vagabond star, and did not settle for long in any one place.

Frederick Hervey was born in 1730, the third surviving son of John, Lord Hervey, and Molly, his wife, and a grandson of the 1st Earl of Bristol. He was well educated at Westminster and Cambridge, but as a younger son his Grand Tour was only a curtailed version of that taken by his eldest brother. He made up for this later by spending years on the continent; he made seven or eight journeys to Italy and frequented the minor German courts where he found the way of life to his taste. At school he was a contemporary of William Hamilton, and as school-children both showed an interest in art and antiquity and laid the basis of a friendship which was to endure for life.

Frederick Hervey's marriage at the age of twenty-two came as a surprise to his family and friends. Elizabeth Davers had no money and her family was identified with the Tory interest in Bury. However, her qualities are summed up by her husband's name for her, 'Excellent', and she very soon won over the kindly old Lord Bristol and her parents-in-law.

Shortly after his marriage, Frederick Hervey decided to become a clergyman. He spent the rest of his life nominally in the Church, but he never showed much enthusiasm for Christianity. He had a long wait for preferment and seized the opportunity of making another visit to the continent, this time in the company of his wife. They visited Voltaire at Ferney who received them graciously, for he was an old admirer of Frederick Hervey's mother, and went on to spend some months in Naples where his school-friend William Hamilton was envoy. In March 1766 Vesuvius obliged and erupted, but with typical over-enthusiasm Hervey approached too close to the edge of the crater and was wounded in the arm by a fragment of lava.

Fortunately for Frederick Hervey, his brother was appointed Lord Lieutenant of Ireland in 1766 and, although he never set foot in the country and resigned after a year, this was time enough for him to secure a bishopric for his impoverished brother. The bishopric of Cloyne to which he was nominated was not the most sought-after in the established Church of Ireland but it was a stepping-stone to the richest see in the land – Derry – which fell to him on the death of the incumbent a year later.

The new bishop was a man of abundant energy, and much to everyone's surprise he began to take a close interest in his diocese; he toured the parishes and carefully inspected the 70,000 acres attached to the see. He began to talk about improvements, new roads and buildings, a spire for the cathedral, a bridge over the Foyle. He took an interest in agriculture and the diocesan accounts. When he arrived the emoluments were in the region of £7000 but under his skilful management these increased to nearly £20,000. So far so good. But eyebrows were raised when the Bishop announced that in future he would appoint only Irishmen to the benefices in his gift, the first step he took along a road, much to the embarrassment of the British Government, which led to complete commitment to Irish nationalism. Throughout his life he was singularly free of sectarianism, and was at pains to placate Catholics and Presbyterians in his diocese. Within a year of his translation to Derry, he was given the freedom of the city which no bishop had ever received before. However, in the eyes of some

The rotunda from the garden.

of his clergy the advantages of the Bishop's rule were outweighed by his eccentricities. When one rich living fell vacant, the Bishop invited the fattest contenders to dinner and afterwards proposed that they run a race to decide who should succeed to it. It amused the Bishop, whose wit was tinged with malice, to run the race across a bog so that none of the competitors had a chance of reaching the winning post.

In 1770 he set off for the continent with his eldest son Augustus. His wife Elizabeth (no longer 'Excellent') was left behind. On this visit he travelled as far as Dalmatia where he saw the remains of Diocletian's palace at Spalato which had so captivated Robert Adam, and no doubt had a decisive influence on Hervey's choice of the neo-classical style when he came to build. But most of his visit was spent in Rome where he tackled the Papal authorities on the subject of religious toleration and enjoyed the entertainments given by the higher Roman clergy.

He was away from his diocese for two and a half years. George III was furious when he was told of the length of his absence, though as the Earl-Bishop's biographer Brian Fothergill points out, there would soon come a moment when the King would be appalled to hear of his return.

In 1775 Frederick Hervey's brother died and left him a legacy of £10,000. He began at once to build a vast mansion known as Downhill on the north coast of Co. Londonderry. He also began to collect works of art and in 1777 he was again in Rome, this time in the company of his wife. He commissioned a portrait of himself by Pompeo Batoni. 'Battoni has taken a striking & pleasing likeness of yr Father,' Mrs Hervey told her daughter. And in marked contrast to Batoni's usual subjects and backgrounds – well clad noblemen and Roman monuments – the Bishop was portrayed in his ecclesiastical dress, bands and lawn sleeves, with a distant view of Derry Cathedral complete with its spire which had not at that date been finished. Characteristically he commissioned a portrait of his wife from a less expensive painter, Anton Maron. The dress he wore for Batoni was sober in comparison with the usual garb he wore about the streets in Rome. Lord Cloncurry saw him riding about 'in red plush breeches and a broad brimmed white or straw hat', and thus attired he spent his time intriguing on behalf of Catholics in Ireland and searching for works of art. 'Tis really a life of Paradise,' he wrote. The Welsh painter Thomas Jones saw him in Naples where he had gone in the company of the architect John Soane; he attended the Bishop's levée which took place at six in the morning. 'I found him,' Jones recalled, 'combing and adjusting a single Curl which was fixed by a String to his own Short Hair. "You see, Mr Jones," said he as I was entering the room, "I am my own Valet."' The Bishop commissioned two paintings from Jones.

In 1779 he succeeded his brother as 4th Earl of Bristol and found his income augmented by about £20,000 a year. As we have seen, he toyed with the idea of building a house at Ickworth, but eventually decided on a site in his diocese on the shores of Lough Beg. Ballyscullion was begun in 1787 and though it no longer exists it is important for it was the prototype of Ickworth. It was inspired by a circular house the Earl-Bishop saw on an island in Lake Windermere – John Plaw's Belle Isle which was built in 1775. Ballyscullion had the same domed rotunda and pedimented portico which projected on the entrance side, but at Ballyscullion the rotunda was oval and curved corridors were planned to lead to wings on either side which were intended as galleries for his collection of German and Italian pictures respectively. The design was probably by Michael Shanahan, a Cork architect, but it was carried out by the brothers Francis and Joseph Sandys who later worked at Ickworth. The rotunda at Ballyscullion was roofed and furnished, but the Earl-Bishop then lost interest in the house and work was abandoned.

The truth was that the Earl-Bishop now had enough money at his disposal to indulge freely in all his favourite pursuits. His renown as a traveller, and as a connoisseur of food and wine, was so great that in time 'Lord Bristol's hotel' became synonymous with excellence and Hotels Bristol sprang up all over Europe. He led a peripatetic existence; in the last eleven years of his life he did not visit his diocese once, which was a relief to the British Government for, in 1783, he had publicly thrown in his lot with the Volunteer movement. He travelled in Germany and in 1793 met Goethe who described the Earl-Bishop's extensive knowledge of the world of men and books.

He lived principally in Rome. The traveller Joseph Forsyth gathered together all the stories he heard on his visit to Italy about this most capricious prelate. 'His conversation ran generally in support of atheism,' wrote Forsyth, 'yet when others attacked revelation he would for the moment defend the religion which doubled his income ... With artists he was either close or lavish never correctly just... He would sometimes talk divinely on art, and then relapse into affected absurdity. His conversation was obscenity itself, no modest woman could talk with him or go up his staircase at Rome, where the frescoes were most indecent...'

His wife Elizabeth had remained quietly at

The Pompeian room. This was decorated by J.D. Crace for the 3rd
Marquess of Bristol in the late 1870s. The design is based on the
wall-paintings discovered in 1777 at the Villa Negroni in Rome,
and later acquired by Frederick, 4th Earl of Bristol, Bishop of Derry.

The entrance hall, showing the sculpture by
John Flaxman of 'the Fury of Athamas'.

Ickworth after their quarrel, and although they had been married for thirty years, they never spoke again. Evidently Elizabeth was relieved to be rid of her infuriating spouse. 'I leave him to Heaven,' she told her daughter, 'and to those thorns that in his bosom lodge to prick and sting him.' The Earl-Bishop is reputed to have described her as a 'majestic ruin', but offered no apology for reducing her to that state. He remained on reasonably good terms with his children, in particular his daughter Lady Elizabeth, who married and then separated from the Irish politician J. T. Foster, but he was parsimonious when it came to allowances.

In his last years in Italy he was absorbed in plans for his new house and the quest for paintings and works of art to embellish it. He cast around for an architect. Mrs Tudor-Craig has discovered that he approached a young Italian, Mario Asprucci the Younger, who produced a design in about 1794 which was subsequently accepted in modified form. The brothers Francis and Joseph Sandys who had worked at Ballyscullion, were brought in to execute this, and they constructed a papier-mâché model (on view in the Pompeian room) of their final plan in 1796, presumably to send to the Earl-Bishop for his approval. The Earl-Bishop's own contribution to the design was paramount, and he attended to every detail. His daughter Elizabeth had begged him to build in white stone bricks. 'What! Child, build my house of a *brick* that looks like a sick, pale, jaundiced red brick, that would be red brick if it could, and to which I am certain our posterity would give a little rouge as essential to its health... I shall follow dear impeccable old Palladio's rule, and... cover the house, pillars and pilasters, with Palladio's *stucco*, which has now lasted 270 years. It ... deceives the most acute eye till within a foot.' The stucco on the rotunda has caused trouble ever since.

The rotunda at Ickworth differs from that at Ballyscullion for it has two tiers of columns as opposed to one, and lavish sculptural embellishments incorporated in two friezes which encircle the building. The Earl-Bishop had great difficulty finding sculptors to execute these, but eventually he commissioned Casimiro and Donato Carabelli and they created the reliefs in terracotta, modelled on Flaxman's illustrations to the Iliad and Odyssey of Homer.

In Italy, the Earl-Bishop commissioned and collected works of art for his new house. In 1790 he asked the young Flaxman on the advice of Canova to execute a marble group of the *Fury of Athamas*, inspired by the description in Ovid of Athamas demented with rage, in the act of snatching the child Learchus from the arms of Ino,

his wife whom he believes to be a tigress. Unfortunately Flaxman underestimated the work involved when he agreed with the Earl-Bishop on a price of 600 guineas. He was happy enough to start with and wrote: 'Lord Bristol has reanimated the fainting body of Art in Rome, for his generosity to me, I must be silent, for I have not words to express its value.' The Earl-Bishop had struck an excellent bargain and poor Flaxman eventually completed the work much out of pocket. This sculpture dominates the hall at Ickworth. The Earl-Bishop was not so lucky with the bulk of his collection, 'large Mosaick pavements, sumptuous chimney-pieces ... pictures, statues, busts and marbles without end, first-rate Titians and Raphaels, dear Guidos and three old Carraccis – *gran Dio che tesoro*'. In 1798 the French invaded Italy and occupied Rome. His collections were confiscated and he was imprisoned for a time in Milan. He never discovered what became of all his treasures, he never visited England to see his house and he died, on his travels, on the road from Albano to Rome, in 1803 at the age of seventy-six. Lord Cloncurry described how the Earl-Bishop was taken ill with gout in the stomach, and died in an outhouse because of the unwillingness of the peasants to allow a heretic prelate to die under their roof. His body was shipped home in a man-of-war from Naples but as the superstitious sailors would not accept a corpse on board, his coffin was placed in a packing-case and labelled as an antique statue. The Earl-Bishop would have been amused.

Work stopped immediately at Ickworth. The rotunda had a temporary roof and the walls of the wings were only a few feet above the ground. Twenty years later the 5th Earl of Bristol (who became 1st Marquess in 1826) began work on the completion of his father's house. He rethought the plans. He abandoned the idea of galleries in the wings and adapted the east wing for use as the family house (which it has remained ever since). The rotunda was furnished and decorated for formal entertainment and the family moved into the house in 1829. The west wing and corridor were left unfinished for a time. In 1879 the 3rd Marquess commissioned J. D. Crace to decorate a room in the Pompeian style, the paintings based on antique frescoes discovered in 1777 at the Villa Negroni in Rome and later acquired by the Earl-Bishop. These were engraved by Mengs and others and published with a dedication to their owner. The 4th Marquess and his wife made many improvements between 1908 and 1911. Lady Bristol was a granddaughter of the Victorian railway contractor George Wythes and she spent much of her fortune on the house. They commissioned Reginald Blomfield to reconstruct the main staircase and to finish the west corridor beyond the

John, Lord Hervey, and his friends, by William Hogarth, about 1738. This painting, known as 'The Holland House Group', shows the 3rd Duke of Marlborough, Stephen Fox and his brother Henry, later Lord Holland, who is showing Hervey an architectural plan, and a parson, Peter Lewis Willemin.

Pompeian room; he also refaced the family wing in stone.

Ickworth was finally completed. The Herveys had owned the estate since the middle of the fifteenth century; it had taken 450 years to achieve a grand house. It was worthy of their history, the setting and the treasures they acquired.

The old manor house at Ickworth was in a ruinous state when the 1st Earl of Bristol decided to demolish it at the beginning of the eighteenth century. He established himself in a farmhouse on the estate and gave careful consideration to the question of his new house. He called in William Talman and Sir John Vanbrugh to advise him, but though plans materialized buildings did not and the farmhouse, which was added to from time to time, remained the principal family house until the Earl-Bishop took the matter in hand. The 1st Earl's failure to build was partly due to lack of money, for he had a mass of children – thirteen survived – and there were contemporary rumours of gaming losses; but it was also due to his growing attachment to life in the farmhouse for he was devoted to country pursuits and as soon as he could escape from court or city, he would return as quickly as possible to his beloved Ickworth. There were pressures upon him to build a grand family house, for he had established the Hervey family fortunes at a national level. Herveys had played a

prominent part in Suffolk affairs and maintained a controlling interest in the borough of Bury St Edmunds for generations; but John Hervey, who was a Whig MP, assiduously supported the Protestant succession and was created Baron Hervey in 1703 and, at the Duchess of Marlborough's insistence, Earl of Bristol in 1714.

He inherited the Ickworth estate in 1700 from an aunt, but the manor house had not been lived in for about eighty years and was uninhabitable. By that time he had been married, widowed, and remarried. His first wife, Isabella Carr, was by all accounts a delightful woman; she was also an heiress. They married in 1688 and divided their time between a house in Bury, her house in Lincolnshire and a house in London which they shared with her mother, a sister of the politician Lord Arlington. John Hervey adored his wife and they were idyllically happy; they had a daughter and a son, but just after she gave birth to a second daughter in 1693 she died. Her husband was shattered by her death and mourned her for the rest of his life. But by nature he was uxorious, and within two years of her death he married Elizabeth Felton. She was also an heiress, but temperamentally she differed from her predecessor and, indeed, from her husband. She never cared for country life for she was a courtier.

Her husband loved to attend to the management

of his estates, to enjoy a quiet domestic life in the country at Ickworth or, if to leave, to go to Newmarket to race meetings. He could not bear to hang about the courts and watering-places which were her natural habitat. She gamed and taught her children to do so; he made a vow, which he solemnly entered in his diary, to give it up. He believed that temperance, exercise and country air would cure most ills; she put her faith in doctors and their potions. For relaxation, he chose to withdraw to the summer-house he built at Ickworth and play the flute, she to gossip at Bath. He was hot-tempered, a little pompous, and warm-hearted towards all men and beasts, she was vivacious, sophisticated and subject to outbreaks of bad temper. And yet their passion for one another lasted for years. When they were separated letters full of extravagant endearments winged their way from one to the other. He describes to 'My ever-new Delight', as he nearly always addressed her, how he lies in his bed with his two children Jack and Betty and drinks her health in chocolate; she fusses over his health and sends to Newmarket 'some biskets ... which I desire you would eat with some sack before you go on to the Heath'. In London, Lord Carlisle was so curious to know the identity of the writer of the letter which made Lord Bristol so excited that he had to be shown that it was from Lady Bristol to avoid further speculation. Sadly, their love for each other died. Lady Bristol was appointed in 1718 a Lady of the Bedchamber to the Princess of Wales, and remained at court until the Princess's death, as Queen Caroline, in 1737. At some point she had a serious disagreement with her husband for the letters no longer begin with endearments, and we find Lord Bristol raging against his wife for her interference in political matters in Bury, but they never formally separated.

In 1731 the amateur architect, Sir Thomas Robinson, spent a day with Lord Bristol and wrote an enthusiastic description of Ickworth to his father-in-law, Lord Carlisle. He found the park most impressive: 'Nature has been so much his friend that little assistance is wanting from Art,' he wrote, but his architect's eye had examined the possibilities – the disposition of the woods, lawns, hills, the abundance of water – and he failed to understand how so large a family had coped for so long in 'so very bad a Habitation'. Lord Bristol filled it with grandchildren and dogs and was most contented. 'My faithful Fanny dyed,' he told his wife, 'who with a much more remarkable constancy than is common to most of her sex loved me with a very particular affection from the first day of our acquaintance to the last, when leaving her little ones before her death just to come and take her leave of me, then returning to them expired.'

Frederick, 4th Earl of Bristol and 48th Bishop of Derry, by Madame Vigée Le Brun, with Vesuvius in the background.

Thus he occupied himself in the last decades of his life at his beloved Ickworth. Lady Bristol died in 1741, Lord Bristol grew stouter and deafer and began to speak of the impending ruin of the country. He was eighty-five when he died in 1751 and survived fourteen of his twenty children.

John, Lord Hervey was his eldest son by his second wife, Elizabeth. He was one of the most handsome men of his time and perhaps the most brilliant member of this gifted family. John was a delicate child and his parents fussed over him from birth. He was precocious and accompanied his father to Newmarket and on visits to country houses from a very early age. He went to Westminster and Cambridge and then set out on the Grand Tour with his tutor.

His Grand Tour was shorter than his eldest brother Carr's partly because his mother would not allow him to visit Italy. But he made his bow at the court in Hanover, prompted by his father who was most dutiful in his royal attentions, and then returned to England and became a hanger-on of the Prince and Princess of Wales's entourage at Richmond.

He was a politician, elected MP for Bury in 1725, and soon gravitated to the Walpole faction. He was also a courtier, and he became, in Walter Bagehot's words, Walpole's '*queen*-watcher ... one of the cleverest men in England ... induced, by

The upper staircase remodelled for the 4th Marquess of Bristol by Reginald Blomfield.

very dextrous management, to remain at court during many years – to observe the queen, to hint to the queen, to remove wrong impressions from the queen, to confirm the Walpolese predilections of the queen, to report every incident to Sir Robert'. Lord Hervey became Vice-Chamberlain of the Royal Household and Lord Privy Seal. And all the time, he was entering in his diary the most detailed account of everything he saw and heard at court. His memoirs of the reign of George II are now his chief memorial. He was a close personal friend of Queen Caroline; he rode by her coach, he told her stories and teased her. 'It is well I am so old,' she said, 'or I should be talked of for this creature.'

He gives us vivid glimpses of court life, sharply

incised portraits of courtiers and politicians, and above all a detailed picture of the private life of the Royal Family. It is a unique historical document compiled by someone who once suggested an armorial device for himself – a *cat* scratchant.

As a very young man he married one of the Maids of Honour who attended the Princess of Wales. Molly Lepell was the daughter of a Danish brigadier-general who came to England with Prince George, consort of the future Queen Anne. She was a popular member of the court, and she was intelligent. She was a friend of Alexander Pope who lived nearby at Twickenham, John Gay sang her praises, and Voltaire addressed some verses to her when he was in England. Years later, Horace Walpole dedicated to her his *Anecdotes of Painting in England*. Lord Chesterfield told his son Philip: 'She has all the reading that a woman should have, and more than any woman need have: for she understands Latin perfectly well, though she wisely conceals it.'

Her marriage with John Hervey was a love match and took place in secret. They told their parents, and after Lord Bristol had recovered from the disappointment, for he felt that his son with his 'advantages of person, wit and beauty', would have found an heiress, he welcomed her with some warmth. When they visited Ickworth, the Bristols fretted over their son's health. He found a diet which suited him, advocated by Dr Cheyne in his book *Health and Long Life*, and for three years according to Hervey's own account 'I ate neither flesh, fish, nor eggs, but lived entirely upon herbs, root, pulse, grains, fruits, legumes and all those sorts of foods'. Hervey believed that his problem was gout in the stomach. His mother could, he wrote, 'quarter the gout upon her pedigree'.

Molly Hervey gave birth to eight children, and though their marriage had been happy, it became progressively less so, and Molly spent more and more time with Lord Bristol at Ickworth.

Although Hervey was friendly with Alexander Pope in the early days of his marriage, political differences drove them apart, and in the early 1730s Pope attacked him in a flurry of pamphleteering which culminated in verses of unparalleled venom and spite. By this time Pope loathed Hervey, and in the *Epistle to Dr Arbuthnot*, he gave him the character of Sporus, 'that thing of silk … that mere white curd of ass's milk' and ridiculed his ambivalent nature, his morals and his principles.

Lord Hervey died at the age of forty-seven in 1743, much lamented by his father who was succeeded by three of his grandsons in turn. The 2nd Earl was a prominent Whig politician, who made no attempt to build a house at Ickworth but called in 'Capability' Brown to advise on the park

and garden. The 3rd Earl was a Vice-Admiral of the Blue; his portrait by Gainsborough – a superb full-length – hangs in the drawing-room at Ickworth.

Five years after the death of the 4th Marquess in 1956, the house and 1792 acres of land including the park and many acres of woodland, together with the greater part of the outstanding collection of paintings, furniture and other works of art were accepted by the Treasury in lieu of death duties and handed over to the National Trust. The 6th Marquess of Bristol who inherited the title from his father, a younger brother of the 4th Marquess, had lived for many years in the private wing surrounded by his magnificent collection of works of art. He has now handed over to his son, and left England to live in Monte Carlo.

Lady Elizabeth Foster, by Angelica Kauffmann. Lady Elizabeth was the daughter of the Earl-Bishop. She was befriended by the 5th Duke of Devonshire and his wife Georgiana, and after the latter's death in 1806 herself became the Duchess.

Lady Aberdeen is a musician. She studied as a pianist at the Royal College of Music and soon after her husband (as Major David Gordon) took over the Haddo House estate in 1946, they gathered together a group of local people to sing carols in the large wooden shed built by the 1st Marquess and Marchioness of Aberdeen as a community centre. From these modest beginnings in the shed – which turned out to be acoustically perfect – the Haddo House Choral and Operatic Society developed over the years and now occupies a major position in the musical life of Scotland. Lord Aberdeen died in 1974, but he and his wife's great partnership (the second 'We Twa') is remembered with great affection and as a source of inspiration by the people of Aberdeenshire, the singers and musicians who performed at Haddo, the audiences and all who came into contact with them.

'When did you first come to Haddo?'

'Just before the war in 1938. David brought me here to visit his uncle George. The house was very formal – still in the Edwardian era – with gas lights and a mass of servants. We were married in 1939 and George made over the estate to David during the war. George went to live in Aberdeen and we moved into the house in 1946. I married David *and* Haddo and I'd always said I didn't want to live north of the Thames!'

'And your Lord Aberdeen loved Haddo?'

'Passionately. He was overjoyed when his uncle asked him to take over. The people here loved him, he was a genial outgoing person and he managed the estate and brought it into the twentieth century. He became Lord Lieutenant of Aberdeenshire as his uncle and grandfather, and was Prior of the Order of St John in Scotland. He was also a great churchman. If only he could have attended the service we held to commemorate the centenary of the Haddo House chapel in 1981! It was ecumenical – for it is the first undenominational chapel in Scotland. Here is the list of participants. The Archbishop of York preached the sermon and the Cardinal Archbishop of St Andrews and Edinburgh, the Chairman of the Synod of the Methodist Church in Scotland, the former Moderator of the General Assembly of the Church of Scotland and the Bishop of Aberdeen and Orkney in the Scottish Episcopal Church all attended so you can understand what I mean by ecumenical.'

'You brought in professional singers as early as 1947 and since then soloists such as Janet Baker, Peter Pears and Heather Harper have performed here and Ralph Vaughan Williams, Benjamin Britten and Michael Tippett have conducted. Did you have great difficulty at first attracting professionals?'

'We had difficulty attracting soloists, musicians and audiences! Most people thought of Aberdeenshire as the Arctic North.'

'What about finances; they have always presumably been a headache?'

'Yes. But we have had help from the Aberdeenshire County Council, The MacRobert Trusts, the Vaughan Williams Trust, the "Friends of Haddo" and the Arts Council, which has enabled us to survive. We have benefited too from the oil industry off the coast here. The directors of Mobil North Sea have given us new lights and a Steinway grand and helped to make improvements to the stage and BP has sponsored major operas and operettas. This has been an enormous help.'

'And there came a point when you and Lord Aberdeen felt you had to approach the National Trust for Scotland?'

'Yes. David had to sell land but he believed that Haddo could have survived in the family for one more generation. However, he had a first meeting with the National Trust in 1973 but although negotiations were finished by the following year he died in September and all the arrangements had to go into mothballs. In the end the National Trust took over the house, terrace and gardens. 180 acres of parkland went to the Grampian Regional Council for a country park. I have this wing for myself and the children but my time is never my own. Of course I don't mind. I am a servant of the National Trust – and Haddo, of course.'

Haddo House: the entrance front.

Haddo House

ABERDEENSHIRE

The National Trust for Scotland:
The Marchioness of Aberdeen and Temair MBE

George, 4th Earl of Aberdeen, took his young bride Catherine to Haddo for the first time in the early autumn of 1806. Lord Aberdeen himself barely knew his Scottish estate, for he had left as a child of eight and visited it once when he came of age. He had been shocked by what he saw on that occasion, for the house was in a miserable state of repair, dung was piled up against the walls, and only a few limes and Scotch firs were visible from the house; beyond stretched acre upon acre of treeless waste, peopled by resentful, poverty-stricken tenants and boorish lairds, for this was a period of extreme economic depression in the Highlands. Lord Aberdeen had been brought up in southern drawing-rooms among politicians and great ladies, he had travelled abroad and been received by Napoleon and Josephine at Malmaison. And this was his ancestral home! Lady Aberdeen loved her husband dearly, and for his sake was prepared to make the best of Haddo on that bleak first visit. 'You need not believe one word of what Lord Aberdeen says about this place,' she wrote to her father Lord Abercorn, 'for I assure you that there is nothing to complain of, I never was so surprised in my life as when I first saw it ... I expected a thing not fit for a human being to live in, placed in the middle of a barren, bleak moor.' Lady Catherine had been well prepared and she was lucky, for the weather was fine. She insisted that though the house was not 'regularly beautiful' on the outside, the inside was comfortable, and with a chair and a sofa or two and new curtains in the drawing-room, she could not wish for anything better.

Thus encouraged by his beloved, Lord Aberdeen began to transform the house of his ancestors, and bring back life to the tired old estate and hope to his tenants. During a career of distinguished public service in London, which

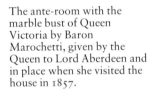

The ante-room with the marble bust of Queen Victoria by Baron Marochetti, given by the Queen to Lord Aberdeen and in place when she visited the house in 1857.

included two terms of office as Foreign Secretary and two years as Prime Minister, he returned whenever he was able to watch the cottages and farm buildings rise, and to see the land drained and sown. He himself would plant trees for stretches of nine hours at a time, and fifty years later he reckoned that he had ploughed £60,000 into the Haddo estate, and some 14,000,000 trees had been planted since he had taken it in hand.

Lord Aberdeen was a Gordon. Haddo House stands on the site of an earlier dwelling, the House of Kellie, but the land has been owned by the family since at least the early fifteenth century. According to the present Lord Aberdeen, the family descends from Jock of Scurdargue, one of two illegitimate brothers who were probably cousins of the Gordon heiress of Strathbogie whose son was created Earl of Huntly in 1445. From him descend the Gordon earls of Huntly, Sutherland and Aboyne, the dukes of Gordon and the present Marquess of Huntly who is the premier Marquess of Scotland.

By marriage the Gordons acquired both Methlick and Haddo, and as soldiers they moved into the mainstream of Scottish life. James Gordon joined his kinsman Lord Huntly in support of Mary, Queen of Scots, and his great-great-grandson, Sir John Gordon, was rewarded with a baronetcy in 1642 by Charles I for his leadership in battle against the Covenanters' soldiers. He defended the House of Kellie against them, but it was sacked and he was captured, taken to Edinburgh, and executed in 1644. His younger son, Sir George, studied law, and practised as an advocate in Edinburgh; he married an heiress and became in 1682 Lord High Chancellor of Scotland and 1st Earl of Aberdeen.

The 2nd Earl of Aberdeen greatly increased the family estates – he married, in turn, a daughter of the Earl of Leven and Melville, a daughter of the Duke of Atholl who produced a son and heir, George, Lord Haddo, and in 1729 when he was almost fifty, the nineteen-year-old daughter of the Duke of Gordon. Shortly after his last spectacular marriage, and with money gained from shrewd dealings in land, Lord Aberdeen was able to consider building a suitable house for his bride. He chose as architect an Edinburgh man, William Adam, who was then in the middle of a highly successful career, but who is better known to posterity as the father of Robert and James.

Haddo House was designed by Adam in the Palladian style under the direction of the antiquary Sir John Clerk of Penicuik. It consists of a central block and two wings linked in the original plan by arcades; the double flight of steps which led to the main entrance on the first floor was removed in the late nineteenth century.

Lord Aberdeen died in 1745 at a propitious moment, because three months earlier Prince Charles Edward had sailed from France for Scotland. He had planted an avenue of limes at Haddo which was supposed to indicate Hanoverian loyalties, but there were plenty of sycamores dotted over the estate to suggest otherwise.

His son, the 3rd Earl of Aberdeen, is known in the family as the Wicked Earl, but he referred to himself as 'Us'. He married a Yorkshire girl and established her and their five children at Haddo. Not content with this, he kept a second ménage at Ellon Castle nearby, a third at Cairnbulg Castle near Fraserburgh, and a fourth at Wiscombe Park in Devonshire. He neglected Haddo, and took a violent dislike to his legitimate children, but as a shrewd man of business he was able to maintain his numerous illegitimate offspring and keep a house for himself in London. He reigned for a

The morning-room. This room was decorated in the style of the Adam brothers in the early 1880s. The National Trust for Scotland arranged for the original carpet to be copied in Bradford. The water-colours on the right are by the 1st Marchioness who was a talented painter.

period of fifty-five years.

His son, George, Lord Haddo, is portrayed in a sparkling portrait by Pompeo Batoni which hangs on the staircase at Haddo. He died tragically young after a fall from his horse, and by doing so was said to have fulfilled a prophecy made by Thomas the Rhymer some five hundred years before:

When the heron leaves the tree
The laird o'Gight shall landless be
At Gight three men a violent death shall dee
And efter that the lands shall lie in lea.

Now it happened that old Lord Aberdeen did make attempts to buy Gight in 1786, and that

The entrance hall. This was
constructed by the 1st
Marquess of Aberdeen and
his wife who made many
alterations to the house in
the early 1880s.

shortly afterwards the herons which had nested beside a pool below the castle flew over the Braes of Gight to Haddo. In the following year, he secured the land and the three deaths which Thomas the Rhymer foretold duly took place; Gight is now a ruin on the Haddo House estate.

The 13th and last Gordon laird of Gight was Catherine, the mother of the poet Lord Byron. Gight was sold to her kinsman Lord Aberdeen to pay the debts of her feckless husband Captain Byron, and as a widow Catherine lived a modest life in Aberdeen, and sent her son to Aberdeen Grammar School where he was entered in the rolls by some Aberdonian clerk as 'George Bayron Gordon'. Mrs Byron struggled to keep her head above water and was, as her son recalled, 'as haughty as Lucifer' about her descent.

After Lord Haddo's death in 1791 his widow was left with seven children, abandoned and penniless, and four years later she died. George

her eldest son, a shy, sensitive child not quite twelve, turned for help not to his grandfather, who remained totally unmoved, but to Henry Dundas, later Lord Melville. Dundas was one of the most powerful men in Scotland, and he responded immediately, receiving the whole family of orphans into his own household. George Haddo had fallen on his feet. He went to Harrow, and later to Cambridge and exercised his right under Scottish law at the age of fourteen to appoint his own guardians or 'curators'. He chose Dundas and William Pitt, who became Prime Minister a couple of years later. His school holidays and Cambridge vacations were divided between his benefactors' houses. At the age of seventeen he became Earl of Aberdeen, but as he would not inherit the Aberdeenshire estates until he was twenty-one, he had time to spare. He chose to go abroad and in the company of his tutor he set out on the Grand Tour. They travelled through

'Dinner at Haddo House', by A.E. Emslie, 1884. This was painted to mark the visit of Mr and Mrs Gladstone to 'We Twa'. Mr Gladstone is on Lady Aberdeen's right and Lord Rosebery on her left. The piper is Andrew Cant.

Below: The drawing-room. Lady Aberdeen uses this room for practices of the Haddo House Choral and Operatic Society.

France, Italy and then on to Greece, where Lord Aberdeen spent two glorious years exploring the country and then settling down to excavate ruins in Ephesus and Athens. He copied inscriptions, and collected sculpture and pottery which he brought back to England.

This interest in classical archaeology remained with him all his life and he published an important book on Greek architecture; he was elected President of the Society of Antiquaries in 1812, and many years later gave the collection of antiquities he gathered on that early journey to the British Museum.

On his return to England, Pitt introduced him to the Marquess of Abercorn and thus Lord Aberdeen came to marry his daughter, Lady Catherine, and to take her to Haddo on that autumn day in 1806. Alas, their happiness was short-lived for Catherine, whom he adored, died in 1812. She left behind three delicate daughters, who died one after the other of tuberculosis, and a husband of twenty-eight who mourned her for the rest of his life.

Lord Aberdeen's political career flourished and he took his seat in the House of Lords on the Tory side as a Representative Peer for Scotland. He went as Ambassador to Vienna in 1813, and signed the Treaty of Paris in the year after. In 1815 he remarried. Pressed by his father-in-law he married his wife's brother's widow and for the next fourteen years he spent his time with his family at

Haddo; he carried out improvements on the estate, and was able to devote himself to many of his varied intellectual pursuits. His second wife never found Haddo congenial, and was reluctant to go there. This caused great anguish to her husband for by this time Haddo had become a passion in his life. He loved to fish and shoot there, to go for seven-hour walks, and hunt with his pack of otter-hounds. He made alterations to the house, he commissioned the Aberdeen architect Archibald Simpson to add the colonnade on the entrance front and to build a courtyard beyond the south wing, and he filled the house with paintings, sculpture, works of art and books.

His second wife died in 1833 and left him with four sons and a daughter. Seven years later his eldest son married Mary Baillie, and Lord Aberdeen lost his heart to her. They remained devoted to each other until his death.

Lord Aberdeen served as Foreign Secretary under the Duke of Wellington in 1828–30, and again in 1841–6 in Sir Robert Peel's second administration. His policy was always cautious and conciliatory; the adjective most commonly attached to his name by his contemporaries was 'just'. After the death of Peel, he became the leader of the Peelites, and, at the end of 1852, Prime Minister of a coalition of Peelite Tories and Whigs. The country drifted into the Crimean War and, ironically he, who had a horror of war, presided over the debacle. The Queen stood by him, and offered him the Order of the Garter as a mark of her support, but his government had fallen before he received it.

From the time of his resignation, Lord Aberdeen spent all his summers at Haddo. The Queen visited him there in October 1857. Lord Clarendon warned her that the house was ugly but comfortable, and she arrived with the Prince Consort in a cavalcade of carriages from Balmoral sixty miles away. As the royal carriage, drawn by four greys with scarlet-jacketed postilions, swept round the curve of the drive, a crowd of mounted tenants, 450 strong, surged forward and cheered the royal pair. The Queen enjoyed her visit; she was fond of her taciturn minister and had always trusted him.

Lord Aberdeen's brothers and sons found him no less daunting than the reputation he had acquired in public life. But close friends, and his grandchildren, penetrated the austere exterior and found a warm heart. He installed his son, Lord Haddo, with his young family at Ranger's House in Blackheath which was a perquisite of office, and at weekends he would drive down to see his grandchildren taking with him the toys which had been requested the weekend before. His grandson, John (later the 7th Earl), tells the story in his reminiscences of Mr Basket the gardener at Ranger's House who was furious with him for trundling the wheelbarrow his grandfather had brought him in such a way as to ruin the edges of the walks. John did this as it reminded him of the way in which the junior postilions at Haddo would sometimes inadvertently pare the edges of the drive with the carriage-wheels. Mr Basket decided to speak to the Prime Minister on his next visit. Lord Aberdeen listened carefully to Mr Basket's complaints and then asked him if he had any children. 'Yes, My Lord, several,' came the swift reply, 'and I would like to get my eldest son into the local bank as a clerk, and I hope your Lordship will kindly help him with your influence.'

Lord Aberdeen died in 1860. He had given back to Haddo the dignity which the house had lost, and enriched the surroundings with avenues, rides and lakes. Although many of his paintings have had to be sold over the years – a Titian, a Tintoretto, the Carracci *Butcher's Shop* – there is much to remind the visitor to Haddo of 'Athenian Aberdeen'. And his house which his contemporaries considered ugly, now shorn of the ivy which he planted and encouraged, has survived intact into an age which cherishes its serene distinction.

His son, the 5th Earl, was the first Lord Aberdeen to live exclusively at Haddo. He was both a painter and an evangelist, and at the time of his father's death he was away in Egypt where he had gone to distribute Protestant tracts to the Coptic Christians. He survived his father by only four years, and left a widow, Mary, and six children.

John, 7th Earl and 1st Marquess of Aberdeen, succeeded his elder brother who was swept overboard in 1870 in a storm while serving under an assumed name in the US merchant marine.

In 1877 he married Ishbel, daughter of the Liberal MP Sir Dudley Coutts Marjoribanks, who later became 1st Lord Tweedmouth. Their partnership is enshrined in the pages of their two volumes of reminiscences, *We Twa* published in 1925 and, by popular request, *More Cracks with We Twa*, which followed four years later. They were devoted and ardent Liberals and dedicated their long married life which was proverbially happy to a variety of humanitarian and social causes. They were mocked and derided by some of their contemporaries, and today nothing could be less fashionable than their philanthropic paternalism and naïve belief in the good intentions of their fellow men. And yet their faith was enviable, and their charity utterly unselfish. They were much loved and their efforts on an international level were of lasting value, his, of bridge-building across the Atlantic, and hers, as President of the International Council of Women which was

View from the house along one of the avenues planted by the 4th Earl of Aberdeen, who planted 14,000,000 trees between his coming of age and his death in 1860.

founded in Washington in 1888.

The list of his appointments – Viceroy of Ireland in 1886, and again between 1905–15, and Governor-General of Canada in 1893–8 – gives no idea of this life-long commitment to public service. They began in a small way on their estate at Haddo soon after they were married. They built a cottage hospital at Tarves, and a hall and recreation room at Methlick, instituted hot penny-dinners for the school-children and founded what later became the Onward and Upward Association which began as a community club for maidservants and girls on the Haddo estate, and spread all over Scotland. In London they played a full part in the social life of the capital but before Lady Aberdeen appeared at a garden party she would almost certainly have attended one of her numerous committees, whether it was in aid of The Provision of Seats for Shop Assistants, The Mission to Costermongers or The Homes for

Working Girls; and after a dinner party, she and Lord Aberdeen were just as likely to set off for Edgware where the Omnibus Men's Suppers began at midnight, as return to their house in Grosvenor Square.

In all their efforts they were supported by their great friend Mr Gladstone whom they worshipped. Gladstone appointed Lord Aberdeen Lord Lieutenant of the County of Aberdeen, and sent him to Dublin as Viceroy. The Phoenix Park murders were still fresh memories, but the Aberdeens threw themselves into the task of reconciliation in their highly unconventional manner.

At the Irish Industries Garden Party at Viceregal Lodge, the guests were asked to use Irish materials for their dress, a request which caused some consternation; and, although they were willing to give the customary Punchestown Ball, they sent a member of their staff to attend the actual race

meeting. Madame Canziani painted two of their sons, Dudley and Archie, about this time: the painting hangs on the staircase at Haddo, entitled *Two Little Home Rulers*. When the Aberdeens went to Ottawa all sorts of rumours preceded them – that Lady Aberdeen dined in the servants' hall at Haddo, and played hide-and-seek with the housemaids and footmen. These stories persisted and grew as they circulated, so that the Queen was concerned enough to ask her Prime Minister, Lord Rosebery, to find out whether it was true that the Aberdeens dined with their servants in Ottawa. Lady Aberdeen dissects these rumours herself in *We Twa*, and speculates on how they arose, but, as the present Lord Aberdeen says, 'They soon learnt to shrug off hostility from Conservatives, Irish gentry, powerful North Americans and smart Londoners.' And many of their good works were fruitful, for in Canada, for instance, Lady Aberdeen founded the Victorian Order of Nurses

which later became a Dominion-wide health service. They loved Canada and established a close friendship with Wilfrid Laurier after he became premier in 1895.

When they left, the Senators and Members of Parliament presented Lady Aberdeen with a china dinner and tea service which is on display at Haddo, painted by members of the Women's Art Association with Canadian birds, flowers and fruit, and places of historic interest. Lady Aberdeen published her memories of this period in *Through Canada with a Kodak*.

Lord Aberdeen's second term of office in Ireland culminated in the Home Rule Bill becoming law in 1914; there were numerous requests for him to remain, and a leading Irish MP wrote that he had converted the lord-lieutenancy from a hateful into a popular institution. Lady Aberdeen set up health clinics and rural industries in Ireland and was photographed with two of her sons at a spinning-wheel wearing a copy of a thirteenth-century Irish dress with a Celtic pattern on the skirt, to extol the Irish industries of wool, flax and silk. Lord Aberdeen was created 1st Marquess of Aberdeen and Temair in 1916.

Haddo was their home and, unless they were abroad, they would spend the autumn and winter there, and return to London for the parliamentary season. Lady Aberdeen did not see the house before her marriage or indeed, until six months after, for they were married in the November of 1877 and her husband was anxious that her first sight of the house should be in the summer. It was a scene which recalled one of over 150 years before. 'Alas for human plans,' wrote Lady Aberdeen, for it was a bitterly cold and windy June day when they drove the twenty miles from Aberdeen to Haddo in a barouche drawn by four horses with postilions. By the time she reached Haddo she imagined her face matched the blue of her velvet dress, but the welcome they received soon banished such thoughts. Two hundred tenants mounted on horses of all shapes and sizes escorted the carriage across the policies, and a host of others waited for them at the front door. A few days later they gave a dinner for over nine hundred tenants in a marquee put up for the occasion, followed by a dinner for the employees, and a treat for the school-children.

Haddo itself was in an appalling state inside. Lord and Lady Aberdeen renovated it from top to bottom, and gave the interior of the house the appearance and character it has today. They removed the steps which landed visitors straight into the drawing-room, and made a hall with an inside staircase. They redecorated all the principal rooms, calling in the London decorators Wright and Mansfield to transform them in the style of Robert Adam, and added a wing with room for menservants, a nursery above and sitting-rooms for themselves. Bathrooms and modern drainage were quickly installed after they found fourteen cesspools in the immediate vicinity of the house. They bought furniture and rehung the paintings, and put up some of Lady Aberdeen's water-colours which can still be seen in the morning-room. G. E. Street was commissioned to design the chapel. This adjoins the house and contains a window by Sir Edward Burne-Jones, and an organ built by Father Henry Willis.

The house was always full of people, for the Aberdeens gave many large house-parties. In 1884 Mr Gladstone and his wife spent a few days there, in a party which included Lord and Lady Rosebery; Mr Gladstone had not stayed at Haddo for forty years, and he was able on the second occasion to open the House for Orphan Girls at Methlick.

There was a price to pay not only for all the rebuilding and redecoration, but also for the charitable works, the money freely given to numerous good causes, the public appointments, the wooden hall they built on their return from Canada beyond the south wing in the style of a Canadian community centre of that time and last but not least, the expenses of their large household. In 1872 the estate extended over at least 75,000 acres. Land was sold little by little to pay the bills and after Lord Aberdeen's death in 1934 the figure shrank to 15,000. They celebrated their golden wedding in 1927 and three years later handed Haddo over to their son, and departed for the House of Cromar which they had built for themselves on the West Aberdeenshire estates in 1905, and within sight of the mountains she loved. After her husband's death Lady Aberdeen continued the good works, her efforts for women, charities for children, the Red Cross, and the League of Nations. The day after her eighty-second birthday, the Germans entered Prague; her thoughts were duly entered in her diary; just over a month later she was dead.

Their grandson David, who became 4th Marquess of Aberdeen on his father's death in 1972, lived at Haddo with his wife for thirty years. Together they founded the Haddo House Choral and Operatic Society in 1946 which is based in the Canadian hall put up by his grandparents and has played an increasingly important part in the musical life of Scotland. Lord Aberdeen had begun negotiations with the National Trust for Scotland before his death in 1974 and, as he wished, Haddo, its contents and gardens, passed into the care of the Trust in 1979.

David, 4th Marquess of Aberdeen CBE, wearing the uniform of the Queen's Bodyguard for Scotland (the Royal Company of Archers). Lord Aberdeen and his wife founded the Haddo House Choral and Operatic Society. He had begun negotiations with the National Trust for Scotland to take over Haddo House before his death in 1974.

Miles, 17th Duke of Norfolk began life as the Honourable Miles Fitzalan-Howard. He inherited his mother's baronetcy (Beaumont), also his father's (Howard of Glossop) and, in 1975, succeeded his cousin as 17th Duke of Norfolk, Earl of Arundel, Surrey and Norfolk, Baron Maltravers, Fitz Alan, Clun and Oswaldestre; and Earl Marshal, Hereditary Marshal and Chief Butler of England.

'How has Carlton survived in such good condition when so many Victorian houses – and Victorian interiors – have been destroyed?'

'My mother loved Carlton passionately. She was very proud of it. There were eight of us, we were known as 'the eight Ms', Miles, Michael, Marigold, Martin, Miriam, Miranda, Mirabel and Mark, and to my mother Carlton was the ninth, an extra child. She was very economical, everything was sacrificed to keep Carlton going.'

'Were you brought up at Carlton?'

'Yes, it's my home. My father worked in the City, so he and my mother spent the term-time in London, but for short holidays we were all at Carlton.'

'Did your father have a family house?'

'Glossop, a bleak house on the moors in Derbyshire. The Howard of Glossop title is very recent – 1869 – Gladstone making up to the Catholics. My mother's title was the senior one and she always insisted on retaining it. They were known as Lord Howard of Glossop and Baroness Beaumont. My father didn't mind leaving Glossop for Carlton. He ran the farm.'

'Was Carlton modernized in her time?'

'Electric light in 1914 and on the mains in the 1930s. Central heating in the passages but not in the main rooms which has of course helped to preserve them. Carlton is solidly built.'

'Was the house open to the public in your mother's time?'

'No, she wouldn't allow it and would never have let it go to the National Trust. But she loved showing people round it; she was so proud of it and all through the time when it was unfashionable she loved the decoration. She would never hear a word against it. She used to paint as a hobby in the style of mediaeval manuscript painting, and she made vestments and did embroidery. We opened Carlton to the public for the first time for a few weeks towards the end of 1977 and then since 1978 for the whole season.'

'Did your parents entertain much at Carlton?'

'There were often odd people staying but they never had grand house-parties, never, a few people from Doncaster or York Races perhaps, dinner parties and the opening meet of the local hunt was always held at Carlton.'

'Your life has presumably taken you away from Carlton?'

'Yes, sadly. I was in the army – the Grenadiers – for thirty years. I left in 1967. I go for the odd weekend but we have a house near Henley.'

'And what about Arundel Castle since you became Duke of Norfolk?'

'I am there once a week but my eldest son lives there on the Arundel estate and farms.'

'What about your royal duties as Earl Marshal and Chief Butler?'

'State occasions only. It would be my job to organize a coronation, for instance. The Prince and Princess of Wales's wedding was a private occasion, not a state occasion.'

'And what about your position as the senior Catholic peer in Britain? What does this entail?'

'Committees, endless committees, schools, hospitals, charities in aid of everything under the sun, speeches, opening ceremonies, that sort of thing.'

'No wonder you find it difficult to find time to visit Carlton.'

'Sadly, yes.'

Carlton Towers: a view from the west showing the towers which justified the change of name from Carlton Hall.

Carlton Towers

GOOLE, YORKSHIRE

Major-General The Duke of Norfolk CB, CBE, MC

Henry, 9th Lord Beaumont, was a child of six when his father died in 1854. During his long minority his estates were carefully managed by his mother, so that when he came of age both the house and the family finances were in good order. Lord Beaumont was a romantic young man and as soon as the house was in his hands he began to cast around for an architect who would help him transform it in a style which clearly reflected his family's chivalrous past. He found an architect after his own heart and the plans, which were quite modest to start with, became more and more grandiose as the months passed.

The first version which he and his architect agreed upon bore no relationship whatsoever to the means at his disposal, but this did not deter him and he gave the order for work to start. His mother's apprehension can be imagined, but she knew that her eldest son was not content to dream dreams and there was nothing she could do to curb his architectural fancies, his wild financial speculations or his efforts to win military glory in the service of the Carlist Pretender to the throne of Spain. Lady Beaumont was more sympathetic to her son's spiritual interests, however, and the year after he was received into the Catholic Church she

followed. Lord Beaumont's conversion had a decided effect on his plans for the house, but it did not help his speculations in any way other than to encourage them, and four years after he came of age he had run up debts of £250,000. When he died at the age of forty-three, not in battle but from pneumonia, the estate was in the hands of a receiver. His brother Miles was able to buy the house and a hundred acres of parkland, and thus retain ownership of an estate which had belonged to their family for at least 800 years. Henry, Lord Beaumont's pride in his race was justified, for his family, the Stapletons, had had a long and honourable history. Sir Miles de Stapleton was one of the original Knights of the Garter and through an ancestress he traced his descent from John of Brienne, King of Jerusalem. But the position in national life which the Stapletons reached through military exploits in the fourteenth and fifteenth centuries was not maintained, for the family clung tenaciously to the old faith and as Catholics were rigorously excluded from the political and administrative life of the country at both national and local level.

Thus Lord Beaumont returned to the faith of all his Stapleton ancestors except his father who, though he had been born into the Church, left it

The entrance front. The wing on the left is the original Jacobean house with the late eighteenth-century stables to the right, all of which was remodelled by E. W. Pugin for the 9th Lord Beaumont in the early 1870s. The extensive wing which was planned to the right was never built.

when the Catholic hierarchy was restored, and at the same time closed the chapel at Carlton. The 8th Lord Beaumont married a Protestant girl from Northern Ireland (though as we have seen she eventually succumbed to the faith of her husband's family) and they brought up their sons as members of the Church of England and sent them to Eton; he benefited greatly from the removal of those barriers which had penalized members of the faith for some three hundred years. The passing of the Catholic Relief Bill of 1829 took place when the Duke of Wellington was Prime Minister. His successor the Whig Lord Melbourne cast a favourable eye in the direction of those Catholics who laid claim to ancient titles.

Successive heads of the Stapleton family had tried from 1795 to have the ancient barony of Beaumont called out of abeyance, for they descended from the sister of the last holder, William, Lord Beaumont, who died in 1507, and the barony was passable through the female line. After a long delay their claim was admitted during Lord Melbourne's premiership, and Miles Stapleton was summoned to Parliament in 1840 as Lord Beaumont. Five ancient peerages were called out of abeyance about this time, and two other successful petitioners, Lords Camoys and Vaux of Harrowden, were also Catholics.

The young Lord Beaumont's decision to return to the faith of his ancestors undoubtedly owed something to his sense of history and his early memories, but the decisive factor was the influence of the great Catholic revival in England with which he came into contact at Oxford. He was for instance a contemporary of the 3rd Marquess of Bute whose spectacular conversion inspired Disraeli's novel *Lothair*. Archbishop Mathew has described this aristocratic turmoil and the succession of noble souls who switched their allegiance from Canterbury to Rome in waves from the 1830s on. The convert peeresses included the Duchesses of Argyll, Buccleuch and Hamilton who followed in Newman's wake and almost swamped the aura of asceticism which surrounded their hero, and in the 1850s and 1860s men who were distinguished in public life such as the Marquess of Ripon and the Earl of Albemarle strengthened the line of convert peers. Between 1850 and 1910 no fewer than seventy-three peers and peeresses of the realm were received into the Catholic Church.

Henry, Lord Beaumont, was caught on this tide and his Catholicism governed his choice of architect when he began to consider plans for the elaboration of his family home. He chose a Catholic architect, Edward Welby Pugin, the son of Augustus Pugin who had assisted Barry with the designs for the Houses of Parliament and worked

for Catholic patrons such as Lord Shrewsbury and Charles Scarisbrick. After he had quarrelled with Pugin, he replaced him with John Francis Bentley, who is now renowned as the architect of Westminster Cathedral.

The transformation of Carlton Hall into Carlton Towers began in 1873. Although a branch of the Stapleton family had made their principal home at Carlton in 1394 and there must have been a house on this site before the seventeenth century, the modesty of their building efforts over the years is explained by their steadfast refusal to abandon their faith; they were excluded from all those offices which extended the influence and wealth of other families, and enormous fines were inflicted on them. A compact and unambitious Jacobean building survives which forms the carcase of one block of the present house. Pugin retained part of the decoration surrounding the original entrance door on the west side and this is one of the few indications of the ancient core which lies beneath the stucco.

This Jacobean house was built by Elizabeth Stapleton in her widowhood. Her husband, Richard Stapleton, died in 1612 and she survived him by thirty-six years, holding the estates in her own hands throughout this period. She was a

The outer hall. This was arranged as a temporary chapel when Cardinal Manning visited Carlton in 1876.

Opposite: The chimney-piece in the Venetian drawing-room, with the armorial bearings of the 9th Lord Beaumont.

Below: The inner hall.

formidable lady, and a granddaughter of the great Tudor matriarch, Bess of Hardwick, with whom she shared a passion for building. Whether or not Elizabeth became a Catholic is uncertain, but she must have been sympathetic to the faith, for in the attic of the house she constructed a priest's hole which is entered through a loose floorboard inside a cupboard, and can be seen by visitors to the house today.

Her grandson, Miles Stapleton, was made a baronet in 1662. He owned Carlton from 1659 until his death in 1707 during a period in which Catholic influence at court waxed, waned and was finally extinguished, and deep hostility to Catholicism lingered in country districts. We gain a picture of the life lived by a Catholic member of the country gentry from his detailed account books. These are full of references to sums of money made to priests 'to pray for mee' which meant no doubt to celebrate a Mass. Priests at that time were constantly on the move to avoid

suspicion, travelling generally on foot and by night from one community to another, and living under a variety of aliases. Communicants tended to cluster together; in the village of Carlton for instance there were twenty-six Catholics in 1604 and a further fourteen in the adjacent parish. Sir Miles kept a chapel furnished; he bought vestments and other necessary items such as 'six pounds of white bleached wax candles at London. 12s'. For a time he made payments to a kinsman, Thomas Thwing, who was ordained at Douai in 1665 and shortly afterwards sent on the English mission. He spent many years in Yorkshire and was arrested at the same time as Sir Miles in the aftermath of the discovery of the so-called Popish Plot. Thwing was refused trial by jury, unlike Sir Miles who had the good fortune to appear before country neighbours who respected him. Thwing was martyred at York in 1680; Sir Miles fared better, for after an hour's consideration, the jury acquitted him of the charge of high treason and

The Venetian drawing-
room. This was decorated by
John Francis Bentley and is
one of the most complete
Victorian interiors in
existence.

allowed him to return a free man to Carlton. His accounts show the high price he had to pay for this freedom. He settled the heavy recusancy fines when they were imposed but from time to time he had to take other steps to ensure that he retained his property intact and was able to live his life in peace, and these evidently included bribery; on one occasion he paid the High Sheriff's son 'two ginny pieces of gold to be favourable to mee'. In 1688 when Protestant fury was at its height, a mob of some sixty people burst into Carlton in search of a priest. They did not find one, and held Sir Miles captive instead; they remained in the house for the night and infuriated Sir Miles for they drank a hogshead of his wine and beer and consumed quantities of bread, cheese and meat.

Sir Miles led a varied social life among the Yorkshire squirearchy, both Catholic and Protestant. The distance between houses in that country district meant that he and his wife made visits for one, two or three nights to their neighbours. We gain an idea of these from the tips he entered in his account books. He paid 13s 6d to the servants at Sir Thomas Wharton's where he and his wife spent

one night, and gave 3s to Lady Dawnay's coachman and footman when they brought them back from her house to the Carlton Ferry. After three nights at Danby with the Scropes, he gave the fiddlers 6s. Sir Miles and his wife visited Harrogate in the summer of 1672 to drink the waters for ten days, and at least once a year he went to London. He varied his means of travel; sometimes he set out from Doncaster in the hackney-coach which was a four-wheeler drawn by two horses with seats for six passengers. The journey to London took four days and the fare was £2; on these occasions he was generally accompanied by his French valet, Pullaine, who rode on horseback beside the coach. At other times, Sir Miles rode with his servant; he would sell the horses on his arrival in London and purchase others for the journey back, and sometimes he made a profit on the transaction. In 1669 he spent seven weeks in London, but he wrote home regularly for the carriage of his letters over that period cost 10s 3d. He was a theatre-lover and, as a young man, interested in dress. But he was always careful about money, and one typical entry, 'two peaces of

taffaty ribbin for fancyes for my suit £1 15s', appears beside another no less typical 'for altering my black suit 3s 6d'. As he grew older, his expenditure on dress decreased; he no longer bought cloaks trimmed with thirty-six yards of silver ribbon as he had as a young man, and from one of his last entries it is evident that he was content to buy holland cloth to cover his woollen night-cap.

Sir Miles was succeeded by his sister's son Nicholas who took the name Stapleton. The latter's grandson Thomas was master of Carlton for over seventy years from 1750 until 1821. He was a most successful breeder of racehorses and raced in partnership with Sir Thomas Gascoigne; together in 1778 they won the first St Leger with Hollondaise, and in the following year Thomas Stapleton won on his own with Tommy. Pictures of some of his racehorses with their names inscribed – Tuberose, Miss Skeggs, Magog and Cannibal – hang at Carlton today. Appropriately, his attentions to Carlton consisted of the addition of a wing to the east of the main house with a chapel at one end and stables at the other. This new wing was transformed subsequently by Henry, 9th Lord Beaumont, into the entrance front of the 'new' Carlton Towers and contains the three rooms Bentley decorated for him: the Venetian drawing-room, the card room and the picture gallery.

Despite the elaborate plans drawn up by Pugin, the actual building occupies the same amount of space today as it did in Thomas Stapleton's day. This was not Lord Beaumont's intention, although according to Mark Girouard, Pugin's first plans for Carlton, dated 1871, are relatively modest. By 1873 the architect, aided and abetted by his patron, had produced a vast scheme which would have grown to the right of the present entrance front. A massive grand staircase contained in a keep-like structure was envisaged, together with a hall of the barons and a large chapel. Pugin encased old Carlton Hall in stucco and built the clock-tower which is 133 feet from the ground to the ears of the Stapleton talbots which crown it. Lord Beaumont quarrelled with Pugin before he had begun any of the interior decoration or progressed with the new addition,

Henry, 9th Lord Beaumont, from a stained-glass window in the inner hall. He commissioned the Victorian decorations at Carlton.

Detail of the decoration in the Venetian drawing-room. The painted panels
by N. H. J. Westlake show figures from *The Merchant of Venice*.

and dismissed him. The doors to the east in the picture gallery lead nowhere and mark the point beyond which Lord Beaumont's dreams remained dreams. He called in an infinitely talented young man, John Francis Bentley, who lavished care on the embellishment of Carlton over a period of fifteen years.

It was Bentley's only major county-house commission, for most of his work was concerned with ecclesiastical buildings. He designed the decorative schemes, and also the chandeliers, chairs and upholstery, wallpapers and curtains. No detail was too small to engage his attention. His work at Carlton culminates in the Venetian drawing-room which is one of the most complete Victorian interiors in existence. The walls are covered in moulded plaster with a pattern of pomegranates gilded to look like leather. The room is dominated by a magnificent chimney-piece which, like the cornice, is decorated with quantities of armorial bearings and heraldic beasts which bear witness to Lord Beaumont's mighty descent. This was carefully investigated by General de Havilland, a man whom Lord Beaumont met during his military adventures in Spain. The General was York Herald and thus a professional genealogist, and he drew up the elaborate heraldic scheme which is a major feature of the decoration. The display cabinets were designed to house the collection of Venetian glass from which the room derives its name and the theme is continued in the dado panels which depict figures from *The Merchant of Venice*. The Venetian drawing-room which is light and airy

with huge windows facing south is entered from the inner hall, where ecclesiastical gloom prevails, with windows of stained glass. The right-hand panel depicts Lord Beaumont himself.

As soon as money began to run out, Lord Beaumont engaged in disastrous property speculations in London. He turned to the age-old expedient and married an heiress. He chose quite mercilessly a young girl named Violet Wootton Isaacson whose father was a Member of Parliament and mother the owner of a dress shop in Regent Street called 'Madame Elise'. Miss Isaacson brought her husband £120,000 when she married him in 1888. But she was not her mother's daughter for nothing and she refused to allow the solid future derived from 'Madam Elise' to disappear in a sea of debt. Most of the Carlton estate was sold in 1888–9. Four years later, Lord Beaumont died. His brother Miles saved the house, and greatly enriched it through his marriage to an heiress who brought with her the paintings which now hang in the picture gallery. He died in a tragic shooting accident three years later. His daughter Mona succeeded him at the age of one, and to her, Baroness Beaumont as she was known throughout her life, is due the preservation of Carlton and its great Victorian interior, for she presided over the fortunes of the house for a period of seventy-six years until her death in 1971.

She was succeeded by her eldest son, Miles, who inherited the Beaumont barony, his father's Howard of Glossop barony and, in 1975, succeeded his cousin as 17th Duke of Norfolk.

Appendix

A further selection of historic houses open to the public in Great Britain.
Information regarding opening times and admission charges can be obtained from the owners.
All photographs in this Appendix by courtesy of the National Trust and the National Trust for Scotland.

England

AVON

Clevedon Court
The National Trust

1½m E of Clevedon off M5 and Bristol rd (B3130). 14th cent. manor house, 12th cent. tower, 13th cent. hall, 18th cent. terraced garden.

Dodington House
Major S.F.B. Codrington

A46, 3m S of Chipping Sodbury rd (A432), 10m N of Bath. 18th cent. Classical; magnificent staircase; grounds landscaped by 'Capability' Brown; carriage museum; passenger railway.

Dyrham Park
The National Trust

8m N of Bath, 12m E of Bristol, approach from A46. Late 17th cent.; Blathwayt furniture; Dutch paintings; panelled rooms; deer park.

BEDFORDSHIRE

Luton Hoo
The Wernher Family

Luton, entrance at Park St Gates (A6129). Exterior 1767; interior remodelled early 20th cent. in French style; magnificent art collection includes Fabergé jewels and unique Russian collection; park landscaped by 'Capability' Brown.

Woburn Abbey
Marquess of Tavistock

Woburn, 8½m NW of Dunstable on A50. Formerly home of the dukes of Bedford, rebuilt mid-18th cent., added to early 1800s; 3000 acre deer park; private art collection; French and English 18th cent. furniture and silver collections, and Sèvres dinner service.

BERKSHIRE

Basildon Park
The National Trust

Nr Pangbourne, 7m NW of Reading on A329. 1776 Classical; unusual Octagon room; important collection of paintings and furniture; fine plasterwork.

BUCKINGHAMSHIRE

Ascott
The National Trust

½m E of Wing, 2m SW of Leighton Buzzard, S side of A418. Rothschild collection of pictures; oriental porcelain; French and Chippendale furniture; gardens.

Chichely Hall
Trustees of the Hon. Nicholas Beatty

2m E of Newport Pagnell, 11m W of Bedford on A422. 1719–23, Baroque; panelling; naval pictures; unique hidden library.

Claydon House
The National Trust

Nr Middle Claydon, W of East Claydon, 3½m SW of Winslow. 18th cent.; unique rococo carvings in state rooms; Florence Nightingale Museum.

Hughenden Manor
The National Trust

1½m N of High Wycombe, W side of A4128. Bought and rebuilt by Benjamin Disraeli in 1847, and lived in until his death in 1881; fine example of the Victorian gentleman's country seat.

Waddesdon Manor
The National Trust

W end of Waddesdon village, 6m NW of Aylesbury on A41. Built late 19th cent. for Baron Ferdinand de Rothschild; French decorative art and furniture; important paintings; 18th cent. style aviary; Sika deer.

West Wycombe Park
The National Trust

W end of West Wycombe S of A40, 3m W of High Wycombe. 1750 Palladian; frescoes and painted ceilings; 18th cent. landscaped gardens with Roman and Greek temples.

CAMBRIDGESHIRE

Anglesey Abbey
The National Trust

Lode, 6m NE of Cambridge on B1102. Founded Henry I; rebuilt as Elizabethan manor; Fairhaven art collection; gardens.

Wimpole Hall
The National Trust

8m SW of Cambridge, signposted at New Wimpole (A603). One of the most elegant houses of the 18th cent.; magnificent state rooms; gardens designed by the country's leading landscapists.

CHESHIRE

Capesthorne
Lt Col Sir Walter Bromley-Davenport

6½m N of Congleton, 7m S of Wilmslow on A34. 1722 Jacobean style, later alterations by Blore and Salvin; paintings; furniture; Georgian chapel.

Dunham Massey
The National Trust

3m SW of Altrincham off A56. 18th cent. house and park; portraits of Lady Jane Grey; Huguenot silver; house and stables restored.

Peover Hall
Randle Brooks

4m S of Knutsford off A50. 1585; Caroline stables; Mainwaring chapel; 18th cent. landscaped park.

Tatton Park
The National Trust

3½m N of Knutsford (A50).
Georgian (Wyatt); good
collections of furniture, paintings
and glass; 50 acre garden; 1000
acre deer park.

CORNWALL

Cotehele House
The National Trust

W bank of Tamar, 2m W of
Calstock, 8m SW of Tavistock.
Mediaeval; original collections of
armour, furniture, tapestries;
terraced garden.

Lanhydrock
The National Trust

2½m SE of Bodmin on B3268. 17th
cent.; picture gallery; kitchen
quarters; fine plaster ceilings;
formal garden.

St Michael's Mount
The National Trust

½m from shore at Marazion,
A394, connected by causeway, 3m
E of Penzance. Mediaeval and
early 17th cent.; alterations and
additions in 18th and 19th cents.

Trerice
The National Trust

3m SE of Newquay, A392, &
A3058. Elizabethan; plaster
ceilings and fireplaces; garden.

Trewithen
Mr and Mrs A.M.J. Galsworthy

1½m E of Probus, just S of A390.
Early Georgian; period furniture;
pictures; landscaped gardens.

CUMBRIA

Holker Hall
Mr Hugh Cavendish

½m N of Cark, off the
Haverthwaite rd, 4m SW of
Grange over Sands. 16th cent.
with 19th cent. additions; gardens
and deer park; special monthly
park events.

Levens Hall
Mr O.R. Bagot

5m S of Kendal on Milnthorpe
Road, A6. Elizabethan; fine
furniture, plasterwork, panelling;
topiary garden; collection of
steam engines.

Muncaster Castle
Sir William Pennington-
Ramsden, Bt

1m SE of Ravenglass village on
A595. 13th cent.; fine collections
of paintings, china, tapestries and
furniture; rhododendron and
azalea gardens.

Sizergh Castle
The National Trust

3½m S of Kendal, NW of A6/A591
interchange. Family home for 700
years; 15th, 16th and 18th cent.
additions; gardens.

DERBYSHIRE

Haddon Hall
His Grace the Duke of Rutland

2m SE of Bakewell, 6½m N of
Matlock on A6. One of England's
best examples of a mediaeval
manor; terraced rose gardens.

Hardwick Hall
The National Trust

2m S of A617, 7½m NW of
Mansfield, 9½m SE of Chesterfield.
Elizabethan; furniture,
needlework and tapestry
collections; gardens.

Kedleston Hall
The Viscount Scarsdale

4½m NW of Derby on
Derby–Hulland Rd. Mid 18th
cent.; Robert Adam's most
prestigious work in England;
unique Marble Hall; collection of
Old Masters.

Melbourne Hall
The Marquess of Lothian

8m S of Derby on A514. Home of
former Prime Minister Lord
Melbourne; art and furniture
collections; formal gardens.

Sudbury Hall
The National Trust

Sudbury, 6m E of Uttoxeter off
A50. 17th cent. brick; some of the
most distinguished craftsmen of
the period contributed to the
magnificent rooms.

DEVONSHIRE

Bradley Manor
The National Trust

W end of Newton Abbot, W of
A381. 15th cent. manor house;
great hall; buttery; perpendicular
chapel.

Castle Drogo
The National Trust

2m NE of Chagford, 1m S of A30.
Early 20th cent., designed by
Lutyens; overlooking Teign gorge
with views of Dartmoor; terraced
garden; walks.

Compton Castle
The National Trust

Nr Paignton, 1m N of Marldon off
A381. 1320, 15th and 16th cent.;
fortified manor house; Great
Hall.

Knightshayes Court
The National Trust

2m N of Tiverton, turn off A396.
1870, William Burges; collection
of Old Masters; gardens.

Powderham Castle
The Earl and Countess of Devon

8m SW of Exeter off A379 to
Dawlish. Mediaeval c. 1390;
restored 18th and 19th cents;
music room by Wyatt; deer park.

Saltram House
The National Trust

2m W of Plympton, 3½m E of
Plymouth, between A38 and A379.
George II, incorporating late
Tudor remnants; Great Kitchen;
orangery; octagonal summer-
house.

Ugbrooke
Lord and Lady Clifford
of Chudleigh

A380, 8m S of Exeter, 7m N of
Torquay. 18th cent., Robert
Adam; collections of needlework
and uniforms; park designed by
'Capability' Brown.

DORSET

Forde Abbey
Trustees of Mr G.D. Roper

4m SE of Chard, off B3162. 12th
cent. Cistercian monastery;
Mortlake tapestries; gardens.

Sherborne Castle
Mr Simon Wingfield Digby

Sherborne (A30). Built by Sir
Walter Raleigh in 1594; fine
paintings, porcelain, furniture;
'Capability' Brown gardens.

EAST SUSSEX

Bateman's
The National Trust

½m S of Burwash on A265 nr
Heathfield. 1634; Rudyard
Kipling's home; water-mill.

Firle Place
Viscount Gage, KCVO

4m SE of Lewes on A27. 15th cent., altered 1730s; collection of Italian, Dutch and English pictures; fine furniture; Sèvres china.

Glynde Place
Viscount Hampden

4m SE of Lewes off A27. 16th cent.; pictures; bronzes; historical documents.

Great Dixter
Mr Quentin Lloyd

½m N of Northiam, 8m NW of Rye off A28. 15th cent. half timbered manor house; restoration and gardens designed by Lutyens.

HAMPSHIRE

Beaulieu Abbey and Palace House
The Lord Montagu of Beaulieu

Beaulieu, 14m S of Southampton, 6m NE of Lymington. Cistercian abbey, 1204; Palace House formerly gate house, converted to private residence 1538; historic car, motor cycle and cycle museum; gardens.

Broadlands
Lord Romsey

Romsey, 8m N of Southampton (A3057). 1536; landscaping and architecture by 'Capability' Brown in 1767; home of Lord Palmerston and Lord Mountbatten.

Mottisfont Abbey
The National Trust

4½m NW of Romsey off A3057. 12th cent. Augustinian Priory, south front 18th cent.; drawing-room by Rex Whistler; gardens, trees, roses.

Stratfield Saye House
The Trustees of the Duke of Wellington

1m W of A33, between Reading and Basingstoke. 1630; home of the dukes of Wellington since 1817; furniture, paintings belonging to 1st Duke; wild fowl sanctuary.

The Vyne
The National Trust

4m N of Basingstoke between Bramley and Sherborne St John. Early 16th cent., classic portico, 1654. Tudor panelling, 18th cent.; ornamented staircase; gardens.

HEREFORD AND WORCESTER

Croft Castle
The National Trust

5m NW of Leominster just N of B4362. 14th/15th cent. Welsh border castle, modified 16th and 17th cents.; Gothic staircase and ceilings added 18th cent.; tree avenues.

Eastnor Castle
The Hon. Mrs Hervey-Bathurst

2m E of Ledbury on A438. 1814; collections of paintings, tapestries and armour; arboretum.

HERTFORDSHIRE

Gorhambury House
The Earl of Verulam

2½m N of St Albans near A5. 1774–84 mansion, modified classical style; 16th cent. enamelled glass; historic portraits.

Hatfield House
The Marquess of Salisbury

Hatfield, opposite station. Jacobean/Tudor 1611, built by Robert Cecil, 1st Earl of Salisbury; Queen Elizabeth I's childhood home; fine portraits and furniture; gardens.

HUMBERSIDE

Burton Agnes Hall
Trustees of Burton Agnes Hall, Preservation Trust Ltd

Burton Agnes, 6m SW of Bridlington on A166. Elizabethan; impressionist art collection; carved ceilings and overmantels.

Burton Constable
Mr J. Chichester Constable

Burton Constable, 1½m N of Sproatley, 7½m NE of Hull (A165), 10m SE of Beverley (A1035). Elizabethan House, 1570; 'Capability' Brown parkland.

Sledmere House
Sir Tatton Sykes, Bt

8m NW of Great Driffield at junc. of B1251 and B1253. Georgian, 1787; Adam ceilings; 100ft long library; gardens.

KENT

Hever Castle
Lord Astor of Hever

Midway between London and S coast, 3m SE of Edenbridge off B2026. 13th cent. moated castle; home of Anne Boleyn; formal Italian garden and lake.

Ightham Mote
Mr C.H. Robinson

Ivy Hatch, 2½m S of Ightham off A227, 6m E of Sevenoaks. Ancient moated manor house, one of the most complete still in existence.

Leeds Castle
Leeds Castle Foundation

6m SE of Maidstone, B2163 Leeds to Sutton Valence Rd. Mediaeval; surrounded by lake, recently restored; landscaped parkland.

Quebec House
The National Trust

Junc. of Edenbridge and Sevenoaks rds (A25 and B2026). Originally 16th cent., now mainly 17th cent.; relics of General Wolfe.

Squerryes Court
Mr J. St A. Warde

Western outskirts of Westerham on A25. William and Mary manor house; objects of interest connected with General Wolfe; grounds and lake.

LANCASHIRE

Hoghton Tower
Sir Bernard de Hoghton, Bt.

5m E of Preston on A675. 16th cent. fortified hill-top mansion; Banqueting Hall; Old English rose garden.

LEICESTERSHIRE

Belvoir Castle
His Grace the Duke of Rutland

7m WSW of Grantham, between A607 (to Melton Mowbray) and A52 to Nottingham. Home of dukes of Rutland since Henry VIII's time, rebuilt by Wyatt, 1816; Military Museum of 17/21st Lancers.

Quenby Hall
The Squire de Lisle

7m NE of Leicester. Jacobean Hall c. 1620; fine ceilings and panelling; pictures; furniture.

Stanford Hall
The Lord and Lady Braye

7½m NE of Rugby off B5414, 3½m from A5 at Swinford. William and Mary House built in 1690; car and motor cycle museum; walled rose garden; Old Forge.

LINCOLNSHIRE

Belton House
Lord Brownlow

2m NE of Grantham on A607. 17th cent. treasure house attributed to Wren; Old Masters including a 'Mona Lisa'; Grinling Gibbons carvings.

Doddington Hall
Mr and Mrs A.G. Jarvis

Doddington, 5m W of Lincoln. Elizabethan manor house; Tudor gatehouse; walled rose gardens.

Gunby Hall
The National Trust

2½m NW of Burgh-le-Marsh, 7m W of Skegness on S side of A158. Built 1700; portraits by Reynolds; walled gardens.

LONDON

Apsley House
Victoria and Albert Museum

149 Piccadilly, Hyde Park Corner. Built 1771–8; art collections; relics of 1st Duke of Wellington.

Chiswick House
Department of the Environment

Burlington Lane, Chiswick, W4. 1725 villa derived from Palladio's Villa Capra; rooms decorated by William Kent.

Fenton House
The National Trust

W side of Hampstead Grove, 300yds N of Hampstead Tube Station. 1693; Benton Fletcher collection of early keyboard musical instruments.

Ham House
The National Trust

S bank of Thames opposite Twickenham, 1m S of Richmond. 17th cent.; portrait gallery; Charles II and early Georgian furnishings.

Hampton Court Palace
Department of the Environment

N bank of Thames. Built in 1514 by Cardinal Wolsey; royal palace with additions by Henry VIII and Wren; state rooms; gardens.

Kenwood
(Iveagh bequest)
Greater London Council

Hampstead, NW3. Remodelled by Adam in 1764; contains Iveagh Collection of English and foreign paintings.

Marble Hill House
Greater London Council

Twickenham. English Palladian villa; early Georgian paintings and furniture.

Osterley Park House
The National Trust

½m N of Great West road, turn off at Thornbury Road near Osterley Station. Adam state rooms; Gobelins tapestry room; Tudor stable block.

NORFOLK

Blickling Hall
The National Trust

1½m NW of Aylsham on N side of B1354. Jacobean, altered 1765–70; Russian tapestry; state rooms; formal garden 1729; temple and orangery.

Felbrigg Hall
The National Trust

2m SW of Cromer on S side of A148. 17th cent. country house; Georgian interiors; 18th cent. library and orangery; walled garden and park.

Holkham Hall
Viscount Coke

2m W of Wells, S of A149. Palladian mansion; art collection; formal garden laid out by Sir Charles Barry.

Houghton Hall
The Marquess of Cholmondeley

13m E of King's Lynn, 10m W of Fakenham. 18th cent. mansion; interior decoration by Kent; state rooms; parkland.

Oxburgh Hall
The National Trust

7m SW of Swaffham, S side of Stoke Ferry Rd. Late 15th cent. moated house; needlework by Mary, Queen of Scots; gatehouse tower; French parterre c. 1845.

NORTHAMPTONSHIRE

Althorp
The Earl Spencer

6m NW of Northampton on A428. 1508, alterations 18th and 20th cents.; art and porcelain collections.

Burghley House
The Dowager Marchioness of Exeter

1m SE of Stamford. Late Elizabethan; state apartments; silver fireplaces; painted ceilings.

Hinwick House
Mr R.M. Orlebar

3½m S of Rushden, 6m SE of Wellingborough, 3m from A6 at Wymington. Queen Anne house; art collection; tapestries and needlework.

Lamport Hall
Lamport Hall Trust

8m N of Northampton on A508. Mainly 17th and 18th cent.; Music Hall; 18th cent. plasterwork.

Rockingham Castle
Commander Michael Saunders Watson

2m N of Corby, 14m from Stamford on A427, 8m from Kettering on A6003. Built by William the Conqueror; 12 acres of wild and formal gardens.

NORTHUMBERLAND

Alnwick Castle
His Grace the Duke of Northumberland, KG

Alnwick, 30m N of Newcastle off A1. 12th cent. mediaeval fortification, restored by Salvin; paintings by well-known artists; Meissen china.

Bamburgh Castle
The Lord Armstrong

16m N of Alnwick, 6m from Belford, 3m from Seahouses. 12th cent. Norman keep, restored.

Callaly Castle
Major A.S.C. Browne, DL

2m W of Whittingham, 10m W of Alnwick. 17th cent. mansion with 13th cent. Pele tower, and Georgian and Victorian additions; 18th cent. plasterwork.

Cragside House
The National Trust

½m E of Rothbury, 28m N of Newcastle-upon-Tyne. 1870–84; experimental apparatus; Pre-Raphaelite pictures; first house in the world to be lit be electricity generated by water power; country park.

Wallington Hall
The National Trust

From N – 12m W of Morpeth on B6343, from S – A696 from Newcastle, 6m NW of Belsay (B6342). 1688, alterations 18th cent.; Central Hall added 19th cent.

NORTH YORKSHIRE

Beningbrough Hall
The National Trust

8m NW of York, 3m W of Shipton on A19. Baroque house c. 1716; major restorations; portrait collection from National Portrait Gallery; Victorian laundry; gardens.

Newby Hall
Mr R.E.J. Compton

4m SE of Ripon on B6265, 3m W of A1. Adam house; collections of tapestries and sculpture; 25 acres of gardens.

OXFORDSHIRE

Broughton Castle
The Lord Saye and Sele

2m SW of Banbury on B4035. Moated Tudor mansion; part early 14th cent., plasterwork ceilings; arms and armour of Civil War period.

Buscot Park
The National Trust

3m NW of Faringdon on A417. Built 1780 in Adam manner; Burne-Jones room; grounds and lake; Italianate water gardens.

Mapledurham House
Mr J.J. Eyston

4m NW of Reading off A4074. Late 16th cent.; oak staircase; private chapel; grounds with 18th cent. water-mill.

Milton Manor House
Surgeon Capt. and Mrs E.J. Mockler

Milton village, 4m S of Abingdon, 1m from Sutton Courtenay on B4016. 17th cent.; Georgian wings, (Inigo Jones); walled garden.

Stonor Park
Lord and Lady Camoys

B480, 5m N of Henley-on-Thames, 5m S of Watlington. Dates from c. 1190 with frequent additions and alterations; Italian sculpture collection; chapel; wooded deer park.

SHROPSHIRE

Attingham Park
The National Trust

Atcham, 4m SE of Shrewsbury, N of A5. 1785; Nash picture gallery; park landscaped by Repton.

Benthall Hall
The National Trust

4m NE of Much Wenlock, 6m S of Wellington, 1m NW of Broseley on B4375. 16th cent. stone house; alterations 17th cent.; oak staircase; mullion windows; small garden.

Weston Park
The Earl of Bradford

Weston-under-Lizard A5, 5m from Shifnal, 12m from Wolverhampton. Fine Restoration period house (1671); collection of Old Masters; gardens and parkland by 'Capability' Brown.

SOMERSET

Brympton d'Evercy
Mr Charles E.B. Clive-Ponsonby-Fane, JP

2m W of Yeovil, A30 or A3088. Tudor west front; late 17th cent. south front; state rooms; Felix Dress Collection; gardens; vineyard; Priest House Museum.

Dunster Castle
The National Trust

Dunster, 3m SE of Minehead, on A396. 13th cent., remodelled 19th cent. (Salvin); 17th cent. staircase; deer park; terraced gardens.

Hatch Court
Commander and Mrs Barry Nation

6m SE of Taunton on A358. Georgian Palladian style house; Canadian Military Museum; china room; grounds and deer park.

Lytes Cary Manor
The National Trust

W side of A37, 2½m NE of Ilchester. 14th and 15th cent. manor house; chapel; formal garden.

Montacute House
The National Trust

Montacute, 4m W of Yeovil, N of A3088, 3m S of A303. Elizabethan house begun in 1590s; heraldic glass; portrait collection from National Portrait Gallery; formal garden.

STAFFORDSHIRE

Shugborough
The National Trust

5½m SE of Stafford. Built by Stuart and Wyatt; Chinese garden house; classical temple.

SUFFOLK

Melford Hall
The National Trust

Long Melford, A134, 3m N of Sudbury. 1554–78; Chinese porcelain collection; garden and gazebo.

Somerleyton Hall
The Lord and Lady Somerleyton

5m NW of Lowestoft off B1074, 7m from Yarmouth on A143. Early 19th cent. mansion; art collection; wood carving; gardens, maze.

SURREY

Clandon Park
The National Trust

West Clandon, 3m E of Guildford on A247. 1731–5 Palladian house; plasterwork; art collections; Museum of Queen's Royal Surrey Regiment.

Polesden Lacey
The National Trust

3m NW of Dorking A246, Great Bookham. Regency villa, Edwardian alterations; Greville collection of pictures; 18th cent. garden.

WARWICKSHIRE

Charlecote Park
The National Trust

4m E of Stratford-upon-Avon, N of B4086. 1558; Shakespeare supposedly caught poaching here; 16th cent. gatehouse, now museum; deer park.

Coughton Court
The National Trust

2m N of Alcester, E of A435. Central gatehouse 1509; mid-Elizabethan wings; Jacobite relics.

Packwood House
The National Trust

2m E of Hockley Heath (A34), 11m SE of Birmingham. Tudor half-timbered; mid-17th cent. additions; tapestry and needlework; yew garden representing Sermon on the Mount c. 1650; Carolean formal gardens.

Ragley Hall
The Marquess of Hertford

2m SW of Alcester on A435, 8m from Stratford-upon-Avon.

Palladian country house, 1680; paintings; furniture; library; park; lake.

Upton House
The National Trust

1m S of Edge Hill, 7m NW of Banbury on A422. Dates from James II's reign; tapestries; porcelain; paintings; terraced gardens.

Warwick Castle
Madam Tussaud's, Warwick.

Mediaeval castle; 14th cent. towers and armoury; dungeons; state apartments; Old Masters; grounds landscaped by 'Capability' Brown.

WEST MIDLANDS

Hagley Hall
The Viscount and Viscountess Cobham

Off A456, 12m from Birmingham near M5/M6. 18th cent. Palladian house; Italian plasterwork; Lyttelton collection of 18th cent. paintings; park with pools and follies.

Wightwick Manor
The National Trust

3m W of Wolverhampton, A454. William Morris period house; Pre-Raphaelite pictures; Morris wallpapers, tapestries; gardens.

WEST SUSSEX

Arundel Castle
Arundel Castle Trustees Ltd

Arundel, 9m W of Worthing, 10m E of Chichester. Originally built about the reign of Edward the Confessor but rebuilt 18th cent. with further alterations during 19th cent.; 15th cent. furniture; portraits by Gainsborough, Holbein, Van Dyck.

Goodwood House
Goodwood Estate Co Ltd

3½m NE of Chichester, A285, A286, A27. Jacobean with additions; Old Masters; tapestries; French and English furniture; porcelain; park.

Parham
The Hon. Clive and Mrs Gibson and Mr and Mrs P.A. Tritton

4m SE of Pulborough on A283. Elizabethan house; portrait collection – Elizabethan, Jacobean and Georgian; needlework; furniture; gardens.

Petworth House
The National Trust

Petworth, 5½m E of Midhurst. Mainly 17th cent. with additions during 19th cent.; 14th cent. chapel; carvings by Gibbons; deer park by 'Capability' Brown.

Uppark
The National Trust

5m SE of Petersfield, E side of B2146. 1690, romantic house; interior decoration and furnishings dating from 1750; Victorian kitchen; Queen Anne doll's house; garden, landscaped by Repton.

WEST YORKSHIRE

Bramham Park
Mr and Mrs George Lane Fox

5m S of Wetherby on A1. Queen Anne mansion; grounds landscaped in style of Le Nôtre.

Harewood House
The Earl of Harewood

7m S of Harrogate, 8m N of Leeds, junc. A61/659 at Harewood. 18th cent.; Chippendale furniture; porcelain collections; grounds landscaped by 'Capability' Brown; bird garden; adventure playground.

Nostell Priory
The National Trust

6m SE of Wakefield, N side of A638. Early 18th cent. with

additions in 1766 by Adam; state rooms; motor cycle and aviation museums.

Temple Newsam
Leeds Metropolitan District Council

5m E of Leeds, 1m S of A63. Tudor and Jacobean house; Georgian rooms; art collections; belonged to Knights Templar; birthplace of Lord Darnley (husband of Mary, Queen of Scots).

WILTSHIRE

Bowood Gardens
The Earl of Shelburne

2½m W of Calne, 5m SE of Chippenham, 1m S of A4. 100 acre garden; exotic trees; lake; Doric Temple; caves; arboretum; pinetum; Italian garden; exhibition rooms containing collections of classical sculpture, costume and ceramics.

Corsham Court
The Lord Methuen, ARICS

Corsham, 4m W of Chippenham off A4. 1582 Elizabethan manor; Georgian state rooms 1760; 18th cent. furniture; collection of Old Masters; park and gardens by 'Capability' Brown and Repton.

Lacock Abbey
The National Trust

Lacock, 3m N of Melksham, 3m S of Chippenham, E of A350. 13th cent. abbey, converted to house 1540; 18th cent. 'Gothick' additions; mediaeval cloisters; brewery.

Stourhead
The National Trust

Stourton off B3092, 3m NW of Mere on A303. 1722 Palladian house; Chippendale furniture; mid-18th cent. landscaped gardens.

Scotland

BORDERS REGION

Abbotsford House
Mrs P. Maxwell-Scott

3m W of Melrose, S of A72, 5m N of Selkirk. Home of Sir Walter Scott, containing historical relics he collected.

Bowhill
His Grace the Duke of Buccleuch and Queensberry, KT

3m W of Selkirk on A708. 18th/19th cent.; collection of paintings including a Leonardo and a Canaletto; collection of miniatures; restored Victorian kitchen; grounds include a nature trail.

Floors Castle
The Duke of Roxburghe

N of Kelso. 1721 with later additions by Playfair; tapestries; furniture; paintings; gardens.

Manderston
Mr and Mrs Adrian Palmer

2m E of Duns on A6105, 14m W of Berwick-upon-Tweed. Edwardian house in classical style; farm and dairy buildings; garden.

Mellerstain
The Lord Binning

9m NE of Melrose, 7m NW of Kelso. 18th cent. mansion house by Adam family; Adam interiors; library; Italian gardens; lake.

Traquair House
Mr P. Maxwell Stuart

1m S of Innerleithen, 6m SE of Peebles, junc. of B709 and B7062. Associated with Jacobite risings; collections of books, manuscripts, embroideries dating from 12th cent.; 18th cent. library; 18th cent. pavilion in grounds.

DUMFRIES AND GALLOWAY REGION

Drumlanrig Castle

His Grace the Duke of Buccleuch and Queensberry, KT

18m N of Dumfries, 3m N of Thornhill off A76. Castle, 1679–91; collection of art treasures includes a Rembrandt, silver, Charles II furniture; grounds contain woodland walk.

GRAMPIAN REGION

Braemar Castle

Captain A.A.C. Farquharson of Invercauld

½m NE of Braemar on A93. Romantic 17th cent. castle; round central tower; spiral stair.

Brodie Castle

The National Trust for Scotland

Off A96 between Nairn and Forres. Burned 1645 and rebuilt with additions 18th/19th cent.; furniture; porcelain; paintings; gardens.

Castle Fraser

The National Trust for Scotland

3m S of Kemnay off B993, 16m W of Aberdeen. 1575–1636; Z-plan castle; gardens.

Craigievar Castle

The National Trust for Scotland

6m S of Alford on A980, 26m W of Aberdeen. Tower house built in 1626, virtually unchanged; gardens.

Drum Castle

The National Trust for Scotland

10m W of Aberdeen off A93. Late 13th cent. tower with mansion added 1619; gardens.

HIGHLAND REGION

Cawdor Castle

The Earl of Cawdor, FRICS

S of Nairn, B9090 between Inverness and Nairn. 14th cent. keep, fortified 15th cent.; mainly 17th cent. additions; home of Thanes of Cawdor since 14th cent.; gardens.

Dunvegan Castle

John MacLeod of MacLeod

Dunvegan, 23m W of Portree, Isle of Skye. 13th cent.; home of Chiefs of MacLeod; gardens.

LOTHIAN REGION

Hopetoun House

Hopetoun House Preservation Trust

2m from Forth Road Bridge off A904 at Queensferry. 18th cent. Adam house; reception rooms; pictures; landscaped grounds.

The House of the Binns

The National Trust for Scotland

3½m E of Linlithgow on A904. Plaster ceilings; pictures; park.

Lennoxlove

His Grace the Duke of Hamilton

1½m S of Haddington on B6369, 18m E of Edinburgh on A1. Home of Maitland family; Lime Avenue named Politician's Walk after William Maitland, Secretary to Mary, Queen of Scots.

Palace of Holyroodhouse

Royal Palace

Foot of Canongate, Edinburgh. Reconstructed by Charles II; relics of Mary, Queen of Scots.

STRATHCLYDE

Culzean Castle

The National Trust for Scotland

12m SW of Ayr off A719. Adam house; spacious gardens.

Inveraray Castle

His Grace the Duke of Argyll

Just NE of Inveraray on Loch Fyne. 18th cent. built by Morris and Mylne; headquarters of Clan Campbell; great hall; armoury; state rooms.

Torosay Castle

Trustees of Torosay Estate

1½m SE of Craignure by A849 on Isle of Mull. Early Victorian house by David Bryce; extensive Italian terraced gardens.

TAYSIDE REGION

Glamis Castle

The Earl of Strathmore and Kinghorne

12m N of Dundee, 4m S of Kirriemuir, junc. A94 and A928. Mainly 17th cent., some parts older; legend of secret chamber; grounds laid out by 'Capability' Brown.

Scone Palace

Rt Hon the Earl of Mansfield

Just W of Old Scone, 1m N of Perth on A93. Originally 16th cent., rebuilt 1803; French furniture; Vernis Martin vases and *objets d'art*; bed hangings worked by Mary, Queen of Scots; pinetum; woodland garden.

Wales

CLWYD

Bodrhyddan Hall

Col. the Lord Langford

4m SE of Rhyl. 17th cent. manor house; portraits; garden.

Chirk Castle

The National Trust

½m W of Chirk on A5, 20m NW of Shrewsbury, 7m SE of Llangollen. Border castle, built 1310, exterior unaltered since time of Edward I; portraits; tapestries; gardens.

Erddig

The National Trust

1m S of Wrexham off A483. Late 17th cent., with 18th cent. additions; original furniture; domestic outbuildings all in working order – laundry, sawmill, bakehouse, smithy; agricultural museum; restored 18th cent. formal garden.

GWYNEDD

Plas Newydd

The National Trust

1m SW of Llanfairpwllgwyngyll on A4080 on Isle of Anglesey. 18th cent. house by James Wyatt; Rex Whistler's largest wall painting; military museum; spring garden.

POWYS

Powis Castle

The National Trust

Just outside Welshpool, A483. 13th–14th cent. castle reconstructed early 17th cent.; fine plasterwork; murals; furniture; paintings; terraced gardens.

Bibliography

Burke's Peerage.
Debrett's Peerage & Baronetage,
1980.
G.E.C.'s Complete Peerage.
Dictionary of National Biography.
Reports of the Historical Manuscripts
Commission.

The place of publication is London
unless otherwise stated
ABERDEEN, MARQUESS AND
MARCHIONESS OF, 'We Twa', 1925
ABERDEEN, MARQUESS AND
MARCHIONESS OF, More Cracks
with 'We Twa', 1929
ALSOP, S. M., Lady Sackville, 1978
ANSTRUTHER, I., The Knight and the
Umbrella, 1963
ARBUTHNOT, H., Journal, ed. Francis
Bamford and the Duke of
Wellington, 1950
ATHOLL, DUCHESS OF, Working
Partnership, 1958
ATHOLL, DUKE OF, Chronicles of the
Atholl and Tullibardine Families,
Edinburgh, 1908.
AUBREY, J., Brief Lives, ed. O. Lawson
Dick, 1949
BALSAN, C. V., The Glitter and the
Gold, 1953
BATHO, G. R., 'Henry, Ninth Earl of
Northumberland, and Syon House,
Middlesex, 1594–1632',
Transactions of the Ancient
Monuments Society, new series,
vol. 4, 1956
BATHO, G. R., 'The Household Papers
of Henry Percy, Ninth Earl of
Northumberland', Camden Third
Series, vol. XCIII, 1962
BEARD, G., Decorative Plasterwork in
Great Britain, 1975
BEAUFORT, DUKE OF., Memoirs, 1981
BERKELEY, M., Beaded Bubbles, 1967
BESSBOROUGH, EARL OF., Georgiana,
1955
BINNEY, M., 'Penshurst Place, Kent',
Country Life, CLI, 1972
BLENCOWE, R. W., Sydney Papers, 1825
BOTFIELD, B., Stemmata Botevilliana,
1858
BOVILE, E. W., English Country Life
1780–1830, 1962
BRENAN, G. A., A History of the House
of Percy, 1902
BRISTOL, EARL OF, 'The Diary of John
Hervey, and Letter Books of John
Hervey, 1st Earl of Bristol
1681–1750', ed. S. H. A. Hervey,
Suffolk Green Books, Wells, 1894
BRITTEN, J., The Sloane Herbarium,
ed. J. E. Dandy, 1958
BURNETT, D., Longleat, 1978
BURY, A., Syon House, 1955
CANNADINE, D., 'The Landowner as
Millionaire: the finances of the
Dukes of Devonshire, c. 1800–
c. 1926', Agricultural History
Review, 1977
CAREW, R., The Survey of Cornwall,
ed. F. E. Halliday, 1953

CARTWRIGHT, J., Sacharissa, 1893
Catalogue of the Sale of the Library of
the late Sir Clement Cottrell
Dormer collected by Lieutenant
General James Dormer, 1764
CAVENDISH, H., Hary-O: The Letters
of Lady Harriet Cavendish
1796–1809, ed. G. Leveson-Gower,
1940
CECIL, A., Queen Victoria and her
Prime Ministers, 1953
CECIL, D., The Young Melbourne,
1954
CHILDE-PEMBERTON, W. S., The Earl
Bishop, 1924
CHURTON, R., A Memoir of Sir Roger
Newdigate, Bart., Leamington,
1881
CLARENDON, EARL OF, The History of
the Rebellion, ed. W. D. Macray,
1958
CLARK, K., The Gothic Revival, 1962
COATE, M., Cornwall in the Civil War
and Interregnum, Oxford, 1933
COLLINS, A., Letters and Memorials of
State, 1746
COLLINS, J., A Short Account of the
Library at Longleat House, 1980
COLVIN, H. M., Biographical
Dictionary of British Architects
1600–1840, 1978
CONGREVE, W., Works, Birmingham,
1761
CORNFORTH, J., 'Boughton House,
Northamptonshire', Country Life,
CXLVIII, CXLIX, 1970–71
COSTLEY-WHITE, H., Mary Cole,
Countess of Berkeley, 1961
COX, J. C., 'The Household Account
Books of Sir Miles Stapleton', The
Ancestor, nos. II and III, 1902–03
CROFT, P. J., Autograph Poetry in the
English Language, 1973
DALE, T. F., The Eighth Duke of
Beaufort and the Badminton Hunt,
1901
DEFOE, D., A Tour through England
and Wales, 1724–26, ed. G. D. H.
Cole, 1928
DE FONBLANQUE, E. B., Annals of the
House of Percy, 1887
DELANY, M., The Autobiography and
Correspondence, ed. Lady
Llanover, 1861–2
DE L'ISLE, VISCOUNT, 'Penshurst
Place', Connoisseur, 1980
DEVONSHIRE, DUKE OF, Handbook of
Chatsworth and Hardwick, 1844
DOWNES, K., English Baroque
Architecture, 1966
DOWNES, K., Hawksmoor, 1959
DUFF, D., Victoria in the Highlands,
1968
DUNCAN, A. I. M., A Study of the Life
and Public Career of Frederick
Howard, Fifth Earl of Carlisle,
unpublished thesis, Oxford, 1981
DURANT, H., Henry, 1st Duke of
Beaufort, and his Duchess, Mary,
Pontypool, 1973
DURANT, H., The Somerset Sequence,
1951

ELIOT, G., The George Eliot Letters,
ed. G. S. Haight, New Haven,
1954–5
ELIOT, G., Scenes of Clerical Life,
Edinburgh, 1858
EVELYN, J., The Diary, ed. E. S. de
Beer, 1959
EWALD, A. C., The Life and Times of
the Hon Algernon Sidney, 1873
FALK, B., The Berkeleys of Berkeley
Square, 1944
FARINGTON, J., Diary, ed. J. Greig,
1922–8
FIELDING, D., Mercury Presides, 1954
FIENNES, C., The Journeys, ed.
C. Morris. 1947
FORD, B., 'The Earl-Bishop: an
eccentric and capricious patron of
the arts', Apollo, 1974
FORMAN, S., Scottish Country Houses
and Castles, Glasgow, 1967
FOSBROKE, T. D., Berkeley
Manuscripts, 1821
FOTHERGILL, B., The Mitred Earl,
1974
GIROUARD, M., Life in the English
Country House, New Haven, 1978
GIROUARD, M., The Return to
Camelot, New Haven, 1981
GIROUARD, M., The Victorian Country
House, Oxford, 1973
GREEN, D. B., Blenheim Palace, 1951
HADFIELD, M., A History of British
Gardening, 1979
HAGUE, D. B., 'Penrhyn Castle',
Transactions of the
Caernarvonshire Historical Society,
vol. 20, 1959
HAIGHT, G. S., George Eliot, Oxford,
1969
HALSBAND, R., Lord Hervey, Oxford,
1973
HASKELL, F. Rediscoveries in Art,
Oxford, 1976
HASKELL, F. AND PENNY, N., Taste and
the Antique, New Haven, 1981
HENLEY, D. G., Rosalind Howard,
Countess of Carlisle, 1958
HILL, O., Scottish Castles of the 16th
and 17th Centuries, 1953
HOLLAND, B. H., The Life of Spencer
Compton, 8th Duke of Devonshire,
1911
HOWARD, H., Indications of
Memorials . . . of the Howard
Family, Corby Castle, 1834–6
HUSSEY, C., English Country Houses,
early Georgian 1715–60, 1955; mid
Georgian 1760–1800, 1956; late
Georgian, 1800–40, 1958
HUSSEY, C., English Gardens and
Landscapes, 1967
HUSSEY, C., 'Berkeley Castle,
Gloucestershire', Country Life,
LXXI, 1932
IREMONGER, L., Lord Aberdeen, 1978
JACKSON, J. E., History of Longleat,
Devizes, 1857
JACKSON-STOPS, G., Ickworth, 1979
LEES-MILNE, J., English Country
Houses, Baroque, 1685–1715, 1970

LEES-MILNE, J. AND CORNFORTH, J.,
'Chatsworth', Country Life,
CLXIV, 1968
LESLIE, A., Edwardians in Love, 1972
LEVER, T., The Herberts of Wilton,
1967
LEWIS, W. S., Horace Walpole, 1961
LINDSAY, J., History of the North
Wales Slate Industry, Newton
Abbot, 1974
LINKLATER, E., The Music of the
North, Aberdeen, 1978
LONGFORD, E., A Pilgrimage of
Passion, 1979
LYTTON, EARL OF, The Life, Letters
and Literary Remains of Edward
Bulwer, Lord Lytton, 1883
LYTTON, EARL OF, The Life of Edward
Bulwer, First Lord Lytton, 1913
MCFARLANE, K. B., The Nobility of
Later Mediaeval England, Oxford,
1973
MARCHANT, L. A., Byron, 1971
MARKHAM, V. R., Paxton and the
Bachelor Duke, 1935
MATHEW, D., Catholicism in England,
1955
MONCREIFFE, I., The Highland Clans,
1967
MONCREIFFE, I., The Story of the
Atholl Highlanders, Derby, n.d.
NEWDIGATE-NEWDEGATE, LADY, The
Cheverels of Cheverel Manor, 1898
NICOLSON, N., Portrait of a Marriage,
1973
NIMROD (C. J. APPERLEY), Hunting
Tours, 1835; Hunting
Reminiscences, 1843
NORTH, R., Lives of the Norths, ed. A.
Jessopp, 1905
OSBORNE, D., The Letters of Dorothy
Osborne to William Temple, ed.
G. C. Moore, Oxford, 1928
PEMBROKE, EARL OF, Catalogue of the
paintings and drawings . . . at
Wilton House, 1968
PENNANT, A. DOUGLAS, Catalogue of
the Pictures at Penrhyn Castle,
Bangor and Mortimer House in
1901, Bangor, 1902
PENTLAND, M., A Bonnie Fechter, 1952
PEPYS, S., The Diary, ed. R. Latham
and W. Matthews, 1970
PEVSNER, N., The Buildings of
England, 1951, et seq.
PHILLIPS, C. J., History of the Sackville
Family, 1929
PÜCKLER-MUSKAU, PRINCE H. L. H.
VON, Tour in England . . . in the
Years 1828 & 1829, 1832
ROBERTS, C. H., The Radical
Countess. The history of the life of
Rosalind, Countess of Carlisle,
Carlisle, 1962
ROWSE, A. L., The Early Churchills,
1956; The Later Churchills, 1958
ROWSE, A. L., Tudor Cornwall, 1969
SACKVILLE-WEST, V., The Diary of the
Lady Anne Clifford, 1923
SACKVILLE-WEST, V., English Country
Houses, 1946

SACKVILLE-WEST, V., *Knole and the Sackvilles*, 1958

SAXL, F. AND WITTKOWER, R., *British Art and the Mediterranean*, 1948

SIDNEY, M. S., *Historical Guide to Penshurst Place*, Tunbridge Wells, 1903

SIDNEY, P., *Memoirs of the Sidney Family*, 1899

SIDNEY, P., *The Sidneys of Penshurst*, 1901

SMYTH, J., *The Lives of the Berkeleys*, ed. J. Maclean, Gloucester, 1883

STONE, L., *The Crisis of the Aristocracy, 1558–1641*, Oxford, 1965

STONE, L., *Family and Fortune*, Oxford, 1973

STRONG, R., *The Renaissance Garden in England*, 1979

STROUD, D., *Capability Brown*, 1957

STROUD, D. *Humphry Repton*, 1962

STUART, D. M., *Dearest Bess*, 1955

SUMMERSON, J., *Architecture in Britain 1530–1830*, Harmondsworth, 1963

THOMPSON, F. L., *A History of Chatsworth*, 1949

THOMPSON, F. M. L. *English Landed Society in the Nineteenth Century*, 1963

Treasures from Chatsworth: The Devonshire Inheritance, Washington, 1979

WAGNER, A. R., *English Genealogy*, Oxford, 1960

WALPOLE, H., *The Letters*, ed. P. Cunningham, 1857

WARD, L., *Forty Years of 'Spy'*, 1917

WHINNEY, M. AND MILLAR, O., *English Art 1625–1714*, Oxford, 1957

WHISTLER, L., *Sir John Vanbrugh*, 1938

WHISTLER, L., *The Imagination of Sir John Vanbrugh*, 1954

WILLIAMSON, G. C., *Lady Anne Clifford*, Kendal, 1922

WISE, C., *The Montagus of Boughton*, Kettering, 1888

WITTKOWER, R., *Palladio and Palladianism*, New York, 1974

WOOD, A. C., 'The Diaries of Sir Roger Newdigate, 1751–1806', *Birmingham Archaeological Society, Transactions and Proceedings*, vol. 78, 1962

WOOD, M., *The English Mediaeval House*, 1965

WOOLF, V., *Orlando*, New York, 1928

YOUNG, F. B., *Mary Sidney, Countess of Pembroke*, 1912

Index

Picture credits

Derry Moore has taken most of the photographs but the author and publishers would like to thank the following for supplying illustrations:

the Marchioness of Aberdeen 219; the Duke of Atholl 159 right, (Cooper-Bridgeman Library) 157, (Scottish National Portrait Gallery, Tom Scott) 151, 154, 158 above; the Marquess of Bath 37, 41 left and right; the Duke of Beaufort (the Courtauld Institute) 135 right, 142 below, 143 below, (the Royal Academy of Arts) 139; Mr John Berkeley (the Courtauld Institute) 17, 21; the Duke of Buccleuch (Tom Scott) 68 left, 71 below; Sir John Carew Pole (the Courtauld Institute) 118, 123 below; from the Castle Howard Collection 93 right, 99, 101, 102 above and below, (the Royal Academy of Arts) 95; the Trustees of the Chatsworth Settlement 74 left, 78 above, 80, 83, 87 above; the Hon David Lytton Cobbold 183 below, 186, 187; Mr Charles Cottrell-Dormer 131 right, (the Courtauld Institute) 128 left, 130 above; the Viscount De L'Isle 27, 28, 29, 61 below; Mr H. FitzRoy Newdegate (the Royal Academy of Arts) 163 left, (John Wright Photography) 166 below; His Grace the Duke of Marlborough 107, 113, 115; the National Portrait Gallery 215; the National Trust 206, 207, (A. C. Cooper) 196, (Jeremy Whitaker) 209; the Duke of Norfolk 229 right; the Duke of Northumberland 179 (Country Life) 175, 178, (Photo Studios Ltd) 174; the Earl of Pembroke 63, (the Courtauld Institute) 61 above; the Lord Sackville 55 right, (Horst Kolo Photography) 50 below, (the Royal Academy) 50 left; Miss Diana Thorne 197.